RAILWAYS AND INDUSTRIES IN
NORTH EAST WALES AND DEESIDE

Fig 01: View along the GWR branch to Brymbo passing a Mile Post. Brymbo East signal box is ahead which originally was Brymbo Station box, The Station closed to passengers in 1943 but freight services to Brymbo Steel Works were maintained until 1980; the branch is now closed and the signal box disused.

RAILWAYS AND INDUSTRIES IN NORTH EAST WALES AND DEESIDE

ROB SHORLAND-BALL

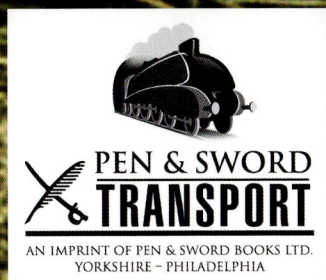

PEN & SWORD
TRANSPORT

AN IMPRINT OF PEN & SWORD BOOKS LTD.
YORKSHIRE – PHILADELPHIA

Illustrations are from the author's collection or, with their permission to him, from those who are acknowledged in the List of Illustrations at the end of the book.

The author, a long-time keen photographer, has accumulated his collection from his time working on BR in the 1950s and 1960s; his time at the National Railway Museum (1987-1994); and as an active member of the Railway & Canal Historical Society and a former member of the Railway Study Association.

He has visited the sites in this book including, in mid-1970s, a detailed guided tour of John Summers & Sons/ BSC Steel Works with Dr Reg Majorcas who was the Works' chemist.

Rob always tries to contact all possible copyright holders and he checks any unacknowledged illustrations with forensic image search engines. He can be contacted at <robsb@wfmyork.co.uk>

First published in Great Britain in 2021 by
Pen and Sword Transport
An imprint of
Pen & Sword Books Ltd
Yorkshire - Philadelphia

ISBN 978 1 52675 377 9

A CIP catalogue record for this book is available from the British Library.

Typeset by SJmagic DESIGN SERVICES, India.
Printed and bound by Printworks Global Ltd, London/Hong Kong.

Pen & Sword Books Ltd incorporates the Imprints of Pen & Sword Books Archaeology, Atlas, Aviation, Battleground, Discovery, Family History, History, Maritime, Military, Naval, Politics, Railways, Select, Transport, True Crime, Fiction, Frontline Books, Leo Cooper, Praetorian Press, Seaforth Publishing, Wharncliffe and White Owl.

For a complete list of Pen & Sword titles please contact
PEN & SWORD BOOKS LIMITED
47 Church Street, Barnsley, South Yorkshire, S70 2AS, England
E-mail: enquiries@pen-and-sword.co.uk
Website: www.pen-and-sword.co.uk

Or
PEN AND SWORD BOOKS
1950 Lawrence Rd, Havertown, PA 19083, USA
E-mail: Uspen-and-sword@casematepublishers.com
Website: www.penandswordbooks.com

CONTENTS

Deeside is the name given to a predominantly industrial area of towns and villages in Flintshire and West Cheshire on the Wales–England border lying near the canalised stretch of the River Dee that flows from neighbouring Chester to Point of Ayr overlooking the Dee Estuary.

PRINCIPAL REFERENCE SOURCES, ACKNOWLEDGEMENTS AND THANKS

I am quite pleased to start this book with the comment that there were and are no 'Principal' reference sources. If I had thought the subject area of the book was already covered, I would never have proposed this title, but I anticipated I might turn to one or more sources as lighthouses to identify hazards and illuminate areas of interest.

I was intrigued to know, before I started serious research, that the NE Welsh village of Brymbo used to have two railway stations – one LNER and one GWR – almost in sight of each other. Shotton, near the River Dee, still has two stations, a Low Level and a High Level, because two railways cross at right angles there and one was originally called the Wrexham, Mold & Connah's Quay Railway which is a fascinating name for a railway-minded geographer like me!

My principal resources have thus been (in no order of priority):

Research visits to Flintshire Record Office, Wrexham, Tata Steel Records Centre on the former John Summers Steelworks site; Brymbo Heritage Centre (BHT) site, BHT offices and a loan of Brymbo Steelworks pictures and records.

My reference collection of relevant books (see Select Bibliography on page 144)

R&CHS 2018 AGM notes and pictures compiled by Ray Shill

Pictures from: my own collection, and loans from Gordon Edgar, John Sloan, Huw Edwards, Jeff Howard, Online Transport Archive (Peter Waller).

Online searches, including *The History of Shotton – Deeside*

Interpretative panels on site and give-away brochures and leaflets from Wrtexham County Borough Council.

And my intention has been to weave together a coherent story about the railways, the major industries and the principal entrepreneurs that made it all happen.

FOREWORD

Putting together the jigsaw

When I started to write this book, I had not intended a 'Foreword' but, as my thinking and writing progressed, I realised that I was putting together a jigsaw. I felt, therefore, that a 'Foreword' was a key to the assembly of that jigsaw which makes up the story of railways, and the industries which were built to serve them, in NE Wales and Deeside.

Originally, I limited the title to be 'NE Wales' but I soon discovered that one of the principal industries, and railway systems, was in England on the eastern banks of the Dee estuary in the huge steelworks created by the John Summers family. And mention of the 'Summers family' introduces another piece of the jigsaw – people or, as many of them were, entrepreneurs who have merited a whole chapter.

As a geographer, I like to investigate the landscapes on which human activities develop which leads me to the shape of the land – Mynydd Hiraethog, Clwydian Range, Halkyn Mountains; river valleys; Dee estuary; NE Wales coastline and maritme activities there – and the minerals underground that may be worth mining or quarrying. And language, too, is one of the social aspects of this jigsaw. I enjoy the sounds of the Welsh language and, when in Wales, I always try to pronounce place names correctly. But it did not seem practical to make this a bi-lingual book so, where necessary, I have offered English explanations of Welsh words – Mynydd Hiraethog is Denbighshire Moors.

The shape of the land may also guide, or even dictate, practical routes for railways which cannot generally be worked up steep hills. The branch line from Prestayn on the coast climbs at 1 in 27 to Dyserth at 213ft above sea-level but is unusually steep for a railway – and the trackbed is now a stimulating foot-and cycle-way. The mainline Chester to Holyhead railway could not, without extensive and expensive civil engineering, take a direct cross-country route so follows the coast.

So the pieces of the jigsaw are taking shape and factors like those above and social history, economic factors, entrepreneurs' intentions and capital resources shape the complete picture from growth, to decline, resurgences and future prospects. I have been writing this book as the Covid-19 pandemic has intensified and has temporarily dimmed future prospects in NE Wales and Deeside, but I hope that by the time this book is published in 2021 there will be a light visible at the end of the present tunnel.

CHAPTER 1

WHY NE WALES AND DEESIDE?

Shrewsbury & Chester Railway; Wrexham, Mold & Connah's Quay Railway
North Wales Mineral Railway .. and others

I have always been interested in areas of the UK that contained unusual or little-known railways and I remember in the 1980s browsing in a Cambridge bookshop and finding *The Cleobury Mortimer and Ditton Priors Light Railway* (W. Smith & K. Beddoes. Oxford Publishing Co. 1980). I bought it, fascinated by the name, and found the railway (1908-60) had been in southern Shropshire. Its principal traffic was granite from Tittersone and Brown Clee quarries, some agricultural produce and a few tourist passengers; unusually it was a rural railway that, at first, generated some income for its promoters.

I explored Shropshire and then looked north into Cheshire and the Welsh Marches and found another

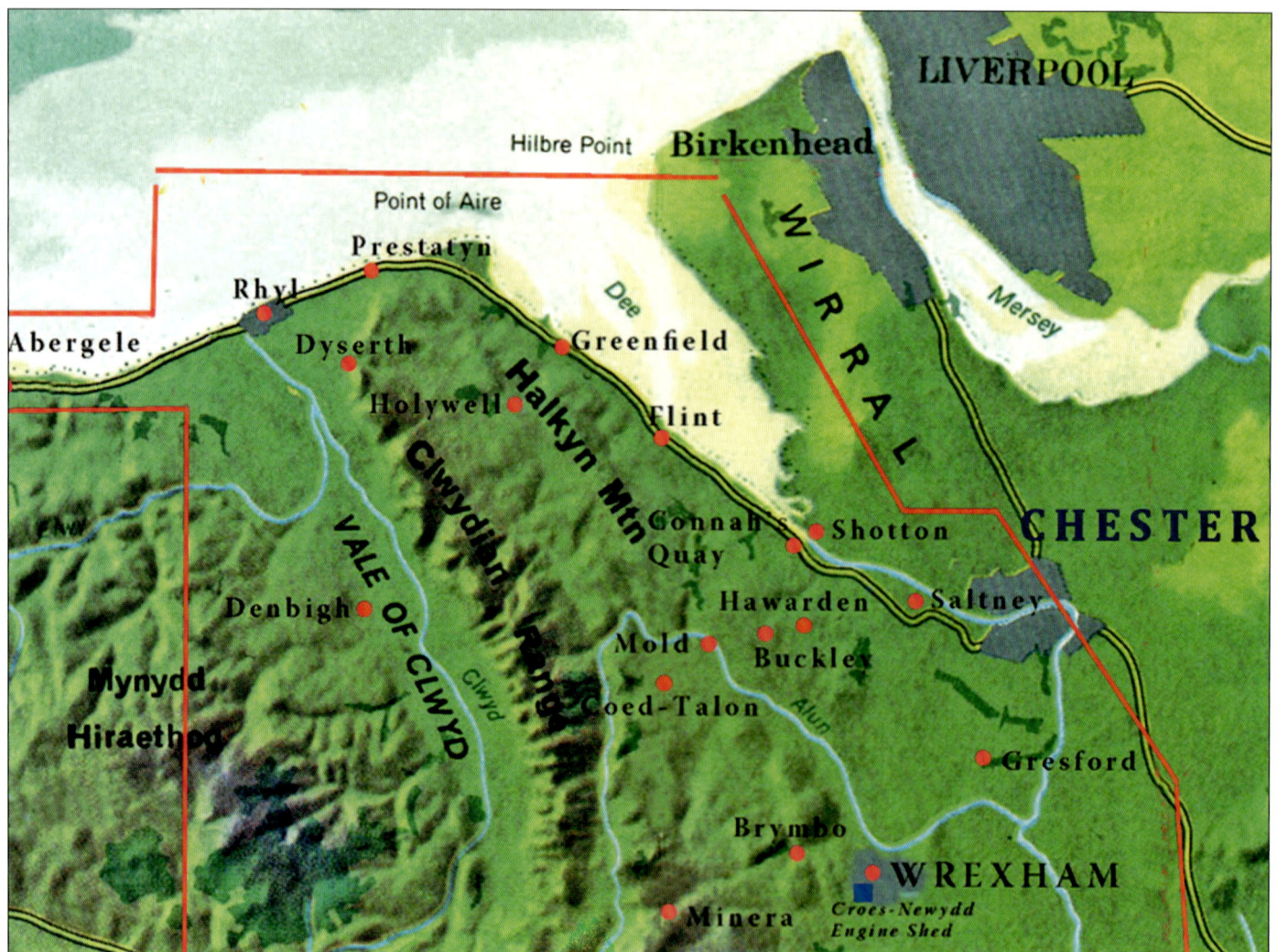

Fig 02: Part of NE Wales and Deeside showing topography, principal railways, industrial centres in this book and the approximate boundaries of interest. (*Author*)

potentially interesting railway, Wrexham, Mold and Connah's Quay Railway. I had never heard of Connah's Quay but correctly assumed it must be on the River Dee estuary. Mold I believed to be the county town of Flintshire and Wrexham was part of Denbighshire.

However, a little further research took me into the complexities of local government re-organisations of 1974, 1996 and further changes made by the Boundary Commission in 2003. The details need not be explained here but **Fig 03** illustrates the contemporary local authority shape of the areas of NE Wales and Deeside outlined in **Fig 02**. I have included 'Deeside' in the title of the book because I needed to embrace part of Merseyside but that name implies the River Mersey, Birkenhead and Liverpool whereas my story only includes the Welsh and English shores of the Dee Estuary. I can do no better than to quote the Wikipedia definition of Deeside:

> **Deeside** (Welsh: Glannau Dyfrdwy) is the name given to a predominantly industrial conurbation of settlements in Flintshire, Merseyside and Cheshire on the Wales – England border lying near the canalised stretch of the River Dee that flows from Chester into the Dee Estuary. These settlements include: Connah's Quay, Shotton, Queensferry . . . Hawarden, Buckley, Ewloe . . . Saltney .

After resolving the past and present local government arrangements for the area I was researching, I turned to the Wrexham, Mold & Connah's Quay Railway (WM&CQR) and discovered that, unlike the CM&DPR which was a branch-line from a main-line junction station, this was a much more complex railway. Nevertheless, for me, it was a key to the NE Wales and Deeside railways and industries jigsaw that I have built together throughout this book. A useful analogy might be a garden plant which grows, at first tentatively but then vigorously, until it is over-shadowed by a larger plant which the Head Gardener seems to favour. More rich compost might be related to wealthy railway company directors who, like the Head Gardener, succeed in grafting the original plant to its larger neighbour.

A logical start to unscramble that analogy seemed to be to consult *Encyclopaedia of British Railway Companies.* (Christopher Awdry. Patrick Stephens Ltd. 1990). I know Christopher and have always admired his

Fig 03: Sketch map showing the current local government administration for the area containing the railways and industries in the context of this book. (*Author*)

work so was not surprised to find that he organised the abundance of nineteenth century railway companies into four groups – GWR, LM&SR, L&NER, SR – plus a fifth group for Independent & Joint Railways and the LPTB. A first puzzle for me, however, was that I found the WM&CQR in the London & North Eastern Railway Group, so I have borrowed from Christopher Awdry's *Encyclopaedia* and added my own research to explain WM&CQR history:

> 'The WM&CQR Company was incorporated on 7th August 1862 to build a railway from Wrexham to the Buckley Railway and thence, via that Railway for goods only, to the River Dee at Connah's Quay. WM&CQR opened for goods on 1st January 1866 and for passengers on 1st May. The Company was soon in financial and legal difficulties because of unpaid bills but some larger railway companies believed there was potential for better business so in 1868 L&NWR offered to work the WM&CQR for 50 per cent of gross traffic receipts but objections were raised by GWR.

'WM&CQR planned extensions from Buckley to the River Dee because the line of the former Buckley Railway included several very sharp curves, difficult gradients and a restricted loading gauge. Parliamentary sanction was finally obtained in 1883 for the Hawarden Loop from Buckley Junction via Hawarden to the River Dee. On the Dee bank there were junctions westerly to Connah's Quay and the former Buckley Railway connections and northerly to Shotton and a meeting with the Manchester, Sheffield & Lincolnshire Railway (MS&LR) via the Hawarden Bridge on the Chester & Connah's Quay Railway.

'In the early 1880s the MS&LR, in agreement with the WM&CQR, had contributed to the construct costs of the Hawarden Loop and on 26th July 1889 MS&LR bought a majority shareholding in the WM&CQR.

'In 1897 the MS&LR, planning for its London Extension to a new station at Marylebone, changed its name to the Great Central Railway (GCR). On 22nd July 1904, by Act of Parliament, the WM&CQR ceased to exist as a separate company and from 1st January 1905 it was vested in the GCR.

'The Railways Act of 1921 stated that:
With a view to the re-organisation and more efficient and economical working of the railway system of Great Britain railways shall be formed into groups in accordance with the provisions of this Act, and the principal railway companies in each group shall be amalgamated, and other companies absorbed in manner provided by this Act.

'GCR thus became LNER in 1923 then British Railways (BR) in 1965 until the gradual privatisation of BR, in stages between 1994 and 1997. Today the two franchises which operate railways in the area of this book are the North Wales Coast Line and the Borderlands Line at present operated by Transport for Wales on behalf of the Welsh Government.

As a Geographer it seems appropriate to illustrate some of the above potted history in two maps:

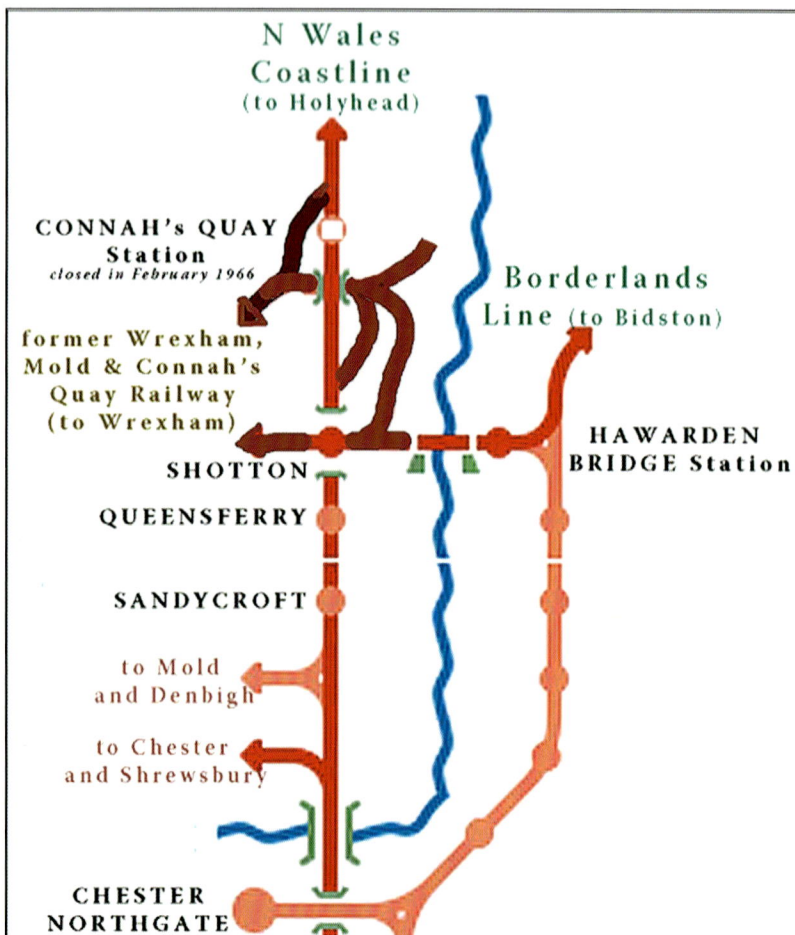

Left: **Fig 04**: (edited from Transport for Wales summary route map). WM&CQR enters from the left-hand side of the N Wales Coastline Railway and joins it North of the site of Connah's Quay Station opened by the L&NWR on 01st September 1870. Shotton Station was opened on 1 October 1891 by the WM&CQR as Connah's Quay & Shotton and became Shotton High Level. Here was an end-on junction with the MS&LR's line from Chester Northgate via Hawarden Bridge. (*Author*)

Opposite: **Fig 05**: Another summary map and a suitable conclusion for Chapter 1 because it illustrates the reasons why the WM&CQR was built and why it offered great minerals potential to LNWR and GCR – who failed to secure it – and GCR/L&NER which owned it from 1904 to 1923. (*Author*)

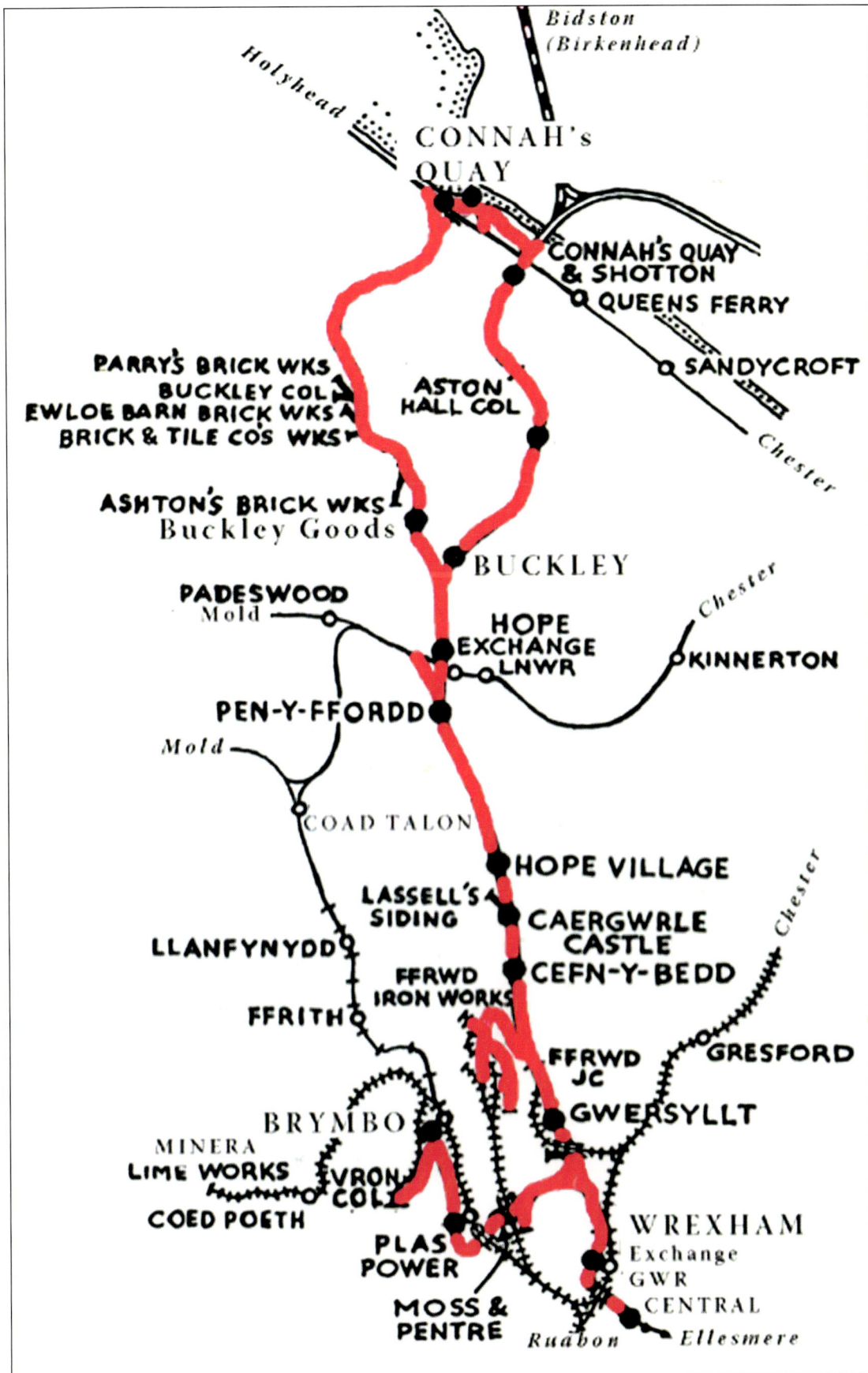

Bidston
(Birkenhead)

Holyhead

CONNAH's
QUAY

CONNAH'S QUAY
& SHOTTON

QUEENS FERRY

SANDYCROFT

Chester

PARRY'S BRICK WKS
BUCKLEY COL
EWLOE BARN BRICK WKS
BRICK & TILE CO'S WKS

ASTON
HALL COL

ASHTON'S BRICK WKS
Buckley Goods

BUCKLEY

PADESWOOD
Mold

Chester

HOPE
EXCHANGE
LNWR

KINNERTON

PEN-Y-FFORDD

Mold

COAD TALON

HOPE VILLAGE

LASSELL'S
SIDING

CAERGWRLE
CASTLE

Chester

LLANFYNYDD

CEFN-Y-BEDD

FFRWD
IRON WORKS

FFRITH

FFRWD
JC

GRESFORD

BRYMBO

GWERSYLLT

MINERA
LIME WORKS

VRON
COL

COED POETH

WREXHAM
Exchange
GWR

PLAS
POWER

CENTRAL

MOSS &
PENTRE

Ruabon

Ellesmere

CHAPTER 2

EXPLORATION

Railways and industries explored in this book

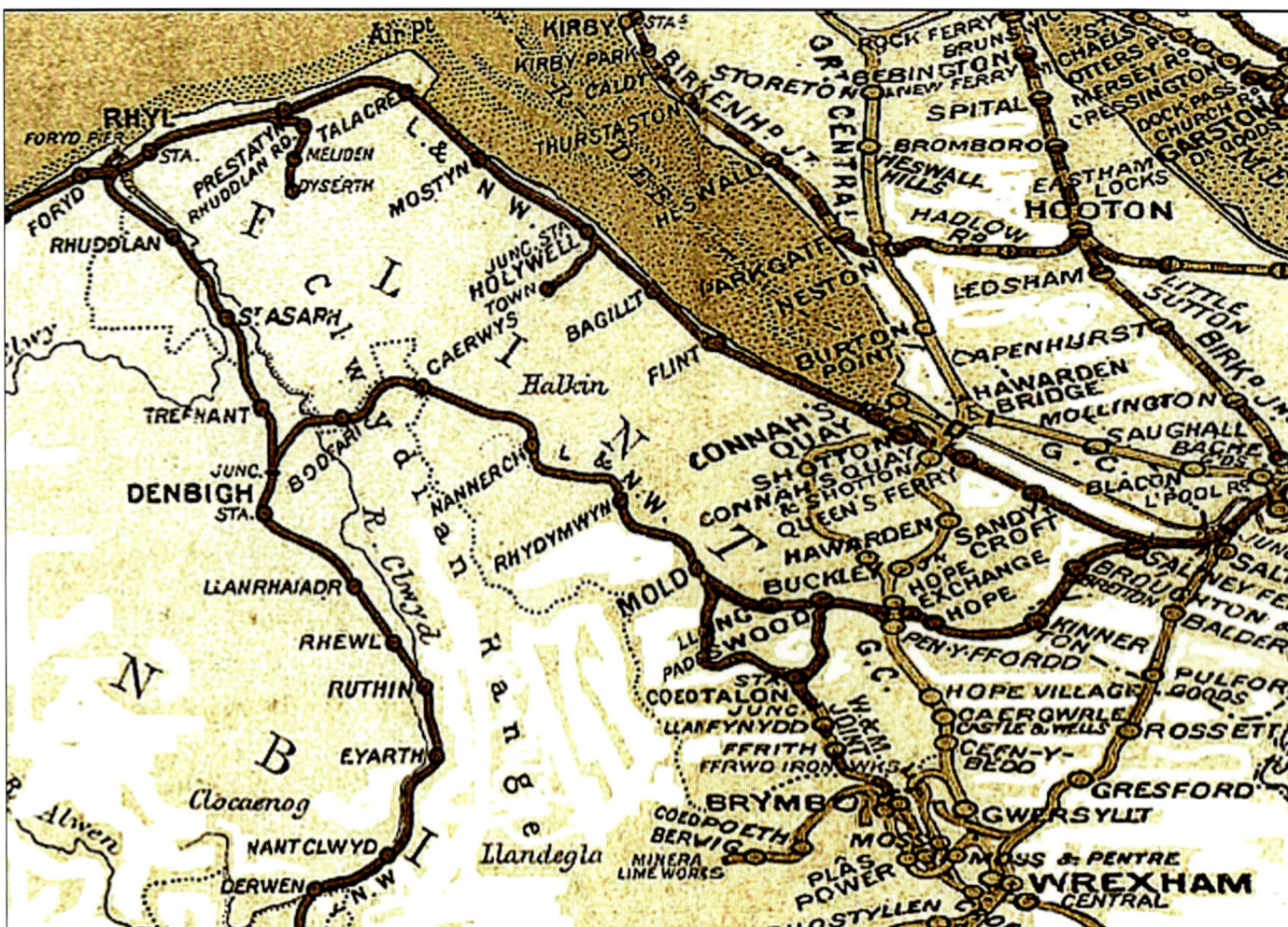

Fig 06: From Railway Clearing House Official Railway Map of England & Wales 1921. (*Author*)

The principal railways on this map in Flintshire, Wrexham and the Deeside area are London & North Western Railway (L&NWR); Great Central Railway (GCR); Wrexham & Minera Joint Railway (W&MJoint) which, by the date of the RCH map, was operated by the L&NWR and the Great Western Railway (GWR). Perhaps the most telling feature of this map is the tangle of railways around Brymbo and Moss to the West of Wrexham.

Fig 02 (page 8) shows the topography of the area and the South-East - North West trending of the Halkyn Mountains and the Clwydian Range, parallel to the shores of the Dee Estuary. The highlands are where most of the industrial minerals were found and where water power was available.

The area was rich in minerals including:

- brick clay
- firebrick clay
- pottery clay
- sandstone – crushed for sand and gravel

- sandstone blocks for building
- limestone
- lead and zinc
- iron ore
- coal

Industries included quarrying, iron smelting, steel making, lead smelting, potteries and terra-cotta works, brickworks for building bricks and fire-bricks for furnace and kiln lining. The industries needed railways for transport and that 'need' encouraged rich railway companies to develop in this area.

Right: **Fig 07**: Sketch map showing Carboniferous limestone – in solid colour – and the Flintshire extent of the NE Wales coalfield – oblique shaded. The coalfield was extensively worked in the nineteenth and twentieth centuries, for industries which developed in this area and for export. The coalfield extended eastwards into England where there were more deep-shaft collieries.

Below: **Fig 08**: Rail connection to Bersham Colliery near Rhostyllen (just visible on Fig 06), Wrexham, opened in 1864 and closed in 1986. Steam engine near entrance is Peckett 0-4-0ST Hornet.

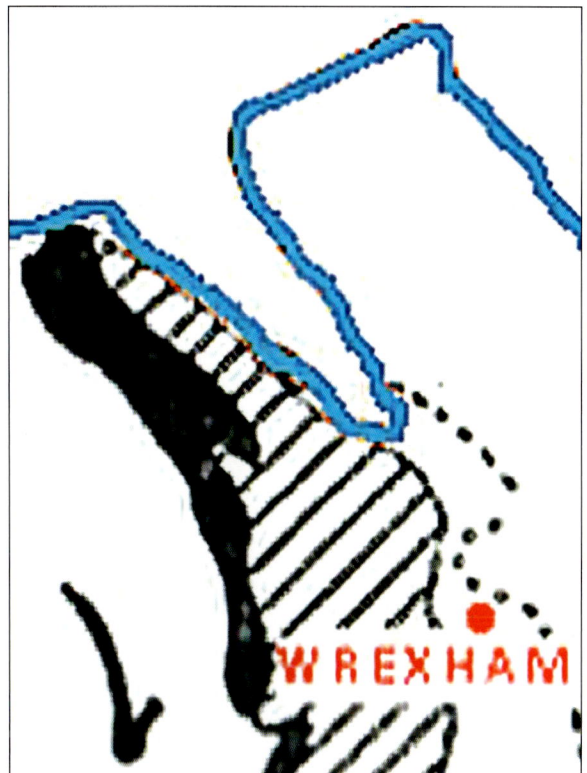

CHAPTER 3

PONKEY

A guide to hidden places

I have explained in some of my earlier books that I like to give a context for the railway, industrial and social history stories I tell. I am sure that I came across the intriguing word 'ponkey' in the first edition of Arthur Ransome's story *We Didn't Mean to Go to Sea* (Jonathan Cape 1937). I seem to remember 'Captain' John explaining various maritime terms to the other children on their boat *Goblin* and that he said a ponkey could help sailors find things.

As a reader you might well be asking, 'What has this to do with the subject of this book?' A very reasonable question because, for me as I was planning the book, ponkey was simply one of those unusual words that linger in my mind. However, research may often wander away from the core subject and a Google search may lead in an unexpected direction. So a search for 'Ponkey' led me to 'Ponciau':

'The Welsh word *ponc*, plural *ponciau*, means "bank" or "hillock", and the village [of Ponkey] probably takes its name from the large number of spoil tips [from collieries and quarries] which formerly covered the area. The village name was spelt using the form "Ponkey" until 1932, when the villagers convened a meeting to petition for its change to Ponciau, feeling the earlier spelling was ugly and did not reflect Welsh language phonetics. While this was based on a belief that "Ponkey" was an anglicised spelling, it in fact probably reflected a local pronunciation of the word in the dialect of Denbighshire, where the word ending *-au* was pronounced *-e* or *-ey*'.

So, to my surprise, my ponkey search had led me to NE Wales and a longer browse through a Google search for 'Ponkey' found a Patent Specification – **Fig 09**:

N° 7329   A.D. 1902

Date of Application, 26th Mar., 1902
Complete Specification Left, 9th June, 1902—Accepted, 31st July, 1902

PROVISIONAL SPECIFICATION.

" Floating Signal to Discover Sunken Ships ".

I, JOHN DAVID JONES, of 92, Johnson Street, Ponkey, Ruabon, North Wales, late Steward aboard ship, do hereby declare the nature of this invention to be as follows :—

5   According to my invention I provide a float or buoy which is normally carried in a loop or cradle supported by stays attached to the funnels of the vessel in such a manner that while it cannot drop down from the cradle it is free to rise therefrom.

Attached to bottom of the float is a wire or other line the other end of which is fastened to a drum. This line is of sufficient length to reach from the surface 10 of the sea to the bottom thereof and it is normally coiled up on the drum. The spindle of the drum is preferably supported on ball bearings. The mode of action is as follows.

If a vessel sinks the buoyancy of the float causes the latter to rise to the surface of the water where it remains anchored to the vessel by means of the 15 line above mentioned, and thus forms a ready guide or signal to locate the position of the sunken ship.

The float may carry a flag or other object easily distinguishable from a distance. The name of the vessel is preferably displayed on the float.

Dated this 30th day of April 1902,

20

CHAS. COVENTRY, C.E.
Patent Expert,
Agent for the Applicant.

Left: **Fig 09**: Provisional Patent Specification No 7329 AD 1902 for a Ponkey – "Floating Signal to Discover Sunken Ships".

Opposite: **Fig 10**: Diagram from the Ponkey Patent Specification.

I was doubly pleased because the Patent Specification included the name of the inventor, David Jones, who lived in Ponkey – which I now knew from my Google searches was correctly so-named in 1902 – and David Jones had a maritime background which might have linked him with Connah's Quay.

So Captain John was correct that a 'ponkey' was a device to help people find things. If we suppose that the burgee in **Fig 10** might carry the name Ponkey then I can justify it here because I have been finding things for my story of railways and industries in NE Wales and Deeside. And here is one such 'find.'

The standard gauge Wrexham Mold & Connah's Quay Railway runs south to north across the map in **Fig 11** and Buckley Station is labelled. From Lane End Brickworks a narrow gauge tramway – Hancock's Tramway – is shown crossing the WM&CQR south of Buckley Station and thence to the River Dee at Aston Quay. Exchange sidings allowed narrow gauge traffic to be transferred to the standard gauge. WM&CQR.

The Buckley Railway was opened in 1860 and the WM&CQ Railway in 1866 but Hancock's Tramway, initially and generally referred to as the Aston Tramroad, dates from c1799. As **Fig 11** shows, the Tramway was initially left in place across the standard gauge Buckley Railway and was used by Hancock's Brickworks but by 1870 the Tramroad had become disused and the exchange sidings were developed by Hancock and shown on the **Fig 11** OS 6in map extract.

Tramway wagons – shipping boxes – were horse-drawn from the Brickworks to the exchange sidings. On the WM&CQ standard-gauge railway shipping wagons (see **Fig 13**) were loaded from the exchange sidings with up to 6 shipping boxes for export. The facility was doubly useful because the shipping boxes could also be used to import coal to fuel the Brickworks.

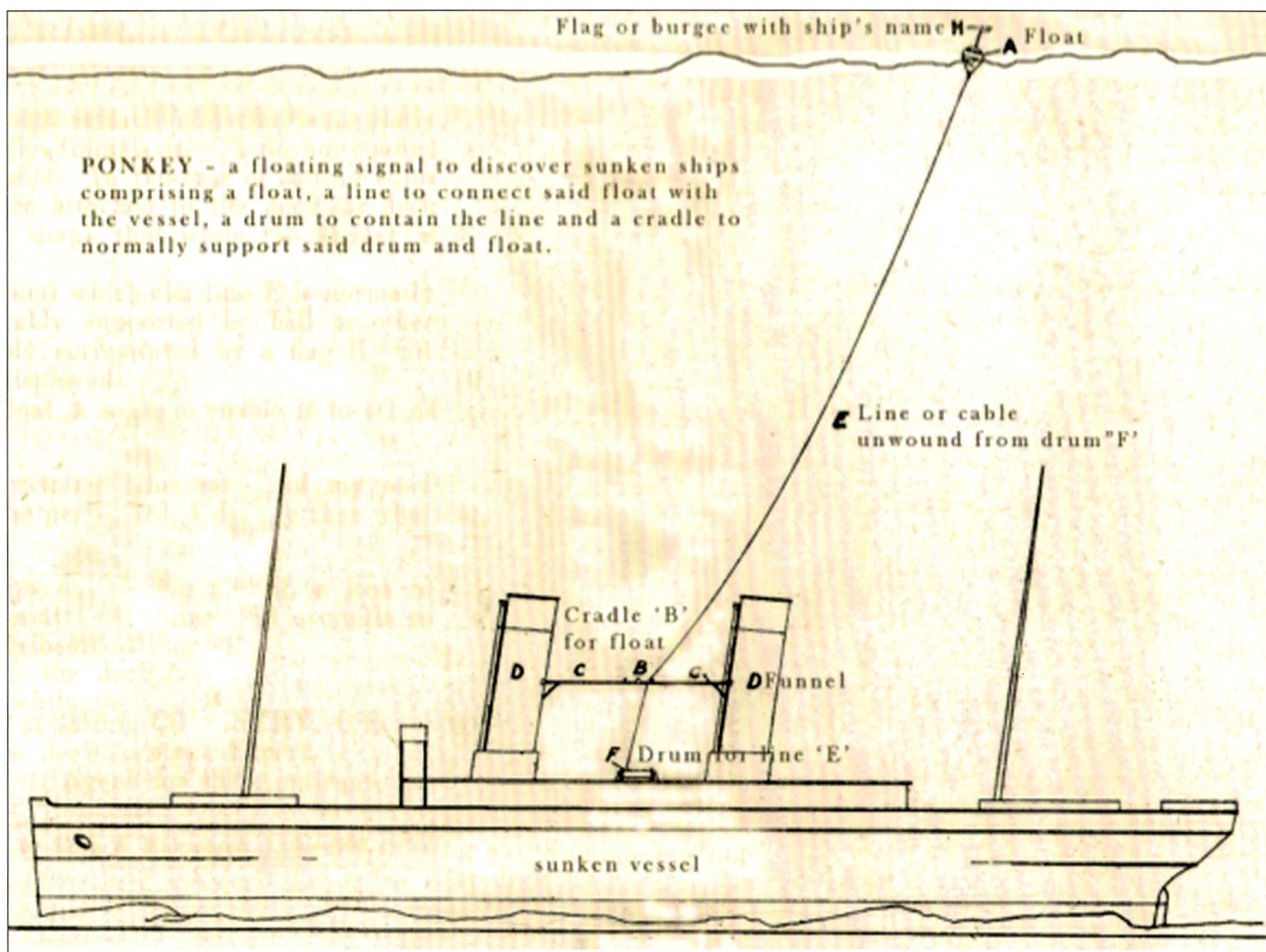

Flag or burgee with ship's name **H** · **A** Float

PONKEY – a floating signal to discover sunken ships comprising a float, a line to connect said float with the vessel, a drum to contain the line and a cradle to normally support said drum and float.

E Line or cable unwound from drum "F"

Cradle 'B' for float

D **C** **B** **C** **D** Funnel

F Drum for line 'E'

sunken vessel

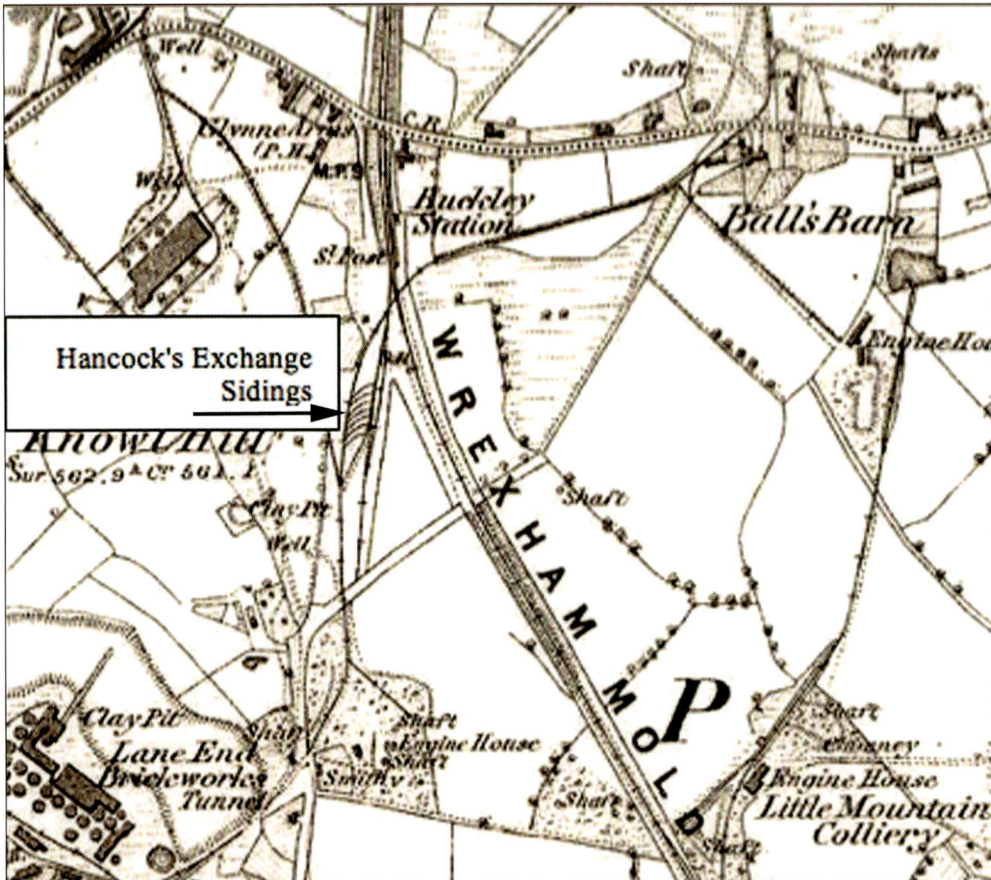

Fig 11: Extract from 1st edition 6in OS © map of 1869 (published 1871). Hancock's Exchange sidings.

Fig 12: Buckley Station was the passenger terminus for the Buckley Railway so the tracks onward to Connah's Quay were goods only. The sidings off to the right are where the narrow gauge Hancock's Tramway goods traffic was exchanged to the standard gauge WM&CQ railway. The photographer is looking towards Connah's Quay.

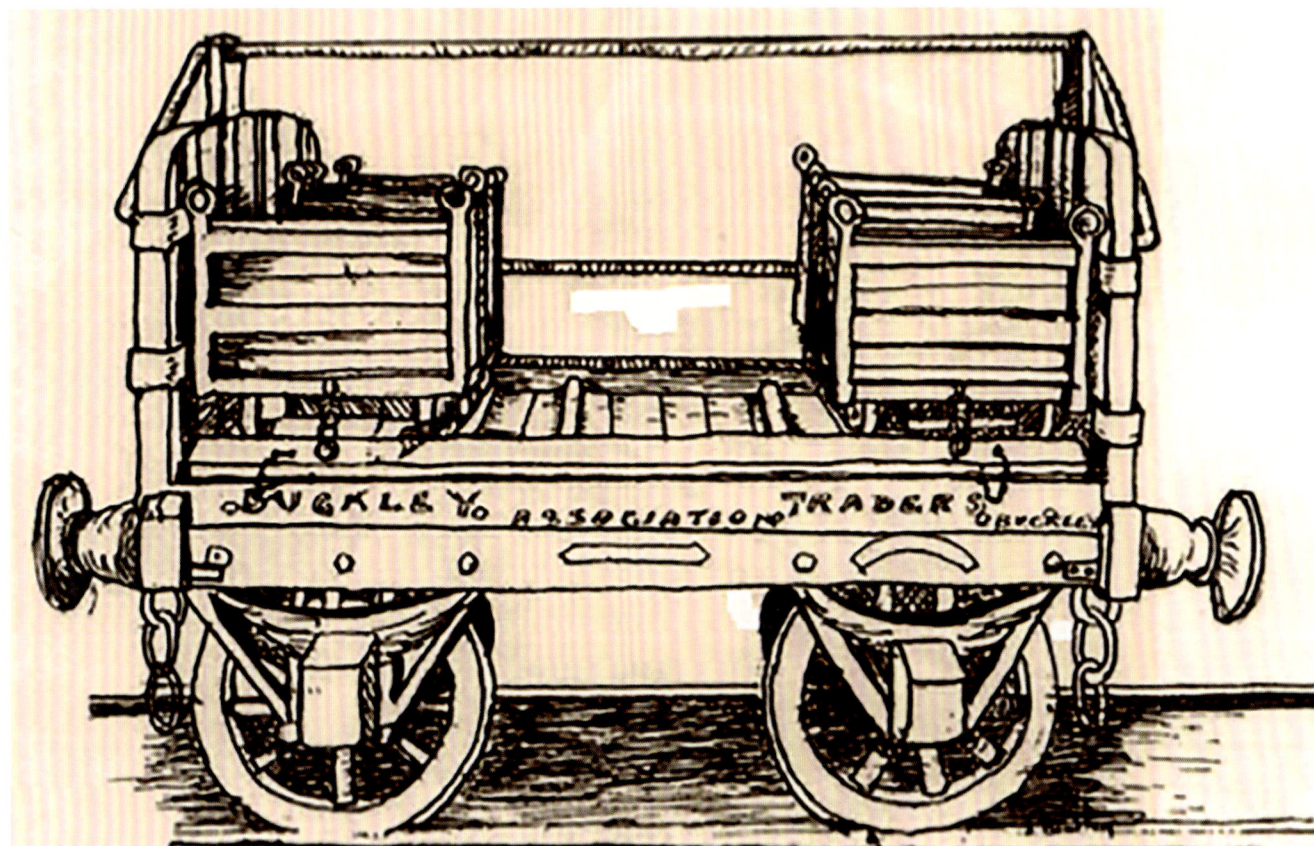

Above: **Fig 13**: Buckley Railway standard gauge shipping wagon designed for 6 shipping boxes. (*Drawn by J. Bentley and courtesy of Buckley Society, Clwyd-Powys Archaeological Trust & CADW*)

Right: **Fig 14**: Sketch map (not to scale) showing the collieries and other industries in and around Ponkey. (*Author*)

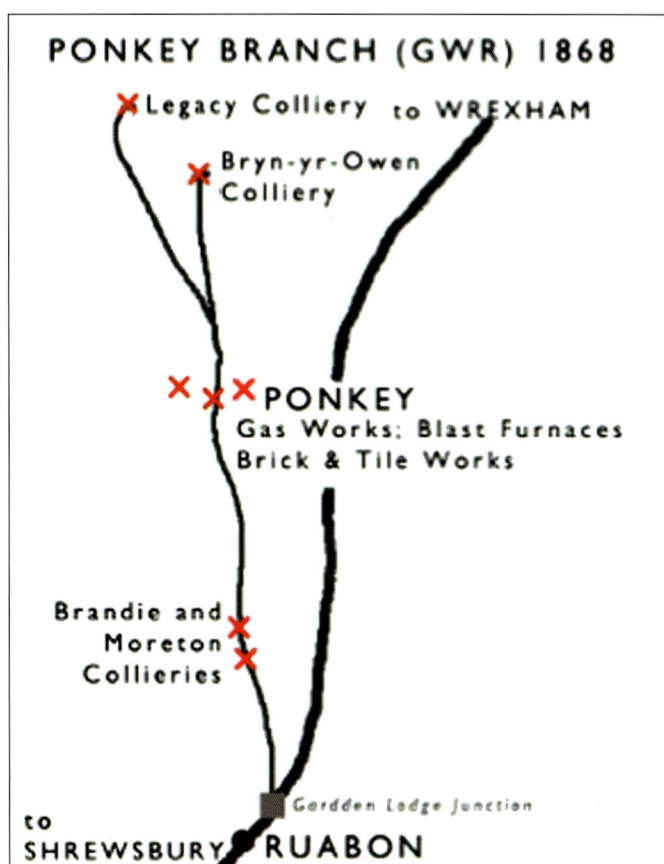

Another Ponkey 'find' and another railway, is the Ponkey Branch opened by the GWR in 1868 off the Shrewsbury-Wrexham railway from Gardden Lodge Junction north of Ruabon to serve the industries in and around Ponkey village.

The industries shown in **Fig 14** are a pertinent segue into Chapter 4 and introduces the interest shown by several railway companies to expand into NE Wales and Deeside.

By 1868 and the building of the Ponkey Branch, tramways and railways were beginning to supersede canal development in this area to provide faster services. The topography, illustrated in **Fig 02**, is not easy for canal-building and a piece of epic canal engineering is Pontcysyllte Aqueduct which carries the Llangollen Canal across the River Dee in the Vale of Llangollen. It is an 18-arch stone and cast iron structure, completed in

Fig 15: Railway viaduct parallel to canal aqueduct across the River Ceiriog valley, Chirk.

1805 after ten years of designing by Thomas Telford and building by William Jessop.

Even more pertinent is the canal and railway developments at Chirk. The Llangollen Canal crosses the River Ceiriog, tributary of the River Dee, in an aqueduct similar to but smaller than Pontcysyllte and parallel to a viaduct supporting the GWR Shrewsbury to Chester railway.

CHAPTER 4

INDUSTRIAL RESOURCES

Limestone, Lead, Coal, Iron Ore, Brick and Pottery Clays

Limestone

Limestone consumption in the 1980s at one industrial site included in this book illustrates the size and scale of the industries which have developed in NE Wales and Deeside – and why tramways and railways were needed to move the raw materials from quarries and mines to manufacturing sites.

John Summers & Sons Ltd developed Shotton Steel works – described in Chapter 7 – and here is the average weekly consumption in the 1980s of limestone flux for blast furnaces and open hearth furnaces:

Blast Furnaces: 1,400 to 1,700 tons
Open Hearth Furnaces: 1,900 to 2,100 tons
so up to **3,800 tons per week** from sources in the 1980s in N Wales and Derbyshire.

Fig 07 (page 13) shows the extensive outcrop of Carboniferous Limestone in the area and it was quarried in the North near Dyserth, which had its own railway branch line and at Minera which was even larger and also rail connected (see **Fig 16**):

The Minera area has been important since Roman times for burning limestone to make mortar, cement, fertiliser, dressed rock carved to order and building stones. The earliest kilns were fired with wood, but it was an obvious advantage if a ready supply of coal was obtainable in the vicinity. Minera, Coedpoeth, Brymbo and the coalmines of the Wrexham area were ideally located both geographically and geologically. When the kiln was burning, limestone and coal were fed in alternately, and the lime and ashes drawn off at the bottom. The kiln could then work continuously for weeks on end.

As lime came into greater demand in agriculture, iron-making in blast furnaces and in the chemical industry, new and larger capacity batteries of kilns were devised and set up in connection with limestone quarries like Minera and Dyserth towards the end of the nineteenth century.

Fig 16: The extensive limestone quarries, lime kilns and brick works at Minera c1905.

Fig 17: The first standard gauge shunting tank engine purchased for work at the Minera Quarry. Built in 1868 by Beyer Peacock (Manchester), noted for their larger locomotives but their high engineering reputation was sustained and enhanced by some smaller locomotives like *Minera*.

W. L. HOBBS [Dyserth] Ltd.

LIMESTONE QUARRIES AND

LIME WORKS

The biggest employers in the district are the W. L. Hobbs (Dyserth) Ltd., Limestone Quarries and Lime Works, who provide employment for 50 persons. The quarries have been in existence for many centuries. Modern kilns and machinery have replaced stone kilns but the ruins of three are still to be seen. Thousands of tons of lime are transported yearly to Steel Works in both Lancashire and Flintshire and also to the Chemical Works of Monsanto at Ruabon and to Petrochemical at Carrington. The limestone is considered of high quality for such purposes as well as for road metal, and for use in the making of cement and for concrete work such as that used in connection with dock development in the Liverpool area

Fig 18: Part of advertisement for W.L. Hobbs' Dyserth Quarry. (*Author*)

The Minera quarries had their own internal 2ft gauge railway system with horse-haulage and gravity inclines which continued in use until 1954 when the 2ft gauge system was supplanted by road haulage. Standard gauge reached the quarry in 1847 via the North Wales Mineral Railway Company which opened to Minera for freight in 1847. There were extensive standard gauge sidings at the quarry. The Minera Lime Company had its own locomotives for shunting the sidings; at first a Beyer Peacock 0-4OST of 1868, *Minera*, which continued in use until 1910. Then a new Beyer Peacock 0-4-OST, *Olwen*, was delivered and in 1949 was registered by BR-WR No 278 because it worked over the 'main line' as well as in the quarry; *Olwen* was scrapped in 1964. In 1942, Hunslet Engine Company 0-4-OST *Swansea*, was bought from Wrexham dealers Cudworth & Johnson and survived at the Quarry until scrapping in 1971.

Dyserth Quarry The main Dyserth quarry opened in the nineteenth century and was first owned by W.L. Hobbs and supplied limestone to Mostyn Ironworks, Shotton Steel works and lime in various forms for the chemical industry, agriculture and as limewash for buildings.

As at Minera, transport in the quarry was by 2ft 7ins narrow gauge tracks, at first horse-powered and then tractor-powered.

The L&NWR mineral branch from Prestatyn to Dyserth opened in 1869 but the spur (shown on OS map in **Fig 19**) was not opened to make a quarry connection until 1885.

Fig 19 OS map shows the quarry served by a short, sharply curved spur which was opened in February 1885. The problem was to get the stone from the quarry to the railway; the quarry narrow-gauge system took trucks to the head of an incline down to the standard gauge siding. The incline was counter-balanced so full trucks down pulled up the empties.

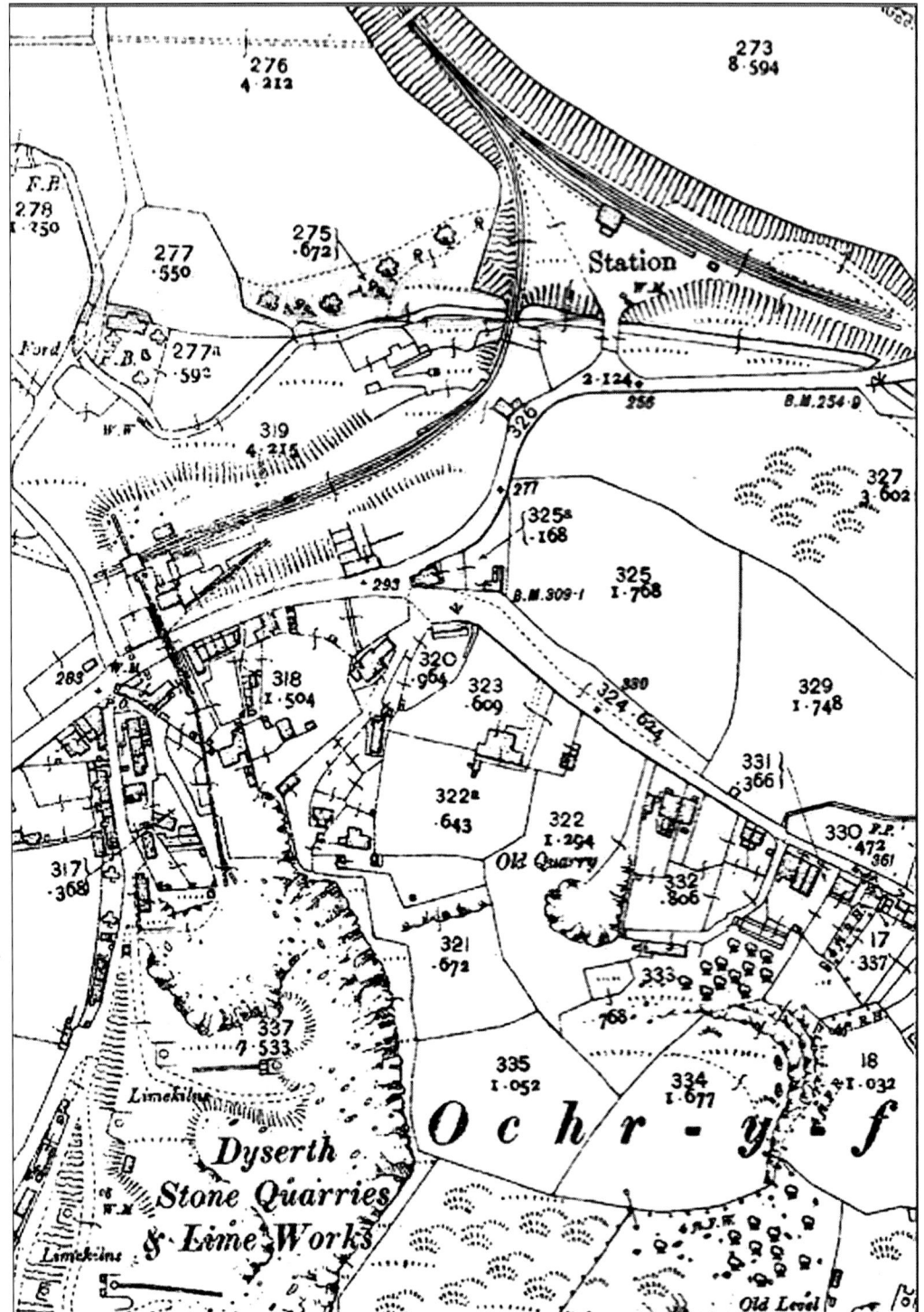

Fig 19: Extract from OS map (reduced from 1:2,500 Dyserth & Meliden 1910) illustrating the problems with loading limestone traffic from the Quarry's narrow gauge railway system and counter-balanced incline to the standard gauge spur north of Dyserth Station.

Fig 20: Main picture: Stanier 2-6-0 'Black 5' 45156 Ayrshire Yeomanry easing empty trucks round the sharp curve of the Quarry spur at Dyserth almost to the loco's limit of shunt.

Inset: loaded trucks shunted to form a train to Prestatyn. September 1963.

Fig 21: Meliden Road bridge in 2019 looking south towards Dyserth; note the sturdy structure of the bridge and the steep gradient. (*Author*)

The standard gauge spur had operating problems for larger locomotives because of the sharp curve and the bridge over the Afon Ffyddion which could not take the weight of a locomotive. So a number of empty wagons were pushed over the bridge, loaded in sidings there and then pulled back to Dyserth Station yard, coupled to a brake van and taken down the branch to the main-line Chester-Holyhead line at Prestatyn.

The quarry closed in the 1980s and the inhabitants of Dyserth were relieved that the frequent blasting at the Quarry would no longer be a problem. On 17 February 1972, Sir Anthony Meyer (MP for Flint, West) said in Parliament:

'Last Friday a shattering explosion at the [Dyserth] limestone quarry . . . sent huge boulders crashing through roofs and windows in the village. 3 schoolchildren were injured in their classroom and a number of cars were totally destroyed; It was a miracle that no one was killed. The people of Dyserth are demanding that no further blasting be allowed at this quarry.'

The whole story of the Prestatyn to Dyserth branch is in Chapter 6.

Lead

Lead has been worked in the area of this book from Roman times to the early twentieth century and, as **Fig 22** demonstrates, was mined and smelted at Minera. By the eighteenth century some rich lead ores were making rich financial gains for several mine owners in and around Minera. This success attracted other speculators until much of the Minera area was being worked by a number of small companies. As the workings deepened, many lead mines had serious problems of flooding. Eventually mine owners co-operated to fund a drainage level and, by the mid-nineteenth century, a railway – **Fig 23** and **Fig 24**.

The railway, described in Chapter 6, was initially a GWR mineral line and extended through Minera Goods Station to the extensive Minera Limestone Quarry. From the Goods Station (see **Fig 23**) the standard gauge New Brighton branch, a private railway not operated by GWR, was opened in 1851 on the west side of the river valley to serve a number of 'mountain' mines to Meadows Shaft (No 12) and finally to the New Minera mine (No 23). Loaded trains, drawn by private quarry locomotives, travelling from these mines, ran to Minera Goods Station then reversed to go onto the line to Wrexham with GWR motive power. In 1919, the New Minera lead mine

Fig 22: Underside of a Minera lead ingot mould. (*Author*)

Lime Works

1. South Minera
2. Sychnant
3. Park
4. Ellerton (810')
5. Andrews (600')
6. Lloyds (660')
7. Speedwell (660')
8. Taylors (810')
9. Roys (945')
10. Oldfields
11. Owen Jones
12. Meadow (1380')
13. Reads (750')
14. Royles (450')
15. Grand Turk (390')
16. Busy Bee (300')
17. Boundary (300')
18. Davies (180')
19. Morgan
20. Cornish
21. Maesyffynnon (480')
22. Eisteddfod
23. New Minera (1050')

Road
Footpath
River
Lead Mine Shaft
Level
Church

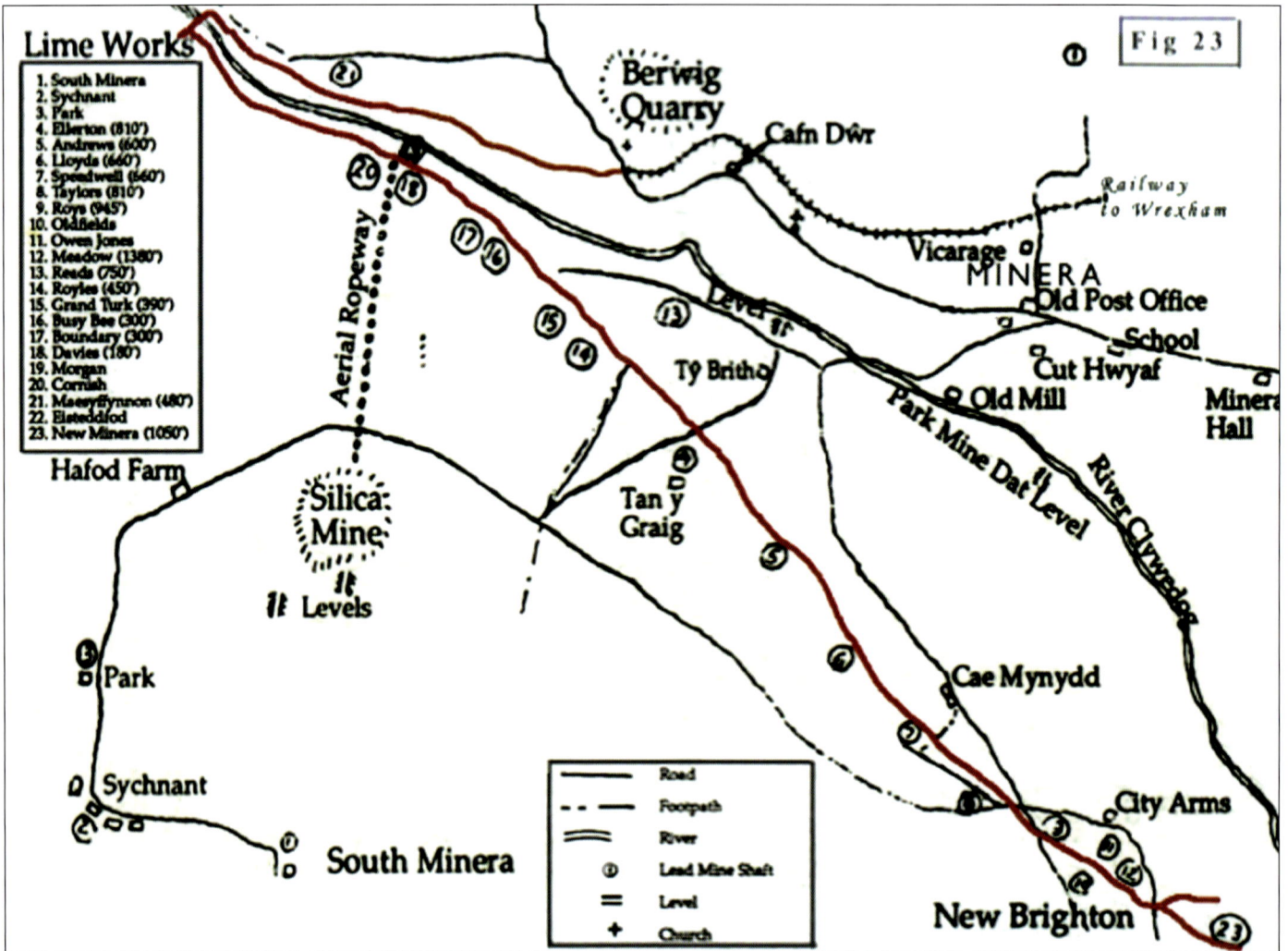

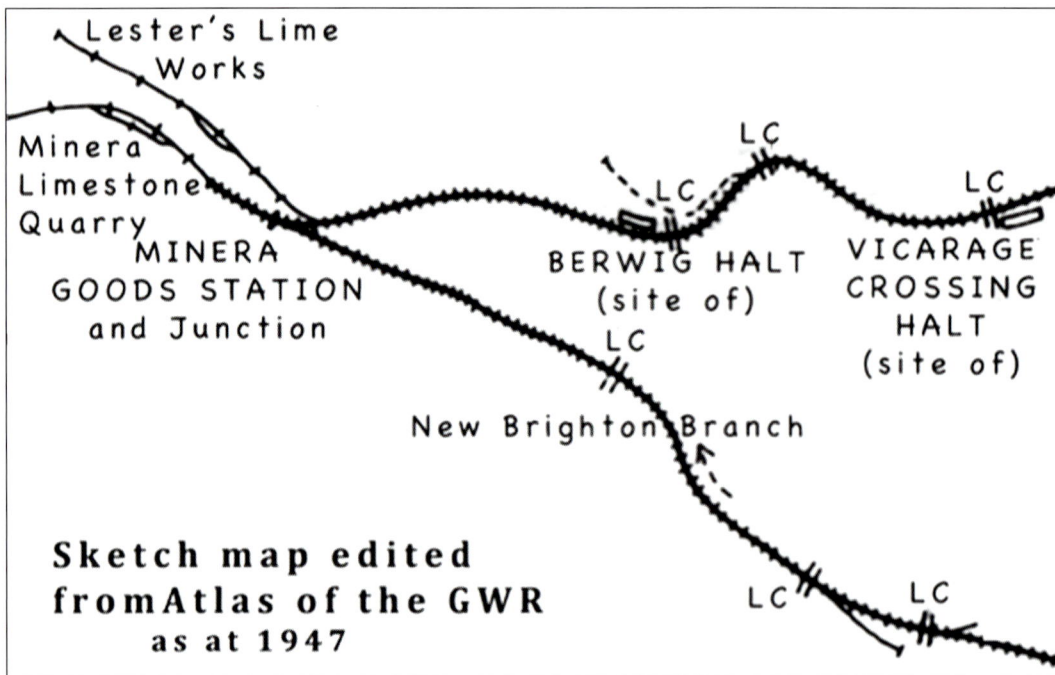

Above: **Fig 23**: Lead mines and railways in the Minera area. (*Edited from 1907 plans courtesy of Glyn Davies 1964 et seq*)

Left: **Fig 24**: Sketch map edited from Atlas of the GWR as at 1947. (*Author*)

Lester's Lime Works

Minera Limestone Quarry

MINERA GOODS STATION and Junction

BERWIG HALT (site of)

VICARAGE CROSSING HALT (site of)

New Brighton Branch

Sketch map edited from Atlas of the GWR as at 1947

Fig 25: Minera Goods Station & Junction looking towards Wrexham; the New Brighton Branch curves in from the right. The passenger train is an SLS Wrexham & District Rail Tour in 1959. (*Author*)

(at New Brighton) closed and the branch that served it was lifted. In the 1920s, part of the New Brighton branch was re-laid to serve newly opened silica clay beds (see **Fig 24**) and remained in use for several more years.

Coal

'Five to seven, Grandpa; there goes the train. And look, the wheels at the pit are going round.'

'Aye Daffyd, it's always the same, every morning. And if the wheels at the pit didn't go round, the five to seven train wouldn't run either.'

'Why not, Grandpa? '

'Because the men going down the pit are getting coal, and the steam winding engine that shows the wheels are going round needs coal to make steam in the pit boilers. And that steam train couldn't run if they had no coal for the loco fire. And we'd have no fire here to warm the house in winter. And no electricity from the steam-powered generating station. 'Coal is the King!''

'Oh yes, I understand. You used to work down the pit, didn't you? What was it like, working over there, underground?'

'Oh boyo, it's better now than when I started; they've made it quite a bit easier with all this machinery they're using, though it's still a man's job down there.'

The N Wales Coalfield (shown in the **Fig 07** sketch map) is 45 miles long, but the exposed field is less than 10 miles wide as illustrated on **Fig 27** and stretches from Point of Ayr Colliery (closed 1996) in the north to pits near Oswestry in Shropshire in the south.

Wrexham was well placed as an industrial and railway centre and much of the network I have later

Fig 26: Grandpa remembers his coal field in 1945.

described as 'Wrexham Railways' embraces Brymbo and Minera where there were a number of early coal mines. Later, deeper mines close to Wrexham were exploiting the concealed coalfield and as early as 1929; Llay Main had an output of 1,057, 592 tons. Gresford Colliery, working the same rich seams as Llay Main is

Left: **Fig 27**: North Wales coalfield, centred around Wrexham. (*Author*)

Below: **Fig 28**: A typical deep shaft colliery, like Llay Main and Gresford. (*Author*)

especially remembered because in 1934, underground explosions there killed 266 miners . At the time it was the worst British coal mining disaster since Sengenydd in S Wales in 1913 when 490 men died. At the Gresford Colliery site (the pit closed in 1973) many of the dead are still underground because, during the recovery of bodies, more explosions killed several rescuers.

While it flourished in the nineteenth and twentieth centuries, the North Wales coalfield was an important producer and exporter of steam, industrial and domestic coal. In the 1950s it was producing one per cent of UK coal and 60 per cent of that output was used in North

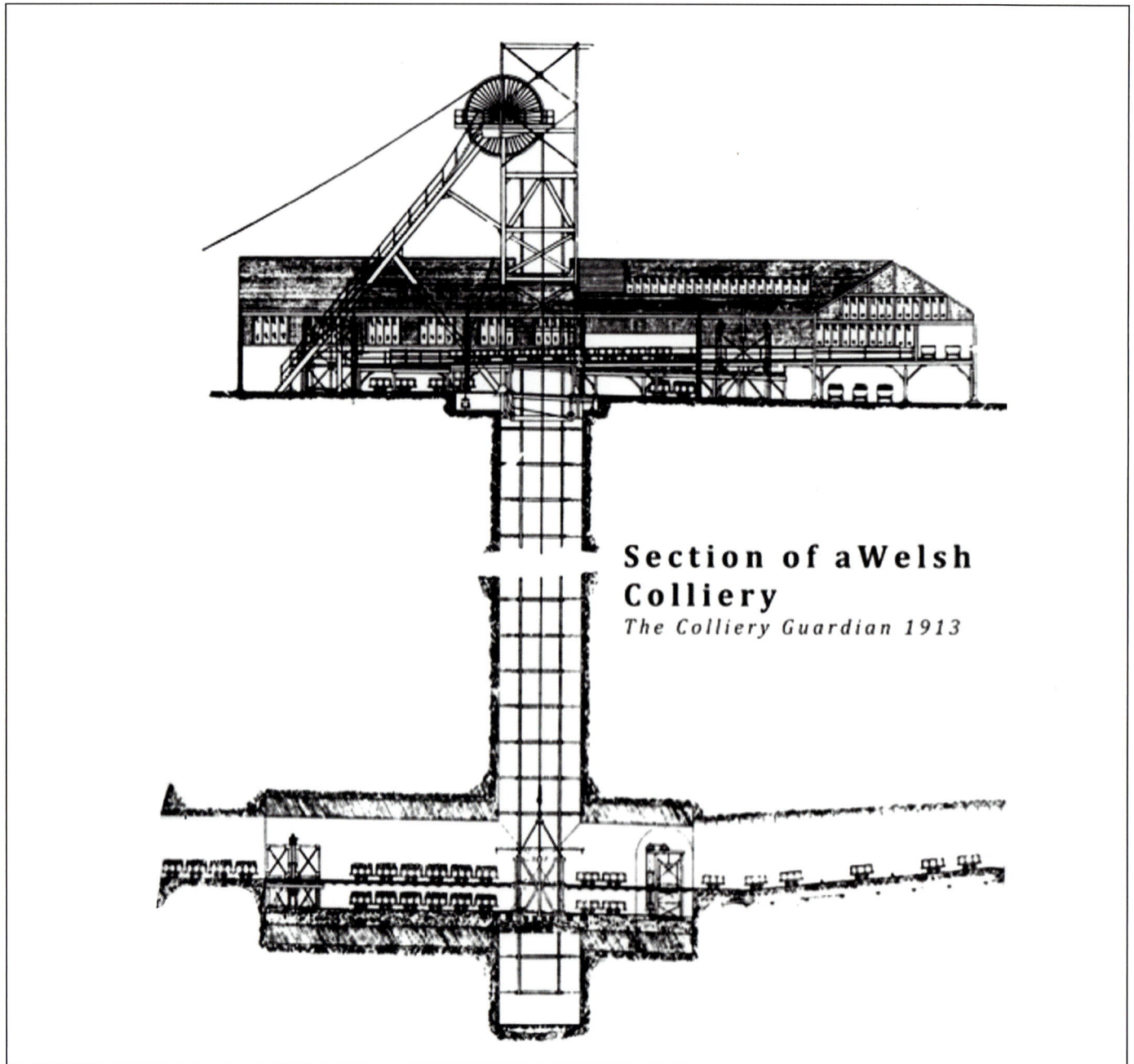

Section of a Welsh Colliery
The Colliery Guardian 1913

Wales with the rest going to Lancashire, Cheshire and Northern Ireland. The coal was used for: industry (including iron & steel making) 40 per cent; domestic consumption 20 per cent; gasworks 10 per cent; railways 8 per cent, others (including chemicals), 22 per cent. By 1978 there were only three pits left in North Wales – Point of Ayr, Bersham and Gresford – and now there are none. The decline of the coal industry has left a legacy of old workings, abandoned shafts, adits, and spoil heaps. Additionally, there are many disused and some extant workings for sand, gravel, iron ore and limestone.

An early the coal mine owner was John 'Iron Mad' Wilkinson who, although his life was before the 1847 railway developments, had works at Bersham and Brymbo and he has an important role in this story (see Chapters 5 and 7). He worked with his father, Isaac, at Bersham Ironworks and, in 1792, purchased the Brymbo Estate, around Brymbo Hall and founded Brymbo Ironworks, which continued as a steelworks late into the twentieth century. Wilkinson learned from his Bersham experience that a blast furnace could be fired with coke rather than charcoal and his extensive Brymbo Estate include coal and ironstone mines but, in the eighteenth and early nineteenth centuries, transport of these heavy minerals and of the iron castings from Brymbo and Bersham needed railways – as did the larger coal mines like Llay Main:

Fig 28 illustrates the railway needs for big collieries, on the surface and underground.

Ironstone/Iron Ore

The most significant mineral resources of this area now are limestone, sand, gravel, and coal. The first three are currently the basis of major extractive industries. Coal mining was formerly important, but no mining or open-casting is active now. There are also several lesser resources, including sandstone, metalliferous ores including iron ore, brick clay and refractory clay but only the clays are now worked.

I have headed this section 'Ironstone' because in the rest of the sections in this chapter are minerals which have been mined, or quarried, to serve various industrial processes. The OED definition of Ironstone is 'any of frequently hard rocks which contain a high proportion of iron minerals'. And Iron Ore is 'especially any iron-rich coarsely banded, or unbanded, sedimentary rock'.

The key importance of the ironstones which were mined in this area is the per cent of metallic iron which

Fig 29: Bodfari Iron Mine headgear. The timber headgear is powered by a horse whim and is a useful comparison with the deep-shaft colliery headgear in Fig 28.

can be economically extracted from them. In North Wales, magnetite and haematite ironstone occur and they may contain 60 per cent or more of metallic iron so are known as 'natural ore' or 'direct shipping ore' which means they can be fed directly into iron-making blast furnaces. Iron ore is the raw material used to make pig iron, tapped from a blast furnace, which is one of the main raw materials used to make steel.

Haematite of a generally earthy nature was mined at a number of localities in NE Wales, principally adjacent to the Vale of Clwyd, such as Cwm and other iron mines near Dyserth and the Bodfari Iron Mine to the northeast of Denbigh.

Ironstone also occurs in the coal measures when it is inter-bedded with shales. It is essentially a hard clay-rock yielding from 25 to 35 per cent of iron so not a 'direct shipping ore'. It may be almost black, due to the presence of much carbonaceous matter, so the ore can be roasted (as a preliminary to smelting) without the use of additional fuel. It is then called black-band ore.

Ironstone mining in areas with a low per cent of iron was often not commercial because the amount of debris was considerable. The workings had to be about 6ft in height but the two or three ironstone beds ranged from less than 2in to about 6in thick so were a small proportion of the material that had to be excavated so there was a considerable quantity to be brought to the surface. This amounted to as much as five or six trams of rubbish to one tram of ore but a number of small mines worked for twenty or thirty years.

Bodfari Iron Mine – active from 1887 to 1909.
The long-disused Bodfari haematite mine survives as two buildings but with all working evidence lost in the dense undergrowth and woodland surrounding them.

There is no surviving archaeological or archival evidence of the transport of ore, and mining debris from the mine. However, the village of Bodfari had a station on the Mold & Denbigh Junction Railway (L&NWR open from 1869 to1968). Bodfari Forge had a long history in the village and the forge was subsumed by the Manchester-based Partington Steel & Iron Company which had railway sidings built to serve it in 1924, so some industry persisted but it was no longer dependent on local iron ore or coal.

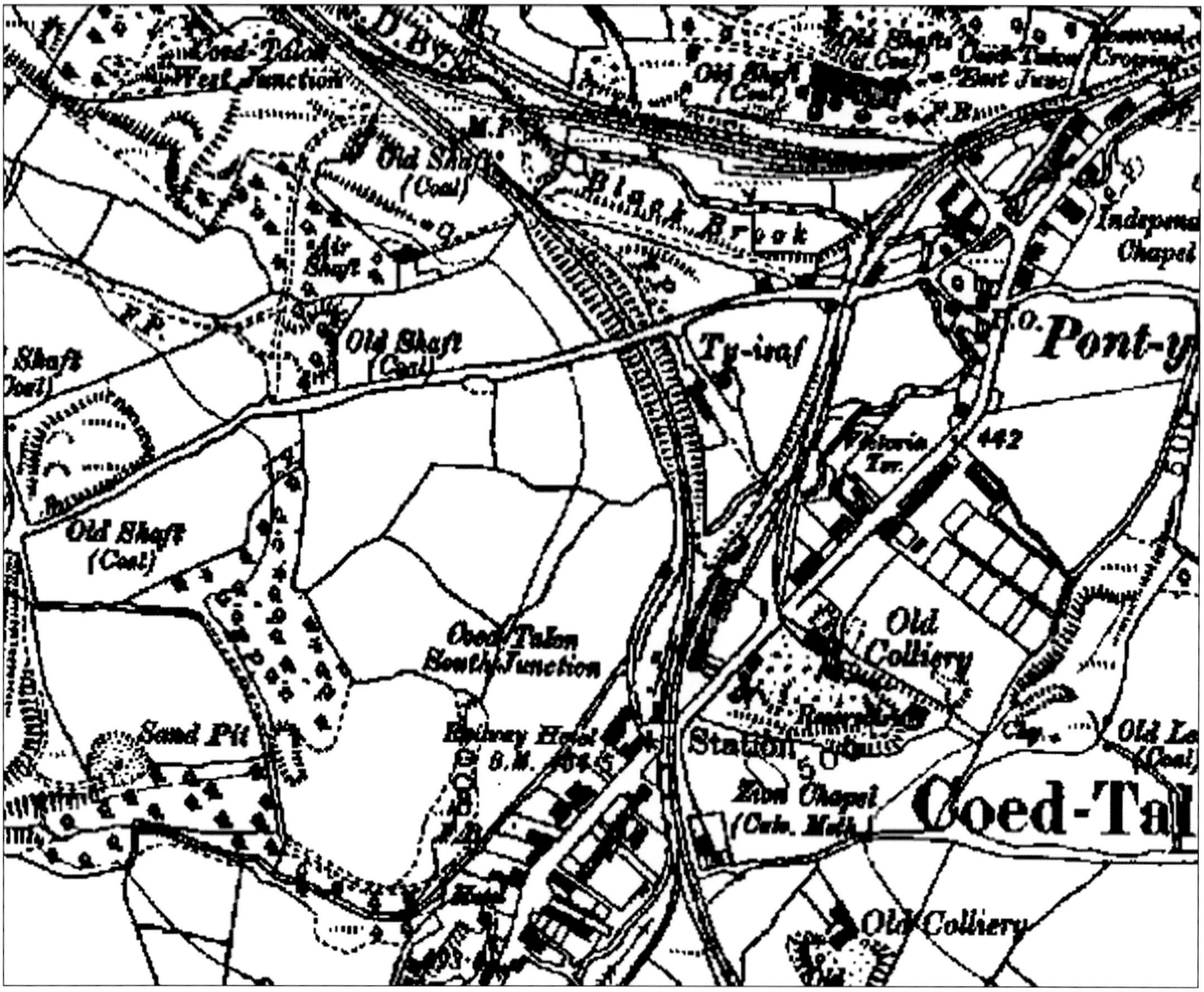

Fig 30: Extract from 6in scale OS © map, 1914. Note the number of 'Old Collieries' and 'Shafts' marked.

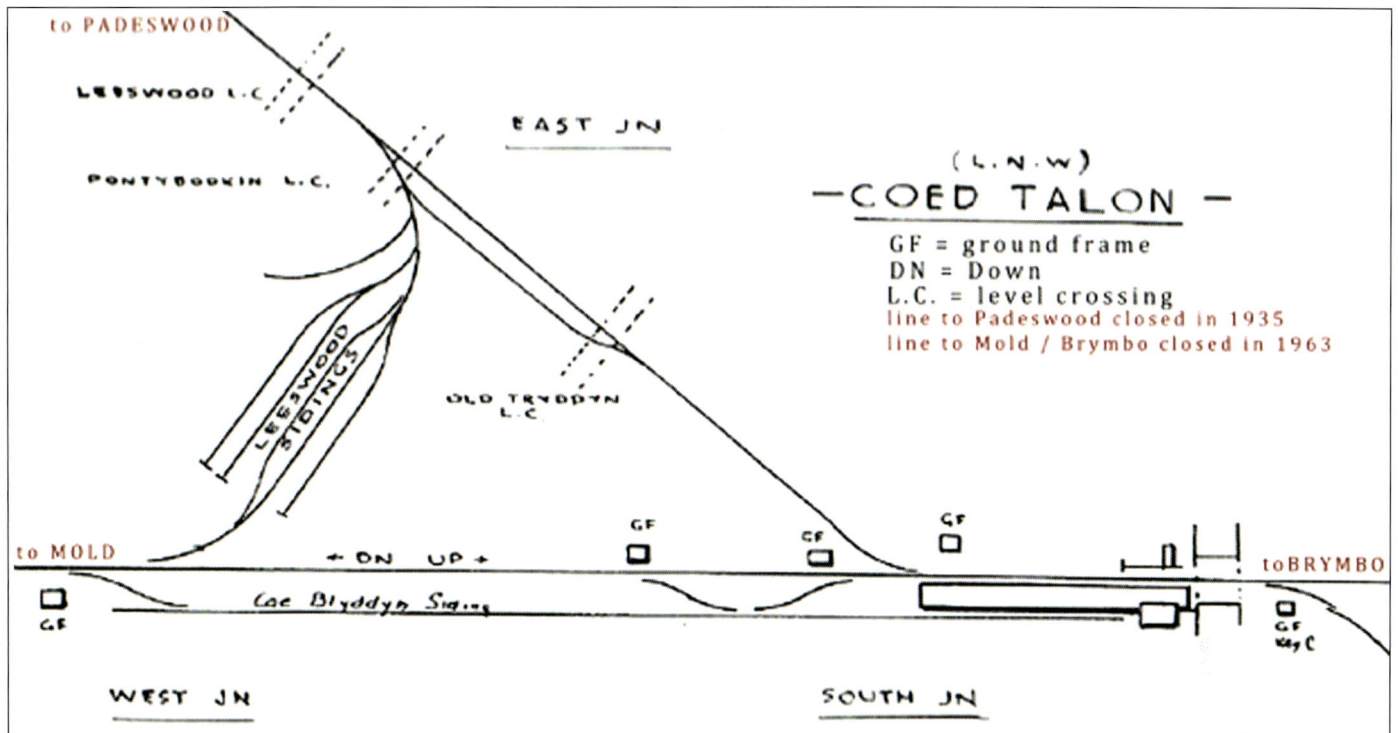

Fig 31: Coed Talon station – courtesy of the Signalling Record Society.

Coed Talon Iron Works The extract from a 6in scale OS map of 1914 (**Fig 30**) shows how a number of small coal mines, some producing black-band iron ore too, could support small works. The Iron Works at Coed Talon drew on local coal and a high-yield iron ore seam and, as the map shows, railway links.

Fig 31 is from a collection of Signalling Record Society signalling diagrams of locations on the former LMSR. in England and Wales. They were created and assembled by John Swift in the course of a railway career of nearly 50 years. He retired in 1982 as Head of Section (Operating and Signalling) in the Chief Operating Manager's Office at Crewe where he was responsible for preparing local and general operating instructions and for the approval of new works and alterations.

The diagrams are very much one man's working documents for use as aides-memoires at meetings about operating problems conducted away from the location. They are based on personal observations. In general, the drawings show the situation in the period about 1955-60 immediately before the many changes and track recoveries of the Beeching era. **Fig 31** shows Coed Talon in the 1930s; the number of sidings emphasises the amount of freight passing through which includes iron ore, coal and clay products. **Fig 32** 1914 OS 6in scale map extract provides evidence of the industries using clay products.

Fig 32 which shows the Erith and Alyn Brick, Tile & Terra Cotta Works is a pertinent segue into the final section of this Industrial Resources Chapter 4.

Fire Brick, Building Brick, Pottery and Terracotta Clay

'The growth of the clay and terracotta industries carried on at the great works [in this area] forms one of those romances of industrial enterprise which is yet, and ought, to be written.'

Anon *Wrexham Advertiser*.
25 June 1892

I found this quotation in the Preface of *Life in the Victorian Brickyards of Flintshire and Denbighshire*. (Andrew Connolly. Gwasg Carreg Gwalch, Llanwrst, Wales. 2003). My researches, like Andrew Connolly's, showed that 'no exploration of this subject has before been attempted'. Conolly's book list locates and illustrates nearly 130 works which 'functioned as commercial brick-making sites' in this area. Some of these works were part of collieries or ironworks and some were independent and run by companies.

Many of the sites, and particularly relevant to this book, had railway connections as illustrated north of Buckley in the 6" OS map extract, **Fig 33**.

It is always encouraging to my teacher-like mind to find that the story I am telling can loop round in virtuous circles of information; Buckley was one of the centres of the clay-based industries and the Buckley Railway was a fore-runner for the WM&CQR. I visited Buckley in 2019 whilst researching for this book, found the new Buckley Library and learned of the work and the publications of the Buckley Society. I bought a copy of *The Making of Buckley and District*. (T.W. Pritchard,

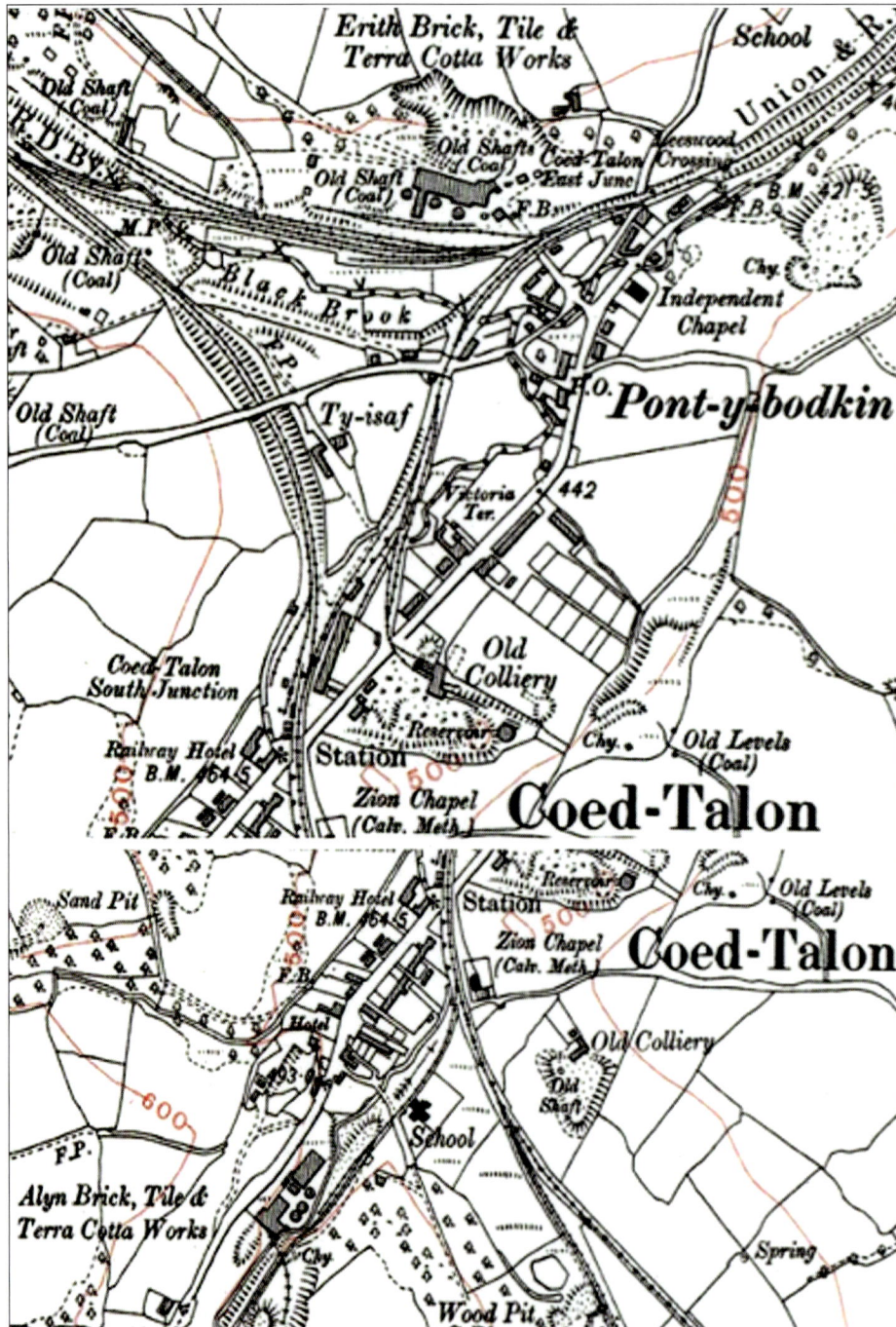

Fig 32: Extracts from 6in scale 1914 OS map showing clay industries north and south of Coed Talon station.

Bridge Books, Wrexham. 2006) and I am pleased to acknowledge a splendid publication and to use it as one of my sources.

Buckley was the heart of the building and firebrick industry in Flintshire. A principal company was Castle Firebrick & Coal Company. In July 1875, this company was registered to bring together the original Castle Works (see north of **Fig 33** map) of 1866 with Plas Bellin and Northop Hall Collieries. The company prospered as the advertisement from *Flintshire News*, December1912 shows (**Fig 34**). In accord with their name, the company began to manufacture high temperature silica bricks for furnace lining and they were bought out in 1916 by John Summers Steel Works nearby at Shotton. Summers

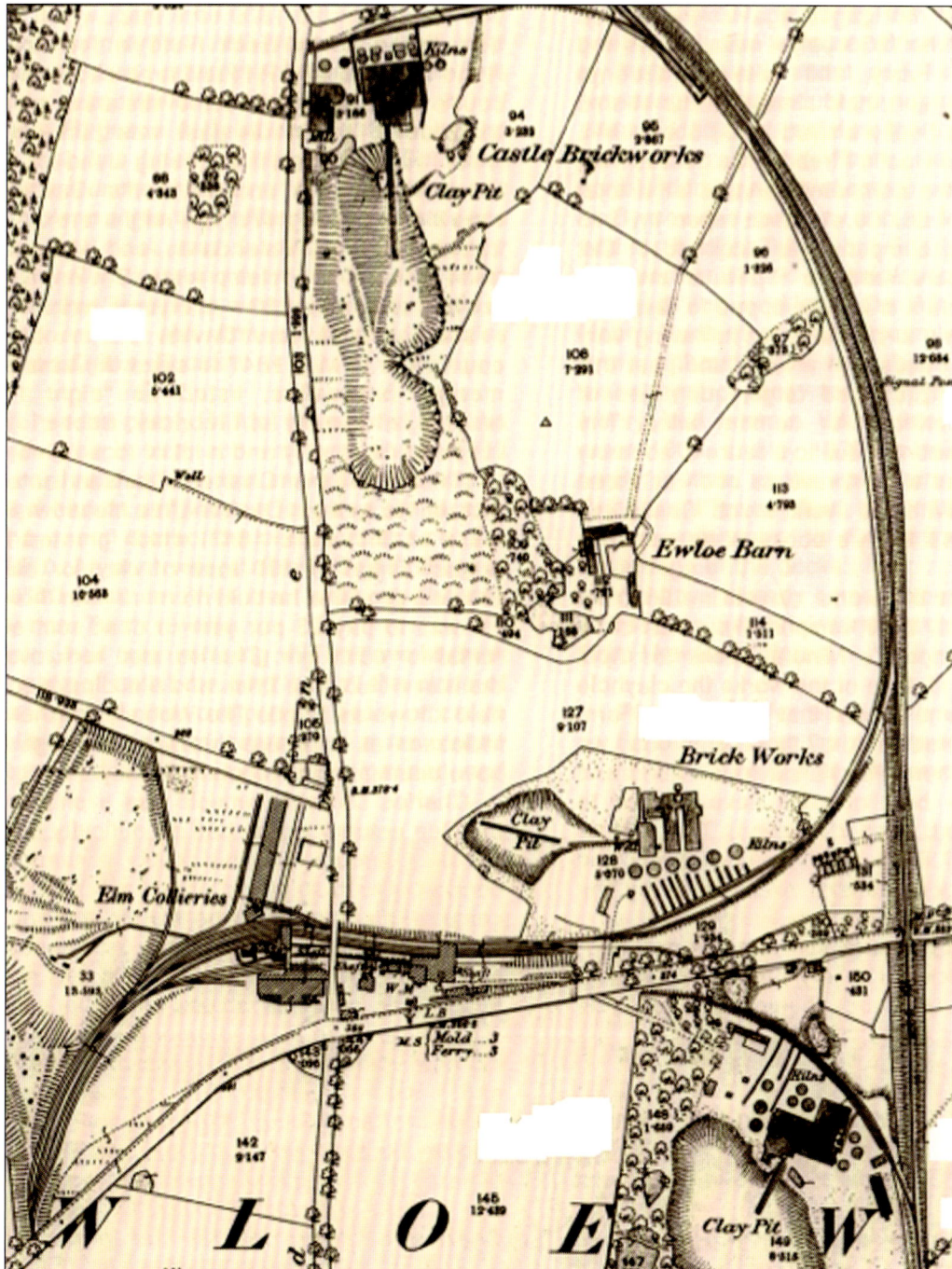

Fig 33: Clay quarries and brickworks north of Buckley served by sidings off the WM&CQR.

Fig 34: Advertisement from Flintshire News, 24th December 1912. (*Author*)

renamed the works as Castle Fire Brick Company and bought up several other Buckley brick manufacturers.

A Works Report of 1930 indicates the scale of the fire and brick making industries and the need for collieries to supply the brick kilns:

'[Fire brick] firing is slow and the period of burning [in the kilns] occupies about 96 hours and the goods are burned at a temperature of about 1,400˚C. The Works also manufactured building bricks; . . . the annual output was 2,500,000 to 3,000,000 firebricks and silica bricks and 3,000,000 to 3,500,000 building bricks.'

Fire clay bricks were high quality with a great mechanical strength and are now defined in British Standard BS ISO 6707-1;2014 as 'fire-clay brick that has a dense and strong semi-vitreous body and which conforms to defined limits for water absorption and compressive strength'. So these 'Engineers Bricks' are very useful but expensive when used in buildings.

To those, like me, unfamiliar with the brick industry, the output quoted above already seems considerable, but the 1930 Report tells of a new brickworks erected by the company in 1925 to make building bricks from Pit Shale of which large quantities were available adjoining the site. The Pit Shale is ground down and then moulded and pressed into bricks in a machine with a capacity of 2,200 bricks per hour. They are then burned in Belgian-type brick kilns 180ft long and containing 190,000 bricks:

'The time occupied by the bricks in the kilns is about 12 days and they are burned to a temperature of 1,100˚C to 1,200˚C. . . The output is approximately 12,000,000 bricks per annum.'

I have described the brick making process at the Castle Firebrick Company's brickworks to emphasis the quantities from one of the 130 brickworks in the Buckley area and the need, therefore, for the Buckley Railway, its branches and successor railways.

Pottery and Terracotta the first of the two remaining items from the clay industries of the NE Wales area in this book is pottery which has a history of at least 600 years.

By the early seventeenth century a group of cottage potters had settled around Buckley Mountain where they exploited local supplies of clay, coal and lead. Unfortunately, there are relatively few reference sources pertinent to this book. Thomas Pennant, a Welsh naturalist, traveller, writer and antiquarian, who spent his whole life in Flintshire recorded the Buckley potteries thus: 'Very considerable potteries of coarse earthenware such as pans, jugs, great pots for butter, plates, dishes, ovens, flower pots, etc. . . The ware is mostly exported to Ireland, and the towns on the Welsh coast, particularly to Swansea.'

The potteries, like Hayes's Pottery established in 1740, continued to produce Buckley pottery and remain

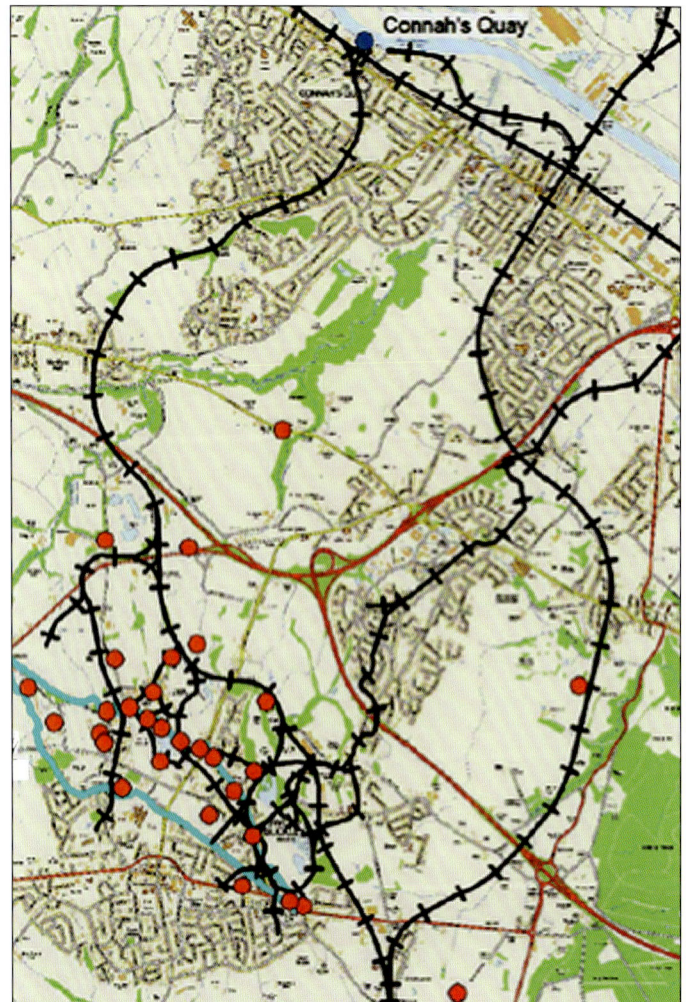

Fig 35: Archaeological sites of Buckley Potteries and railways serving the area from CPAT Report 1246: *The Buckley Potteries. An assessment and survival and potential.* 2014. Railways, branch lines and private sidings have been added to the OS base map by CPAT. Most have now gone.

in the same family ownership until closure in the 1940s. Others, like Powell's Pottery, which was the largest Buckley Pottery until 1914, converted their production line to work in engineering and plastics.

Mass production of crockery and enamel dishes began to pose a threat to Buckley's family-run earthenware businesses. By the late nineteenth and during the twentieth century Stoke-on-Trent white ware was flooding the market so the main Buckley firms such as Catheralls and Hancocks specialised in refractory bricks. These were for a variety of purposes, such as roof furniture, blast furnace linings, malt kiln floors, crucibles, acid resistant pipes and junctions for the lead industry, as well as low value pottery, and crude stoneware. They operated on an industrial scale but by the 1950s they were all closed.

'In 2010 the *North Wales Chronicle* ran a story about John Jonathan (92 years old) who was the last surviving Buckley potter. He left school aged 14 to work in one of Buckley's two remaining potteries. "I left school in 1931 on the Friday, went to see the owner of the company on the Saturday and started work the following Tuesday," he said.

'John was one of 6 workers who worked 10-hour days Monday to Friday from 7am-5pm and Saturday 7am-1pm, for 14 shillings a week.

"I enjoyed working at the pottery," said John. "Things were hard in the [19]30s, but it was no disgrace to be poor because everybody was the same. It took a war for things to pick up. After the war there were lots of jobs in Buckley, plenty of employment, not like now.

"The potteries closed in the end as they couldn't get the flint that coloured the clay as it went toward the war effort. It couldn't have lasted much longer anyway, as people didn't need pottery anymore. We used to make the clay pots in which people used to make hotpots, stews and rice puddings, but things move on and people started to use plastic instead."

'John went on to work at John Summers steelworks, Standard Brick and Pipe Works in Drury and then for the Flintshire County Council until his retirement in 1981.'

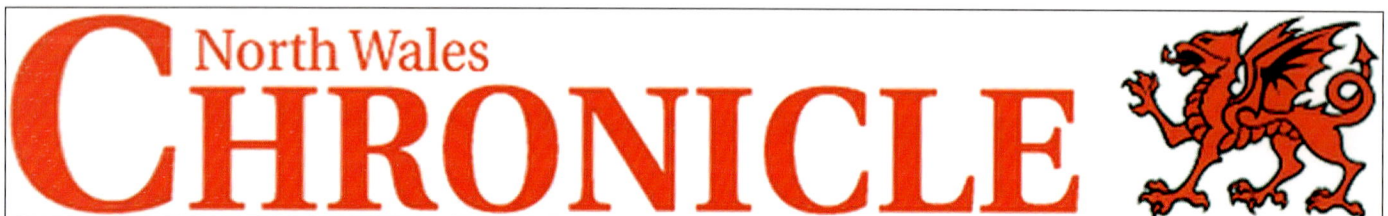

Fig 36: Header from the *North Wales Chronicle.* (*Author*)

Fig 37: Henry Dennis's Red Works, Ruabon. (*Author*)

Terracotta the last of the clay-based industries developed from local resources. Ruabon, on the Shrewsbury to Chester line (part of the GWR to Birkenhead Woodside) was the centre of this industry in an area rich in coal, clay and other minerals. Ruabon was also the junction to the now closed Ruabon–Barmouth line until the 1960s, most of the industries in the area were rail connected.

Ruabon was the centre of the terracotta industry because vast amounts of high quality Etruria Marl clay were discovered, quarried and worked there. The town gave its name to the 'Ruabon tile' which is still the best known quarry tile in the UK and Ruabon Quarry Tiles are still manufactured at Hafod Tileries, Ruabon, Wrexham.

A predecessor of Hafod Tileries, Ruabon Red Works, was founded in 1867 by local entrepreneur, Henry Dennis, and produced ridge tiles, chimney pots and ornamental terracotta. It was here that the famous quarry tile was born – the Ruabon tile, which is today still Britain's best-known quarry tile.

In the early 1980s a major investment and modernisation programme for Hafod Tileries saw the construction of a completely new factory and plant complex with a further major investment to install a modern high speed, computer-controlled tunnel kiln, which is over 100 metres long. Unfortunately, but understandably in the twenty-first century, Hafod Tileries are no longer rail connected and concentrate on tiles and pavers.

In the nineteenth century Ruabon was nicknamed 'Terracottapolis' because several of potteries and tileries were specialising in terracotta building blocks which could be tiles or decorative mouldings which were especially popular with Victoria architects. The frieze round the top of the Royal Albert Hall and the decorated front of the Natural History Museum in London are good examples and the railways used glazed terracotta tiles to decorate some station buildings such as Worcester Shrub Hill (**Fig 38**):

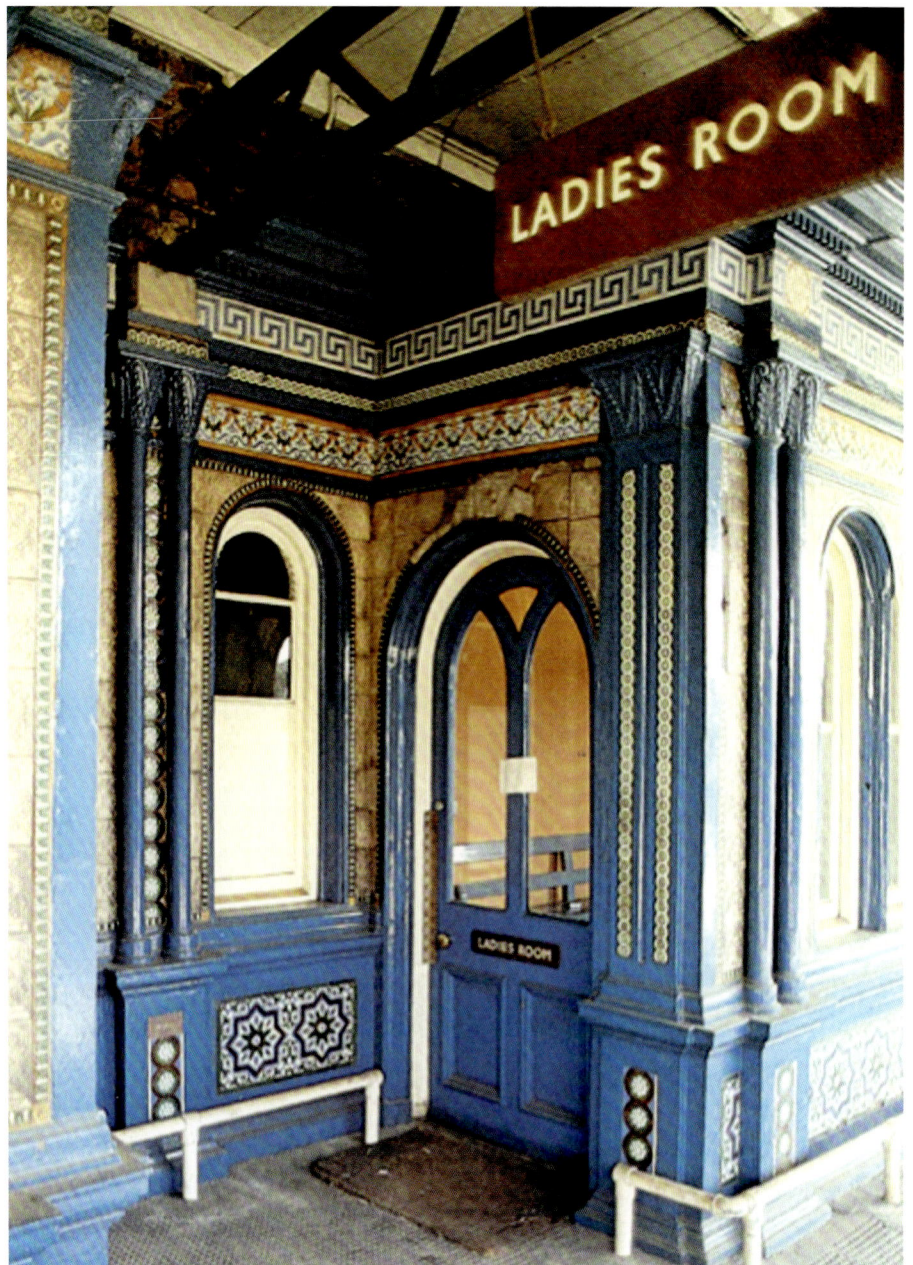

Fig38: Victorian decorative faience – glazed tiles – at Worcester Shrub Hill Station (GWR 1865).

CHAPTER 5

ENTREPRENEURS

Some of the men who developed the resources in Chapter 4 and built the railways which served them

When telling my railway stories, I am always fascinated by discovering and exploring the people – usually men in the nineteenth and early twentieth centuries – who made things happen; they were the engineers of change. I deliberately chose the French word 'Entrepreneurs' for this chapter because it could suggest an outside – or non-Welsh – intervention and all of the men in this chapter are 'outsiders'. Shorter OED (Oxford University Press. Sixth Edition 2007) defines 'entrepreneur' thus – 'A person who undertakes or controls a business or enterprise and bears the risk of profit or loss; a contractor who acts as an intermediary.'

I have chosen to tell the stories of some of these entrepreneurs because their lives, experiences and actions are part of the jigsaw I mentioned in my Foreword and which help to explain the railways and industries this book is exploring. For this chapter I am very grateful for the excellent and very thoroughly researched notes that Ray Shill prepared for the R&CHS 2018 AGM Weekend in Wrexham which I attended. Ray is a railway and industrial historian, a published author and a former Secretary of the R&CHS. From Ray's notes and my own researching I have chosen the names below from the many more who instigated and led many of the railway and industrial developments embraced in this book. They are:

William Henry and Charles Edward Darby – Directors, Shareholders and Managers at Brymbo Iron Works
Henry Dennis – Coal Owner and Brick and Terracotta maker, Ruabon
Daniel Gooch – Engineer and Chairman of GWR
Henry Robertson – Engineer, Coal Owner, Iron Master, MP
Thomas Savin – Contractor
George Stephenson – Engineer
John Summers' family – founders and operators of John Summers Ltd Steel Works

George Hammond Whalley
John Wilkinson – Iron Master
George F. Wynne

Probably the most familiar name is George Stephenson, who was commissioned in 1838 to survey the line of the Chester & Holyhead Railway. The government subsequently accepted Holyhead as the railway terminus for Ireland and many labourers in the NE Wales industries were Irish. Stephenson also surveyed a private mineral railway to Plasmadoc Colliery in 1839 which later was extended to serve other the Ruabon brick and ironworks, adopted by the GWR and formally acquired by the L&NWR about 1896.

I need not expand here on George Stephenson's career which has been well covered in a number of books but, as a County Durham man, he serves as an 'outsider' exemplar as were most of the other names. Stephenson, and the other names, brought experience, contacts, and great energy and foresight to the development of railways and industries in NE Walesa and Deeside.

John Wilkinson and John Summers were two very successful Iron Masters – Wilkinson at Bersham and Brymbo and John Summers at Stalybridge (Lancashire) and subsequently, his sons at Hawarden Bridge (Shotton) Steel Works. They saw opportunities for successful development in NE Wales and Deeside – but they, too were outsiders. Wilkinson was born in Cumberland and died at his Works in Bradley near Wolverhampton, Staffordshire. John Summers came from Lancashire and his sons, especially Harry Summers, created what became a very large steel company with an extensive internal railway system with over sixty steam locomotives on the Hawarden site. Wilkinson died before the Railway Age but his ambitions, and his transport requirements, were considerable so he promoted turnpike roads, canals and tramways for his Bersham and Brymbo works. One measure of his success as a businessman and entrepreneur is that when he died in 1808, his works and estates were valued, in 2020 terms, at £10,500,000. Both Wilkinson's and Summers' Iron and Steel Works are described in Chapter 7.

Chapter 7 and Brymbo Iron and Steel Works points to two more outsider names and, alphabetically, they head the list above. William Henry and Charles Edward Darby were both related to Abraham Darby of Coalbrookdale. Research of the Darby family's industrial history is complicated by their repeated use of Abraham as the name of their eldest son. Suffice it to say here that Abraham Darby I and his son, Abraham Darby II developed the use of coke (burned from coal) as a blast furnace fuel at their Coalbrookdale Foundry and used iron to replace the more expensive brass for cylinders for Thomas Newcomen's steam engines.

Brothers William Henry Darby and Charles Edward Darby were born in Coalbrookdale and were interested in Brymbo Works as shareholders. Both brothers moved to Brymbo, bringing with them Darby knowledge and experience of iron making. They became Directors of a new company set up by Henry Robertson, a Scots engineer, to take over the Works and Brymbo Colliery. Both brothers remained active at Brymbo for over thirty years so were more 'outsiders' who contributed successfully to the development of the area.

Even more important, and mentioned above, was Henry Robertson, who merits a longer entry.

Robertson was a talented engineer, born in Banff, Scotland, and educated at Kings College, Aberdeen University where he matriculated with an MA. He proved to be a brilliant scholar and became a very sound businessman.

He took up engineering and became a pupil of Robert Stephenson and Joseph Locke who were engaged on the Glasgow and Edinburgh railway and lines into England. Robertson helped to level and set out the West Coast main line over Shap Fell. Subsequently, and on his own, he secured an overhead bridge contract for the Glasgow and Grenock Railway. He explained that this work 'made [my] first bit of money . . .[and] . . . gained the most valuable experience . . . in dealing with contractors on the larger works [I] carried out.'

During 1842, Henry moved to the North West of England and entered into a partnership that included himself, Robert Roy and Alexander Ross to take over the Brymbo Ironworks, near Wrexham, which had closed

Fig 39: An engraving of Henry Robertson, copied with thanks from *Henry Robertson, Pioneer of Railways into Wales*, George L. Lerry. 1949.

following bankruptcy proceeding against Alexander Reid.

Brymbo was only then served by the roads and turnpikes although there had been schemes for a canal link (the original Ellesmere Canal Act 1793) and tramway schemes. Robertson was keen to improve those links and set about planning a railway towards Connah's Quay. This scheme was abandoned in favour of another that became the North Wales Mineral Railway. Robertson became its engineer once the Act of Parliament had been granted, although company minutes first refer to his post as 'Acting Engineer' on a salary of £500 per annum.

That railway was the start of grander railway expansion plans that, with Robertson as engineer, was to link North Wales with South Wales and with Liverpool, although the latter line was not achieved in his lifetime.

In 1846 Henry Robertson married Elizabeth Dean, the daughter of William Dean of Shrewsbury They had one son, Harry Beyer Robertson, and three daughters, Elizabeth, Annie and Henrietta.

Robertson began with the North Wales Mineral Railway in creating a line from Saltney Quay to Wrexham and then added an extension through to Ruabon and the all important mineral branches to Brymbo Ironworks, Minera Lime works, Minera Lead Works, Ffrwd ironworks, Vron Colliery and the Westminster Collieries.

Subsequently, as engineer to the Shrewsbury & Chester Railway, he was responsible for making the rest of the railway to Shrewsbury in 1848. On this section were the artistically designed Cefn Viaducts (River Dee) and Chirk Viaduct (River Ceiriog). He then went on

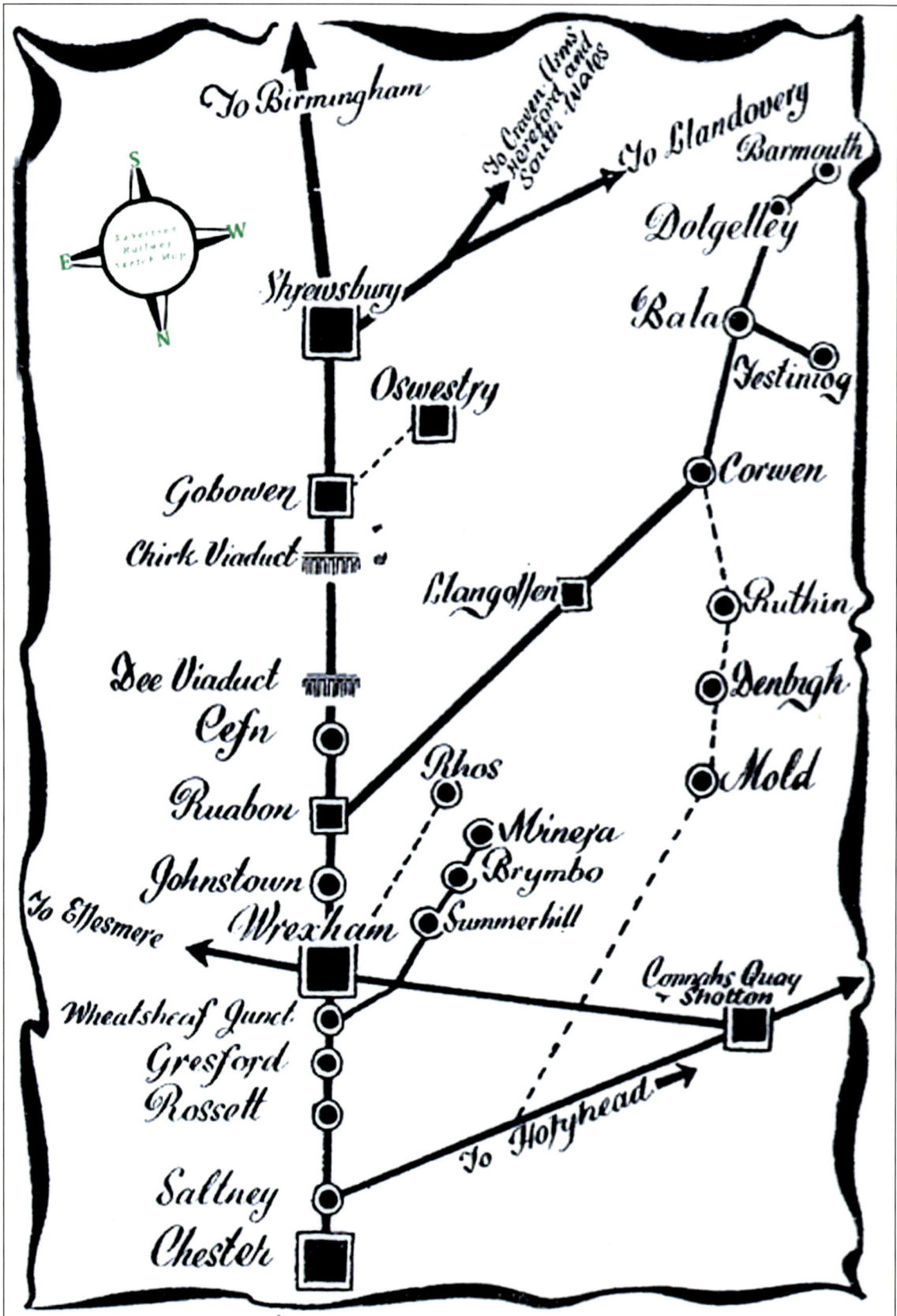

Fig 40: A sketch map illustrating Henry Roberson's railway projects edited with thanks from *Henry Robertson, Pioneer of Railways into Wales*. George L. Lerry. 1949. Note: sketch is South orientated.

to originate and engineer the Shrewsbury & Hereford Railway, which became a joint GWR and LNWR route. Robertson then engineered the Central Wales Railway from Craven Arms to Llandovery (LNWR). In 1850 he became engineer to the Shrewsbury and Birmingham Railway and became responsible for constructing the branches to Coalbrookdale and Horsehay

He fought a bitter battle for a rival scheme to link Ruabon with Llangollen, which received Parliamentary approval as the Vale of Llangollen Railway. He engineered that line and also the connecting Llangollen & Corwen and Corwen & Bala lines. Later he was engineer to the Bala-Ffestiniog Railway.

Henry designed Kingsland Bridge over the Severn at Shrewsbury, which was a single span iron bridge and, at the time of his death, he was carrying out the Dee Railway extensions and Wirral Railways

Robertson continued association with Brymbo until his death and in 1884 he helped to add steel-making to the business there. In January 1885 he oversaw the charging of a Basic Open Hearth Steel Furnace at Brymbo – the first in the British Isles. He also was involved in several colliery undertakings that included the Broughton, Gatewen and Plaspower collieries and

the Old Brandy Collieries (these became the Ruabon Coal & Coke Co.Ltd). He owned Minera Lime Works, which were at the end of the Minera Branch Railway.

Robertson was one of the original partners in the firm of Beyer Peacock, locomotive builders of Gorton, Manchester. He was chairman of Llangollen and Corwen Railway, Corwen and Bala railway, Vale of Llangollen Railway, Minera Lime Company, Broughton and Plas Power Coal Co and the Brymbo Water Co as well as interests in the Wrexham, Mold & Connah's Quay Railway. Robertson consulted on improvements to the River Dee and made a report to the Admiralty in 1849. He later was appointed a River Dee conservator and was involved as engineer for the Seacombe Hoylake and Deeside Railway.

Henry Robertson had homes in Boughton in Cheshire, Shrewsbury, London (13 Lancaster Gate) and finally Palé Hall near Bala in Merionethshire.

Robertson was a Liberal in politics and an ardent admirer of Gladstone. He was elected as MP for Shrewsbury from May 1862 to July 1865 and then for a second term from February 1874 to 1885. Robertson was then elected MP for Merionethshire which post he held from 1885 until 1886, when he differed with Gladstone

Fig 41: Palé Hall from *The Architect*, July 5, 1875: 'The mansion at Palé, Merionethshire, has recently been erected for Mr H Robertson MP from designs and under the superintendence of Mr S. Pountney Smith, Architect, of Shrewsbury'. (*Author*)

on Irish Policy and chose to stand down. His death in 1888 occurred when there was still unfinished business to undertake.

Henry Robertson was a remarkable man who, without inherited wealth or help from powerful friends, won for himself a great reputation as an engineer, ironmaster and businessman. He undertook a variety of projects in a spirit of adventure and confident that the outcome of his hard work would win rewards for himself and benefits for the whole community. He enjoyed life in NE Wales, was a keen fisherman and walker. He could read Latin almost as quickly as English and could reel off many poems by Byron and Burns.

His son, Henry Beyer Robertson, assisted his father in various business enterprises and was involved in many new developments at Brymbo steelworks. During the First World War he ensured maximum production of iron and steel for munitions. Palé was turned into a military hospital (like Downton Abbey!) and a hydro-electric plant was established there in 1918. Henry Beyer Robertson was a director of several companies, including the Great Western Railway Company, and a member of the River Dee Fisheries Board. In 1890, he was granted a knighthood by Queen Victoria as a mark

Fig 42: The late Mr G.H. Whalley MP, edited from a portrait presented by the citizens of Peterborough and placed in Peterborough Museum. (*Author*)

of her gratitude for his father's achievements and his son's hospitality when she stayed at Palé Hall in 1889.

Robertson (senior) was generally very well regarded but some of his projects were vigorously opposed by local land owners and one who can be recalled here is a missed opportunity in Victorian fiction; George H. Whalley. However, had an author like Charles Dickens invented a character who in any way resembled Whalley, a writ would have been served at Dickens' door forthwith.

Whalley lived at Plas Madoc Hall near Ruabon with extensive grounds, known to Whalley as his 'Park'. It was this same park that he claimed with fervour was to be destroyed by Henry Robertson's Vale of Llangollen Railway although the line, when built, skirted the perimeter of Whalley's Park to the south.

As MP for Peterborough, he had considerable political influence and as a former barrister he proved to be a vicious person to cross. He had considerable dealings in railways local to the Wrexham & Ruabon area. There were many attempts by him to pursue new railways, though few schemes he claimed to support came to fruition.

Henry Robertson often requested him to state facts in the many exchanges in which they were engaged. Yet as a politician, facts were only ammunition in an arsenal of many other tools to achieve an aim. That aim was often to the benefit of George Whalley and 'facts', mistruths, evasion and bullying were part of his arsenal of weapons.

Development of railways aided George Whalley in his political and business activities. Once the GWR gained control of Wrexham and Ruabon districts, rates were raised for transport of goods. This encouraged brick and terracotta makers, coal masters, iron masters and quarry masters to find alternate routes for their trade so new railway schemes were proposed. This was fertile ground for Whalley who excelled in chairing meetings so, no matter the scheme, he was there arguing a case.

Whether George Whalley had a genuine feeling for the success of the schemes he supported cannot be established but he profited from these ventures and there are reports of him charging for speaking on each project. Railway speculation had been a sad fact since the first public railways were constructed and it is likely that Whalley profited from such speculation. Robertson called in question Whalley's motives in a disagreement about his own colliery work in the Ruabon district and Whalley's involvement with the Ruabon Coal & Coke Company:

> 'I . . . pay my men for their work in money and not through a "tommy shop" [as you do]; I continue to do so at collieries in Ruabon and Brymbo. You sir (addressing Mr Whalley) were once a coal master . . .[but] you were not one for long. Is that what you call developing the trade of the district?'

A testament to Whalley's nature is evident from a libel case he instigated (and lost) against the *Railway Times* in December1861. This came about through alleged payments during one of Whalley's chairmanships that involved the contractor Thomas Savin. The editor of the *Railway Times* wrote thus:

> 'With regard to the personal position of Mr Whalley, as an MP, as a gentleman of fortune, or as a magistrate we have nothing whatever to say. However, we do find that gentleman at the head of certain railway confederations, in which disputes and no little suspicion exist. . . In this character alone, as representative of these Companies and as individually involved in the transactions which excite so much clamour . . . we have attempted to deal with him.'

The *Railway Times* was 'dealing with' a wealthy land-owner who accumulated a number of local and national posts which put him in a strong position to propose, or oppose, railway development schemes. Whalley was educated at University College, London and was called to the bar in January 1839, although he later relinquished his legal practice. He was a Deputy Lieutenant and JP for Denbighshire, a JP in Merionethshire and Montgomeryshire, Sheriff of Caernarvonshire (1853) and Captain of the Denbighshire Yeomanry Calvary. He was an assistant Tithe Commissioner from 1836 till 1847 and Examiner of private bills for Parliament. During the Irish Famine he established Fisheries on the west coast of Ireland, for which he received the thanks of the British Association. He won an election in Peterborough in November 1852, where there were two seats, but was found guilty of 'treating' and had votes discounted so he lost his seat. He was later re-elected as the second Member of Parliament. Whalley had stood as a Whig in the first election; on the second he became a Liberal.

At Plas Madoc Hall and Park Whalley lived with wife, Ann, and three children. Their servants included a nurse/midwife, dress-maker, butler/footman, cook, scullery maid, dairy maid, house maid, coachman and a general servant, a team that indicated considerable personal wealth. Such wealth enabled him to pursue his career as an MP and the many railway schemes in which he became involved. He remained an MP until his death on 8 October 1878. His will showed an estate value that was nearly £18,000 (purchasing power in 2020 = £32,000,000) so perhaps a testament to his expensive tastes and, too, a dwindling fortune in later years.

Whalley, and Robertson, had business interests in the Ruabon district and Robertson owned the Brandie pits of the Ruabon Coal Company. He gave evidence to a Parliamentary Committee for a proposed GWR railway from Wrexham to Mold in 1861 and, inter alia, deposed that for fifteen years, the successful lines in the district were those owned or operated by the GWR. He believed that the GWR must always be the collector of minerals for Ruabon and Wrexham and that, but for the GWR, the small collieries would cease to exist.

Sir Daniel Gooch, Bart. was Chairman of the GWR 1865 to 1889. In his diaries (published in 1892) Gooch writes:

> '1856: [When he was still Superintendent of Locomotive Engines on GWR] 'In the early part of this year I formed the Ruabon Coal Company. . . It had been impossible to get a regular coal trade on our line and I proposed to my Company to have some collieries of their own, and went to Wrexham to look at those belonging to Mr Henry Robertson . . .
>
> 'I advised the directors to buy Robertson's works, as they were in operation and could be made available for our purpose at once. . . [However] a similar plan in operation on the ECR showed it not be within the powers of the ECR company and stopped our plan. Mr Walpole, our Chairman, then asked me if I could find private parties to form a company and enter into an agreement with the GWR Company to send a large fixed quantity of coal over our line. This I agreed to do, took a large stake in the Coal Company myself, and was to be the chairman.

'Feeling that this might conflict with my position as an officer of the railway company I placed my resignation in the hands of Mr Walpole, but the GWR directors did not think it right to accept it. I, however, left it in the hands of Mr Walpole to accept it at any time should circumstances make it desirable. I felt that there were interests in the coal trade amongst the shareholders of the GWR who would no doubt object to what had been done; and such proved to be the case. For two or three and a half years afterwards it was the cause of a row at our meetings and some parties went to the Court of Chancery to put an end to the agreement. In this they failed and the Court expressed themselves strongly that what had been done was perfectly legal and right. I thus got a great deal of abuse by trying to do a good turn to the shareholders of the Railway and risking a good deal of my own money in so doing.

'The colliery, however, has been a very good investment and has done good to both parties in the arrangement.'

I do not know whether George Whalley was a GWR shareholder but, had he not died in 1878, I am sure he would have been interested to read Gooch's diary entry quoted above but not made public until 1892!

A 1907 obituary from the Institute of Civil Engineers for Henry Dennis provides another example of an 'outsider' with railway and mining experience who came from Cornwall to NE Wales and whose name is still remembered in Ruabon today.

In 1897 he founded the Hafod Brickworks near Ruabon, later to become Dennis Ruabon Tiles Ltd. His ICE Obituary reads:

'Henry Dennis was born in Bodmin, Cornwall, in 1825 and began his engineering career in the office of the Borough Surveyor of Bodmin, Mr. Henry Coom. On completing his training he joined the engineering staff of the Cornwall Railway, which now forms part of the GWR and subsequently he was employed in surveying the coast-line and taking soundings in Padstow harbour with a view to the construction of a break-water. The construction of mineral railways in the south of Spain/' during 1856 and 1857 brought him into contact with the mining and quarrying branch of the civil engineering profession, to which his subsequent career was principally devoted.

Left: **Fig 43**: Henry Dennis, civil engineer specialising in railway, mining and quarrying industries.

Right: **Fig 44**: Hafod Brickworks Quarry, near Ruabon and managed by Henry Dennis. (*Author*)

'Returning to England in 1858 he was entrusted by Messrs. John Taylor & Sons (Mining Engineers) with the construction of railways for the Llangollen Slate and Slab Company's mines in Denbighshire. Having settled in the district, Mr Dennis turned his attention to its mineral resources, and from that time forward he took a prominent part in the development of the Wrexham coalfield, as well as of lead mines and stone quarries in the neighbourhood.

'He became manager of the Bryn-yr-Owen Colliery, and afterwards managing director of the Wrexham and Acton collieries and the Ruabon Coal and Coke Company, director of the Minera Lead Mining Company, and chairman of the Westminster Brymbo Coal and Coke Company, the Snailbeach Lead Mining Company, and other undertakings. He also carried on a private practice, and, as engineer, was instrumental in obtaining parliamentary powers for supplying Ruabon and several other districts with water and gas.

'He built the Glyn Valley Tramway, the Wrexham District tramways, and the Snailbeach Railway. He owned and managed the Cefn freestone quarries, and was identified with various other undertakings in the district. He also acted as consulting mining engineer to several large estates in North Wales. Mr. Dennis was for some time chairman of the North Wales Coal Owners' Association and their Mutual Indemnity Company, and he also represented the Association on the Coal Trade Conciliation Board.

'In 1904 he was President of the Mining Institute of Great Britain. The claims of business left him little leisure for public affairs, but he served for a time as an Alderman of the Denbigh County Council, and was also a Justice of the Peace for the county. Agriculture was his hobby, and he acquired a considerable reputation as a breeder of sheep.

'He was taken ill immediately after a journey by motor-car from his home, New Hall, Ruabon, to his Cornish residence at Bodmin, and died at the latter place on the 24th June, 1906 aged 82.

'Mr. Dennis was elected an Associate Member of The Institution of Civil Engineers on 31st May, 1881.'

Thomas Savin – railway contractor – was only an 'outsider' to the particular area of NE Wales and Deeside on which this book is centred; he was born in 1826 at Llwynymaen between Oswestry and Trefonen.

Fig 45: Thomas Savin, railway, mining and quarrying contractor, speculator, Mayor of Oswestry and bankrupt in 1866 with £2M debts. (*Author*)

Savin was a railway contractor but with a chequered career because he was not always financially wise though any losses were generally out of his own pocket. He started with David Davies contracting to build various railways in Wales but that partnership was dissolved on 29 October 1860 when he undertook railway construction on his own account. He sometimes financed the construction himself and often took shares in payment. At times brother John assisted with the construction and at other times Savin worked with brother-in-law, John Ward. He acted as a railway director from time to time and also operated lines and owned a colliery at Coed y Go, near Oswestry.

David Davies had the greater civil and mechanical engineering knowledge and Savin provided the energy and drive for what was a very difficult business. He, brother John and John Ward effectively became Savin & Co. They generally contracted for a whole railway building package agreeing a set sum for purchase of land, track and infrastructure building.

Savin built at least ten different railways, in Wales and the border area. He was also employed to build the Bishop's Castle Railway (Shropshire) in 1863 but he was already experiencing some monetary problems because he took their £20,500 advance but never built the line. The Bishops Castle Railway directors had to file a bill in Chancery to recover their money and they may not have been surprised to learn of Savin's bankruptcy in 1866.

In 1863, Savin became Mayor of Oswestry but his financial downfall was already looming because he began to build and buy a number of hotels on the Welsh coast. He also took over the lease of the Llanymynech quarries, both the Welsh side owned by the Earl of Powis and the English side owned by the Earl of Bradford; Savin was already operating quarries at Porth-y-waen. Hotels were also built at Aberystwyth and Borth.

Railways

(1) Aberystwyth and Welsh Coast Railway – Savin & Co

(2) Beddgelert Railway – Savin & Co

(3) Bishops Castle Railway – Savin & Co *but no work carried out on site*

(4) Brecon and Merthyr Railway – Savin & Co

(5) Denbigh Ruthin and Corwen Railway – Savin & Co

(6) Hereford, Hay and Brecon Railway – *Savin appointed to succeed a failed contractor*

(7) Kington & Eardisley Railway – *Savin's £16,000 of shares were sold at his bankruptcy in January 1866*

(8) Llanfyllin Railway – Savin & Ward

(9) Nantlle Railway & the Caernavonshire Railway – Thomas & John Savin. *Difficult & expensive project*

(10) Oswestry & Newtown Railway – Davies & Savin (from 1875 - 1860) *Accepted shares as payment*

(11) Oswestry, Ellesmere & Whitchurch Railway – Savin & Co. *Railway lacked money to pay Savin*

(12) Vale of Clywd Railway – Davies & Savin (from 1875 - 1860)

Oswestry would not have become the important railway town it was if Savin had not insisted that the locomotive works for the Cambrian Railways was built in Oswestry, and not Welshpool, as was suggested. His five years of railway building were clearly busy, yet he proceeded very incautiously. In 1865, further responsibility became his when the Cambrian Railway transferred to him the Company's agreement to work the Aberystwyth and Welsh Coast Railway.

In 1866 Savin's mistakes caught up with him. His estimate for the cost of the Machynlleth to Barmouth Railway was wildly low because he had not realised that at Aberdovey the railway would need many tunnels. His other problem was that instead of taking money when he built railways, he often took shares. This meant he had a huge number of shares in a great number of companies all over Britain. But contractors have to buy – and pay for – goods and services so debts accumulated. On

5 February 1866 creditors pressed for an assignment and he was forced to declare bankruptcy. Savin did continue to undertake some uncompleted railway work which included the Oswestry Works for the Cambrian Railway.

During his bankruptcy investigations it was discovered Savin owed over £2,000,000 – a purchasing power of £186,600,000 in 2020. When Savin's finances were sorted out, all his shares were taken from him to pay his debts, except for four small companies, one being the Llanymynech quarries. These companies were tiny in comparison to the ones he had partly owned before his crash, but he seems to have put all his energies into running them. But from now till he died he always seemed to have money problems, either owing money or complaining that he was getting a bad deal.

He obviously still yearned for greater things and for more personal publicity, so he organised two 'Big Bangs' – demonstrations of gunpowder blasting at his Llanymynech quarries, with local dignitaries invited to watch the explosion. The first demonstration was on 17 September 1867, with one and a half tons of gunpowder. An immense mass of rock was brought down, weighing about eight or nine thousand tons, and about half that amount again was loosened. But this wasn't enough for Savin, and he wanted an even bigger demonstration, using electricity to set off the explosive and six and a half tons of blasting powder. An eye-witness on 11 March 1868 described the result:

'A few minutes after three o'clock, Mr Savin gave the final signal for the explosion, which . . .was instantaneous. The effect was terrific. The huge rock was burst from base to summit with tremendous force, and poured down with a fearful roar on to the floor of the quarry; the dull thunder of the explosion caused a tremor to pass through the rock. Some of the debris fell at an immense distance, a portion of the tramway bridge was destroyed on the Oswestry road . . . and a large quantity of powder was carried over a mile distant. The noise of the explosion was distinctly heard at Welshpool, ten miles away. No other experiment of the kind has since taken place.'

In 1878, Savin became embroiled in the great 'Traction Engine Dispute'. He had been unsuccessfully trying for several years to get a railway built along the Tanat Valley to Llangynog, where he owned quarries. Lacking a railway, he used traction engines to take slate away from his works and coal to them, but these heavy vehicles made deep ruts in the road and were smoky and noisy. Several people complained and Savin was taken to court. However, the JP was his old friend Sir Watkin Williams-Wynn and the case was dismissed. A feast was held in his honour with songs in praise of him, as he was a major employer in the region.

Alas, his last ten years were full of petty disputes, about the traction engines, the leases for his quarries, his attempts to see the Tanat Valley Railway built, and about bills he had not paid or paid late.

Thomas Savin was an interesting character; he was hard working, ambitious, inventive, often starting new projects but he frequently overreached himself, lost money and accumulated formidable debts. He died aged 62 on 16 July 1889.

And finally in this chapter, a man who, unlike Savin, was a careful and meticulous worker and never looked for 'Big Bangs' to advertise his activities. He contributed greatly to the successful operations at Minera Lime Works and this success justified GWR building the Minera Mineral Branch from Wrexham and Brymbo to Minera. George Frederick Wynne was another 'outsider' who made good, for himself and the community he served, when he moved to Minera in 1878. The account which follows is edited from Bersham And Clywedog Industrial Trail – Information Sheet N° 6M courtesy of Wrexham County Borough Council and obtained during my research visits to WCBC's Minera Lead Mines and Country Park in 2019

Wynne was born in Stafford and worked in Chester as a teacher and in Manchester in engineering work before coming to Minera as Assistant Secretary to the Minera Mining Company. His interest in machinery of all kinds soon involved him in the design of automatic ore-dressing machinery to replace the obsolete equipment he found at Minera. This work eventually led to the founding of his Record Vanner and Slimer Company in 1915. Vanners were machines used for the separation of ore and they proved very successful with large sales to Cornwall and South Africa.

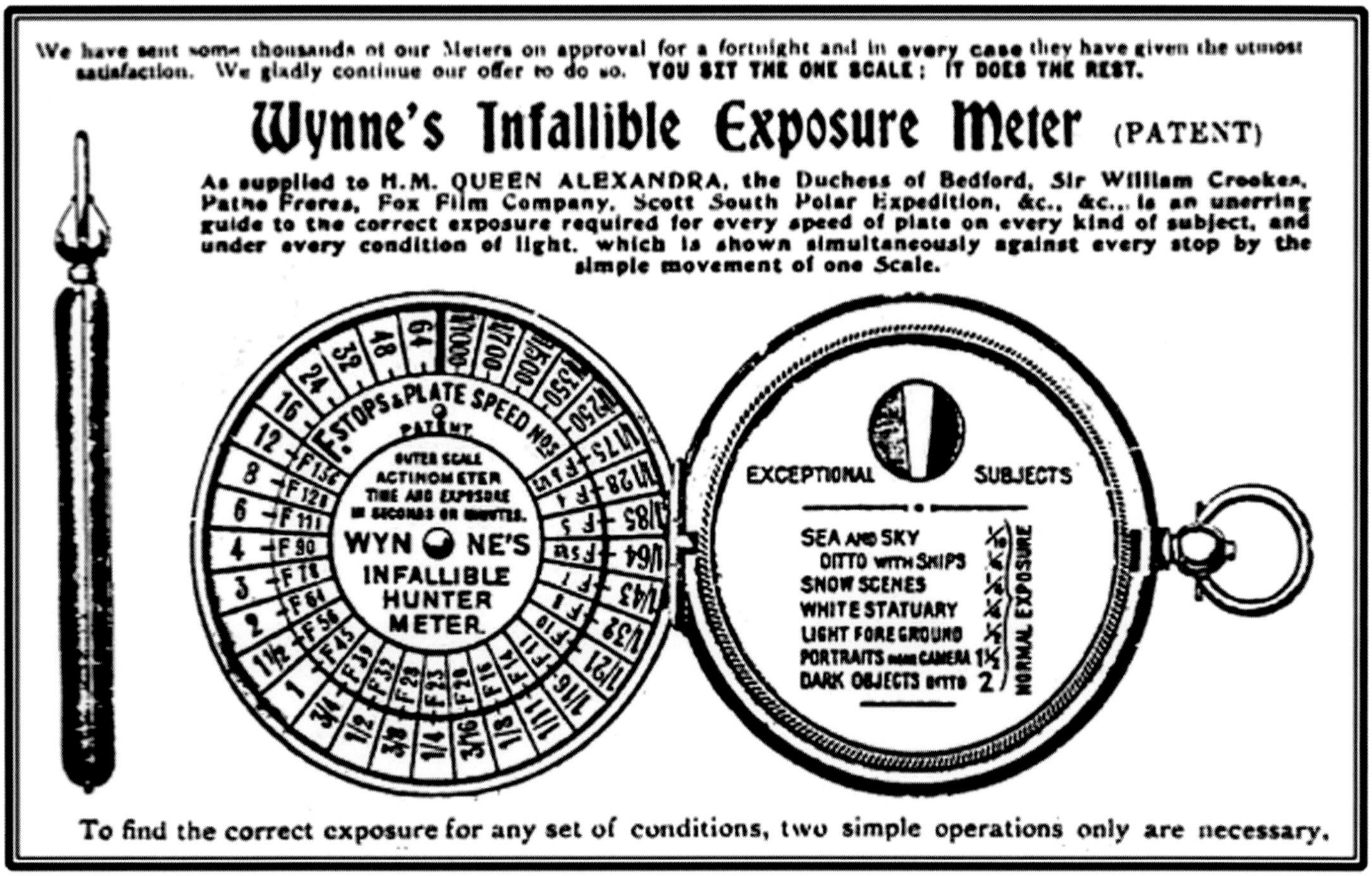

Fig 46: An extract from a brochure advertising George Frederick Wynne's Exposure Meter. (*Author*)

Wynne also invented new or modified types of rock drill and rock-breaking machinery. His 'Excelsior' drill was patented in 1895 and 200 of them were used by the French Panama Canal Company in making the Great Culebra Cut through the Rocky Divide which separated the Atlantic and Pacific Oceans. Excelsior drills were selected following a competition organised by the French contractors of the Canal and they were subsequently used all over the world.

Wynne's inventive skills were also applied to photography; his exposure meter, patented in 1893, proved to be a success for many years following the setting up of the Infallible Exposure Meter Company.

The company's order books, starting in 1912, show the extent of the interest which Wynne's exposure meter had gained, with foreign orders from Belgium, Spain, Switzerland, Russia, USA, Canada and Nigeria. One of the meter's selling points was undoubtedly its simple operation requiring no complicated calculations. At 9/6d (£47 today) in a solid nickel case it seems to have been good value for money.

George Wynne's talents were equally as obvious in his business administration. Soon after starting as Assistant Secretary to the Minera Mining Company he became Company Secretary, and by 1897 had become the largest shareholder and acted as Liquidator when the Company closed in that year. He played a principal role in the formation of the United Minera Mining Company, formed out of the Minera Mining Company and the New Minera Mining Company, which was working lead and zinc blende at the east end of the Minera mines. This company operated up to the final closure of the mines in 1914 when Wynne once again acted as Liquidator. The waste tips, the old smelting works buildings and all the rights still possessed by the mining company were sold to him and he was able to start his Minera Mines Gravel and Concrete Company.

Wynne's personal cash books (part of a collection of his papers deposited with the Clwyd Record Office, Old Rectory, Hawarden) indicate the kind of person he was. The extremely careful and methodical way he entered each item of expenditure and his equally careful analysis of these accounts, suggest a person who was by nature systematic and logical in his approach to any task. He was ideally suited to apply the scientific knowledge he acquired at work or elsewhere. This, coupled with business acumen, assured a successful outcome to his many ventures.

My invaluable industrial locomotives 'Bible' for this book – *Industrial Locomotives of North Wales*. V.J. Bradley. Industrial Railway Society. 1992 – suggests that *Henrietta* probably arrived at Minera in 1897 by which date it had been rebuilt by Hawthorn Leslie, By February 1899, the Minute books record it 'in poor condition'. It had at least four owners before Minera and its previous owner had been contractors Meakin & Dean. They were close associates of Henry Robertson who had a daughter named Henrietta . . .

Fig 47: *Henrietta* standard gauge 0-6-0ST with inside cylinders and probably built by Manning Wardle in 1861. The loco was owned by the United Minera Mining Company so could shunt the quarry lines, which were all privately owned, and work up to and sometimes a little along the GWR Minera Branch where wagons could be exchanged. It is hauling coal for the Limeworks c1900.

CHAPTER 6

RAILWAYS

Narrow gauge mineral tramways Standard gauge industrial and passenger lines

Researching for this chapter led me first of all to *Early Wooden Railways*, M.J.T. Lewis, Routledge & Kegan Paul, 1970 and *Stone Blocks & Iron Rails (Tramroads)*, Bertram Baxter, David & Charles, 1966.

And a reminder for myself, and readers, of the varying terminology which names early railways. In this context 'tram' – or in Wales a dram – is a wheeled truck used underground then on the surface – and sometimes both when day-holes, adits or drifts which sloped underground were used instead of vertical shafts to reach minerals. A railway is defined by Lewis as 'a prepared track which so guides the vehicles running upon it that they cannot leave the track'. That will serve usefully for this book so whether a railway is locally called a woodenway, waggon road, waggonway, barroway, gangroad, plateway, main rail, Newcastle road, trailway, tramroad or tramway it is essentially serving the same purpose, so I have adopted 'tramway' for all early railways.

It may be that there were wooden railways in NE Wales but Lewis does not name any. Baxter, however, records some in an extensive Gazetteer so I have included an edited list as follows:

Denbighshire: three examples in the area covered by this book.

Ruabon Brook – 3.25 miles from the head of the Ellesmere & Chester Canal at Pontcysllte Aqueduct to coal pits at Ruabon Brook. Opened 1806. Owned by the Canal Company. Traffic coal, lime, pig iron, general goods.

Bersham – 2.0 miles from Brymbo Hall to Glascoed Valley. Owned by Ironmaster John Wilkinson. Opened 1757 (proven date of opening not known but referred to in dated documents by 1757). Traffic iron, ironstone.

Ponkey – no details but mentioned in the deeds of Ponkey Furnace which was in blast by 1760. Owned by Ironmaster John Wilkinson.

Flintshire: five examples in the area covered by this book all on or leading to the south bank of river Dee:

Sandycroft Plateway – 4.5 miles from site of later Sandycroft Foundry on the bank of the Dee to Old Colliery near Drury Lane and serving pits at Level Row, Twenty Row, Lane End; collieries at Sandycroft, Lenham Green; Trap Brickworks near Ewloe, Catherall's Brickworks at Knowl Hill, Hancock's Lane End Brickworks at Drury Lane. Opened c1790 (proven date of opening not known but referred to in dated documents by 1790). Owned by (i) Botfield, (ii) from 1801, Rigby & Hancock. Traffic coal, bricks.

Mancott Woodenway – mileage unknown because no traces remain but from River Dee to Pentre and Big Mancott. Opened c1750 (proven date of opening not known but referred to in dated documents by 1750). Owned by Hope & Crachley. Traffic not known

Aston Hall – 1,5 miles from Lower Ferry (now Queensferry) to pits at Aston Hall. Opened 1801 (proven date of opening not known but referred to in dated documents by 1801). Owned by Leach & Co. Traffic coal

Wepre – 1.0 mile from Shotton to Latchcroft Pit. Opened 1740 (proven date of opening not known but referred to in dated documents by 1740). Owned by '. . . a company from Chester' . . (unnamed). Traffic coal.

Dublin Main – 1.25 miles from Connah's Quay to Dublin Main Collieries near Northophall. No other details known.

There are no closure dates shown in the list above, but Baxter assumes that the Tramway Era came to an end in

1830 with the opening of the Liverpool & Manchester Railway and steam traction replacing horse power. However, 1830 is only a convenient date to round-off tramway operation and in some cases – like Minera – horse haulage continued for many years (see **Fig 48**).

The other reason that Baxter did not suggest a likely closure date is that several tramway routes were developed, track was changed to standard gauge and sometimes the name was changed, too, as a branch off a later standard gauge development.

Above: **Fig 48**: Drams loaded with clay on a 1ft 8in gauge tramway (opened 1862) from quarry to Caello Brickworks, Minera, in 1962. (*Author*)

Left: **Fig 49**: A substantial embankment on the Sandycroft Plateway leading to Sandycroft Ironworks/ Foundry and a wharf on the river Dee. (*Author*)

The Flintshire tramways were all carrying heavy minerals, or manufactured goods like cast iron, from collieries and/or ironworks down to the south shore of the river Dee which was navigable upstream from the Estuary to Chester by vessels of various sizes.

Dee river traffic was upstream to Shrewsbury or downstream to the Wirral peninsula, Birkenhead, across the Mersey to Liverpool, along the North Wales coast or across to Ireland. Industries were seeking markets but the geography in which they developed was mountainous and trending North-East/South West parallel to the Dee estuary so not easy to cross. The tramways were man- or animal-powered, gravity-assisted down to the Dee and they were built to a narrow gauge – perhaps the width of a horse or a little

wider – to save money on civil engineering construction. Although some tramway remains prove that they were substantial works for their time (see **Fig 49** on the Sandycroft Railway).

In the 1970s John Bentley, working with historians, archaeologists and the Buckley Society investigated a number of Flintshire tramways, using historic documents and walking along potential sites. His sketch map, edited and reproduced here as **Fig 50,** shows the complexity of the early tramway systems and the industries they served. The map shows the Buckley area before the Buckley Railway was built because the coming of standard gauge railways and steam locomotives supplanted the narrow gauge tramways.

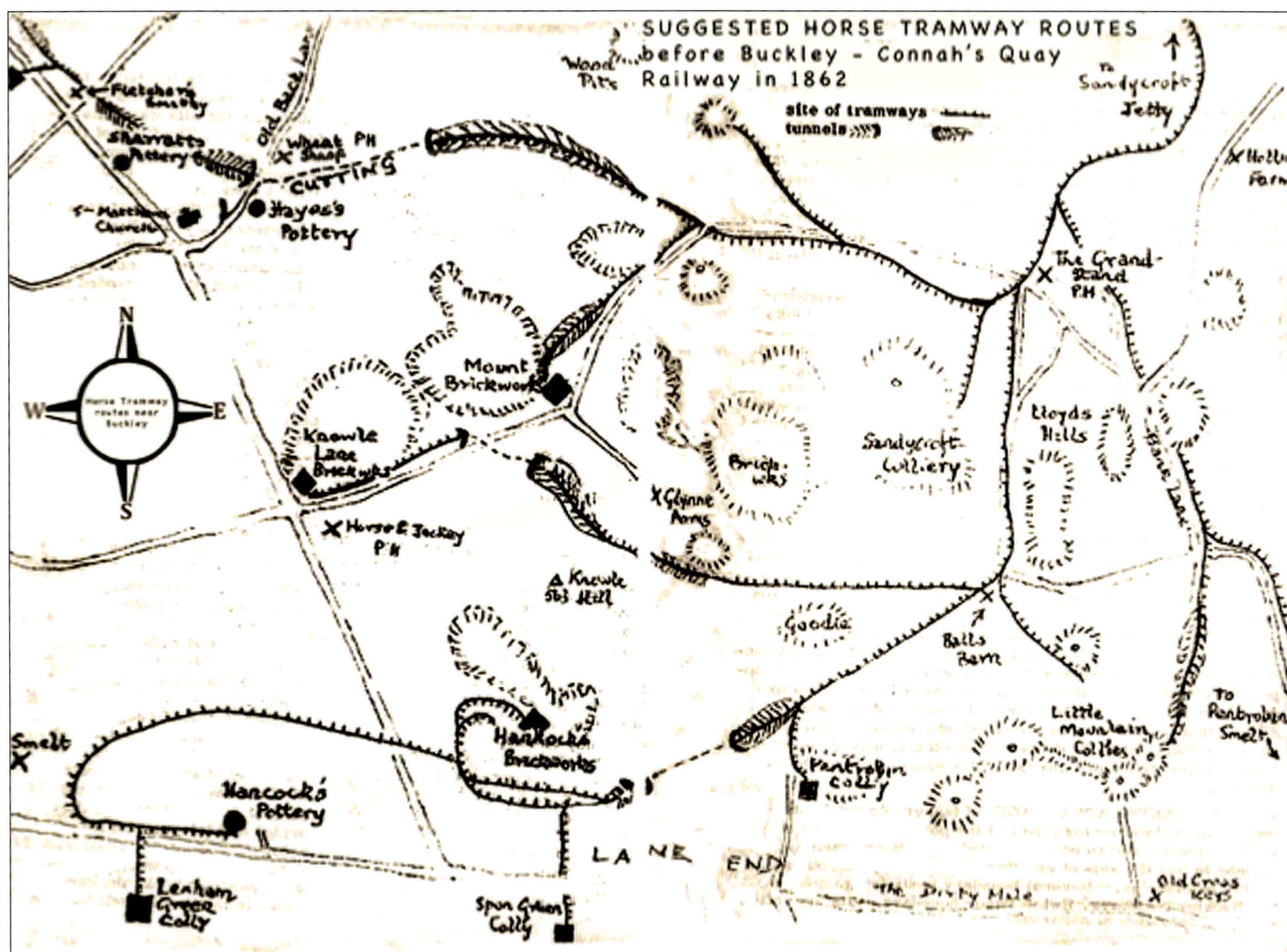

Fig 50: Edited sketch map of tramways in the Buckley area before the standard gauge steam-hauled railways were built. The original was drawn by John Bentley in 1971 and is reproduced here courtesy of the Buckley Society.

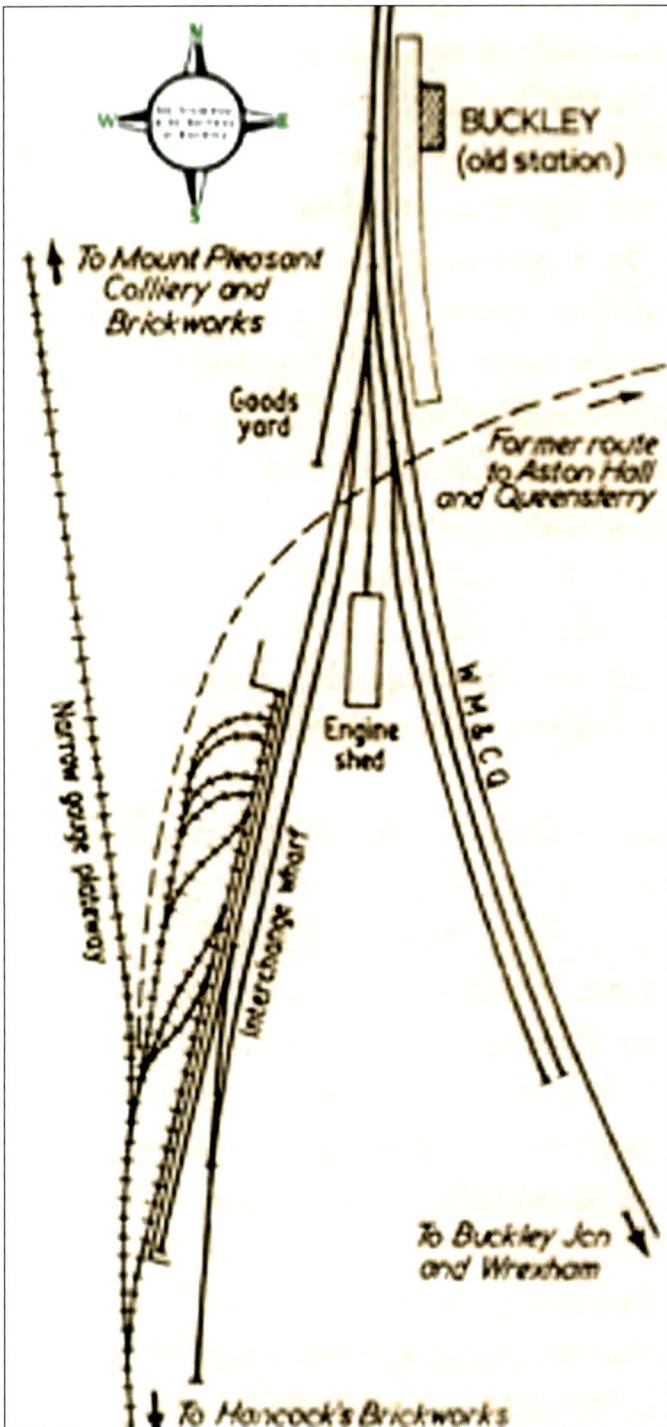

Fig 51: Tramways and standard gauge railways meet south of Buckley Old Station. A crossover is avoided by the building of sidings on an interchange wharf where incoming coal – for the brickworks – is exchanged for outgoing bricks. (*Author*)

And finally, before moving forward in time from the Tramway era, I must refer again to **Fig 11** and **Fig 12** for the Exchange Sidings just south of Buckley Old Station where Hancock's Tramway was intersected

and replaced by the Wrexham, Mold & Connah's Quay Railway.

These are parts of the 'jigsaw' again and can best be understood by re-reading pages 15 to 16 and looking at **Figs 11** & **12**.

A refresher here is **Fig 51** (edited from *Forgotten Railways – North and Mid Wales*, Rex Christiansen, David & Charles, 1976) where the author shows Buckley in detail – 'small, busy and varied.'

Buckley is a jigsaw piece that links together narrow gauge tramways to standard gauge railways, horse haulage to steam and subsequently diesel haulage, mineral traffic to passenger traffic (though none via the original Buckley Railway) and introduces (as marked on **Fig 51**) the Wrexham, Mold & Connah's Quay Railway (WM&CQR). The WM&CQR was one of the elements which started my interest in and research for this book. It is a useful exemplar for railway development in NE Wales because it started bit-by-bit and never reached Mold despite its name. The WM&CQR principal raison d'être was the desire and commercial need of Flintshire and Deeside Iron Masters, Coal Owners and Potters to secure a market for their products via the Dee or the N Wales coastal ports Connah's Quay and Mostyn.

The origins of the line began as several separate railway companies which were progressively amalgamated. Initially some horse tramways were built serving individual works in the late eighteenth and early nineteenth centuries. Main line railways followed from the 1840s but they – like the Chester to Holyhead Railway – skirted the principal areas of production in the Brymbo and Buckley areas. The North Wales Mineral Railway (NWMR) was a tortuous development both in preparing viable proposals to go before parliament and by agreeing a purposeful route. Initially the line was from Wrexham to Rossett and then Saltney on the river Dee and a junction there with the Chester and Holyhead Railway. Finally, an 'extension' from Chester through Gresford and Wrexham then north-westward to Ruabon was sanctioned as were several branches including a line to Brymbo and onwards to Minera. This group of interconnected railways was reconstituted as the Shrewsbury & Chester Railway in 1848 and was merged with the GWR in 1860.

Nevertheless, a direct line from Wrexham through the mineral-rich area NNW of Wrexham and onto tidal water in the Dee Estuary was still missing, so that became the aegis of the WM&CQR.

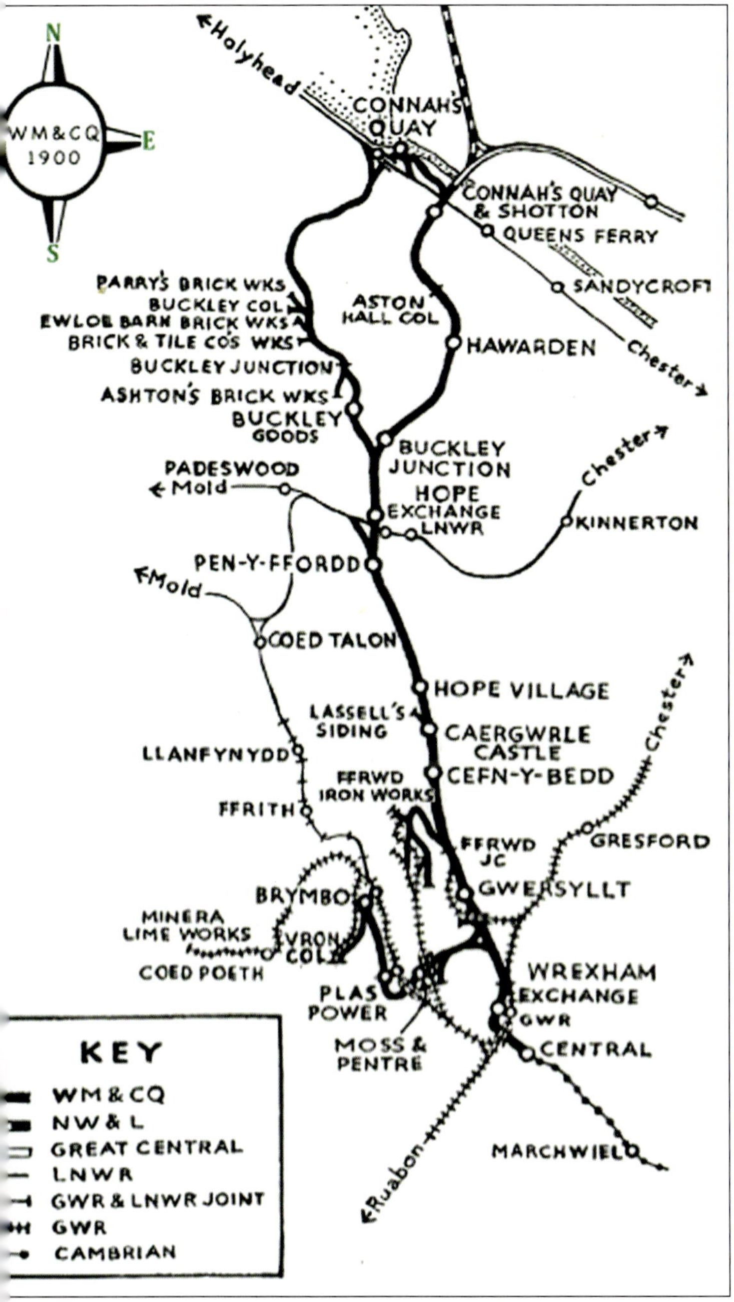

Fig 52: The network of railways which constituted the WM&CQR in 1900. Note that Brymbo had two stations by 1900; one owned and operated by WM&CQR and the other by GWR. (*Author*)

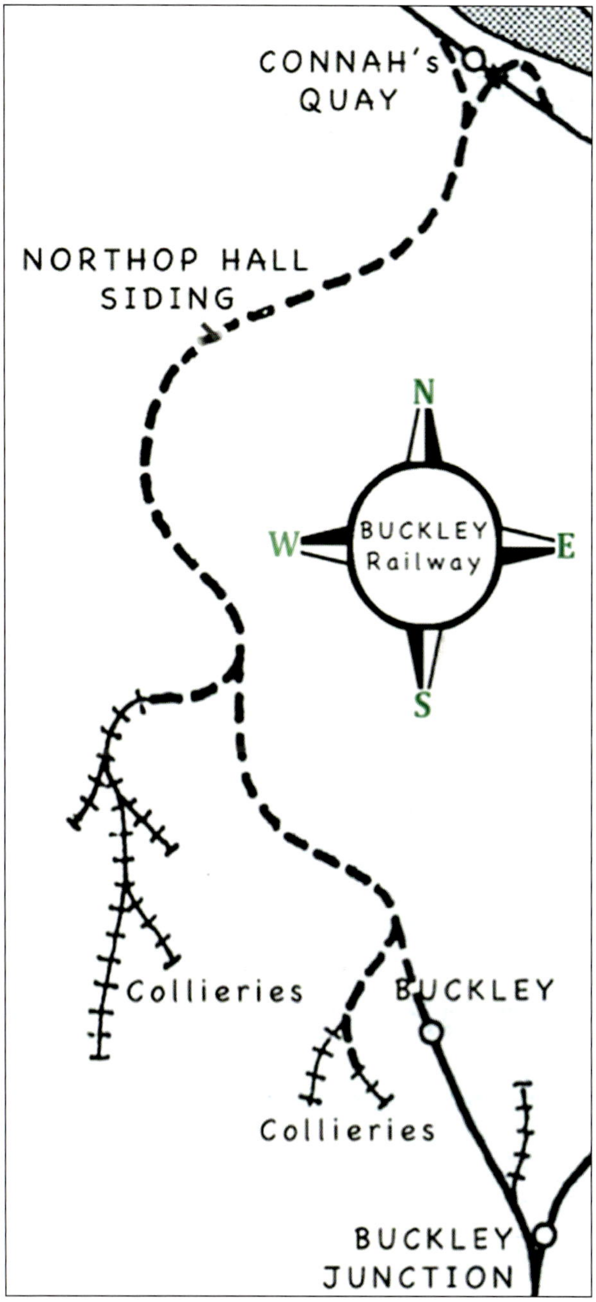

Fig 53: Buckley Railway, an initiative developed in 1860 by local coal owners, brick-makers and potters to secure enhanced market opportunities via the Chester to Holyhead Railway at Connah's Quay or by boat on the river Dee and the Irish Sea. (*Author*)

The entrepreneur who brought it about was Henry Robertson who was at Brymbo Works by 1826. He engineered the Shrewsbury & Chester line and had the far-sighted vision to link together several existing railways into the WM&CQR. The embryo from which Robertson developed his vision was the Buckley Railway which was authorised by an Act of 14 June

1860. It was to be a single track line, 5.5 miles long from near the village of Buckley – a centre of the Flintshire brick and pottery industry – to Connah's Quay on the Dee estuary where there was a small port. Apart from pottery the principal traffic was coal from a number of local collieries and it opened for mineral traffic only on 7 July 1862. At Connah's Quay the Buckley Railway

Fig 54: Buckley Railway's steep descent to Connah's Quay. The weed and litter-strewn trap siding on the right of the picture was intended to trap and contain runaways. (*Author*)

forked to make an up and down connection with the main line Chester to Holyhead Railway (see **Fig 53**).

A strength of the Buckley Railway was its access to Connah's Quay, a tidal port on the Dee estuary which, though relatively small, could handle larger vessels than Saltney Quay further upstream, though that, too, was also rail-connected. One of the operating problems on the Buckley Railway is illustrated in **Fig 54** and in **Fig 55** which is the gradient profile of the whole railway – descending to the Dee but on gradients like 1 in 30 which gives braking problems downhill and haulage problems uphill.

Connah's Quay had been inadvertently benefited by the Dee Navigation Company deepening the navigable channel in the estuary southwards in the eighteenth century. Connah's creek was developed as a quay by the Irish Coal Company in the early nineteenth century. The Buckley Railway, opened to the quay in 1860, made the quay busy for fishing and for exporting coal and bricks in sailing and steam vessels. The Chester to Holyhead railway opened in 1848 and brought more cargoes to the port as did the Buckley Railway which provided direct rail links onto the wharves as illustrated in **Fig 56** and **Fig 57**.

Henry Robertson was established at Brymbo Works from 1826 but with a much wider vision for the development of the NE Wales and Deeside area. He was keen to extend the local railway network and was aware of the potential in the geographically isolated Buckley Railway and its port at Connah's Quay. His solution was the Wrexham, Mold & Connah's Quay Railway (WM&CQR) Company, incorporated on 7 August 1862. The engineer and principal promoter was Benjamin Piercy, who was a very experienced civil engineer and business partner with Henry Robertson in several NE Wales railway projects.

Incorporation of the WM&CQR had been bitterly opposed by several influential bodies, including the GWR, so the Act only permitted a line from Wrexham to Buckley, a junction with the Buckley Railway and running powers over that railway to Connah's Quay. An 'extension' was also sought for a junction at Hope

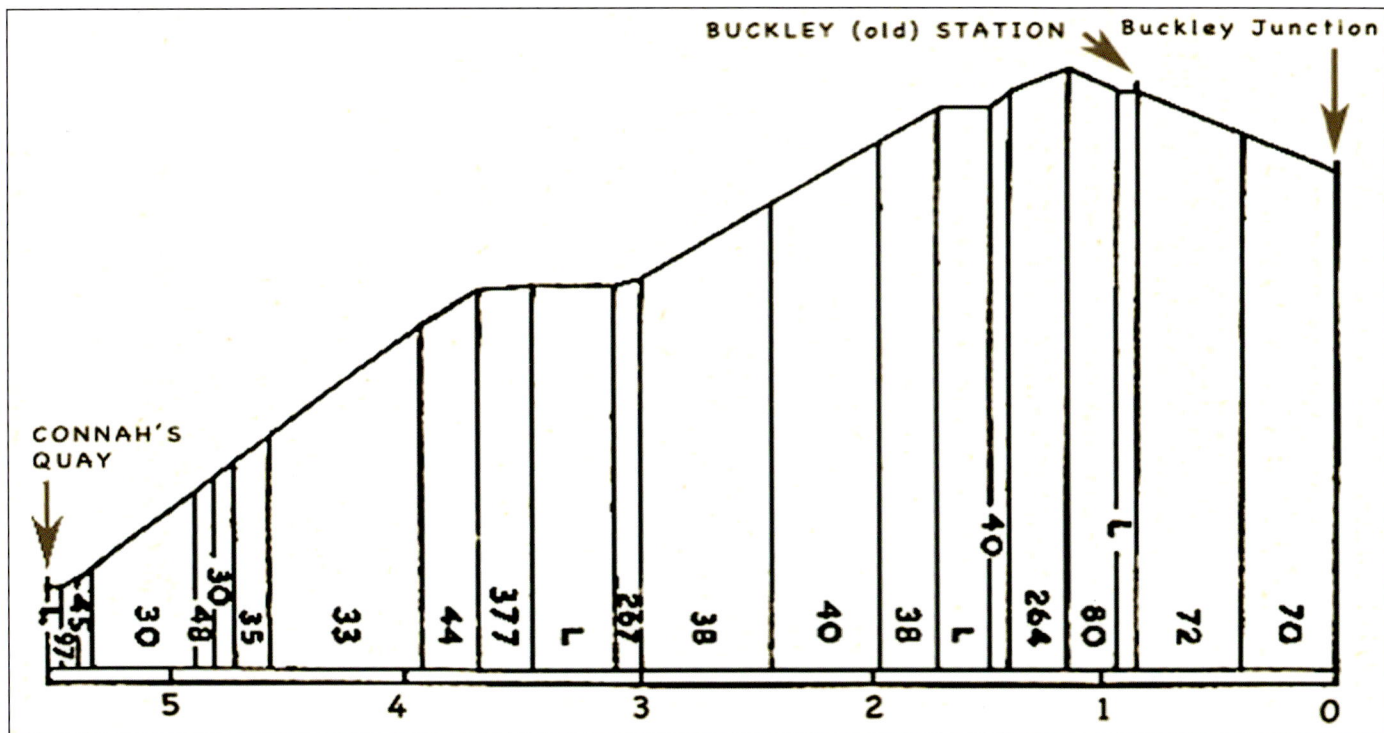

Fig 55: Gradient profile of Buckley Railway from Buckley (old) Station to Connah's Quay. (*Author*)

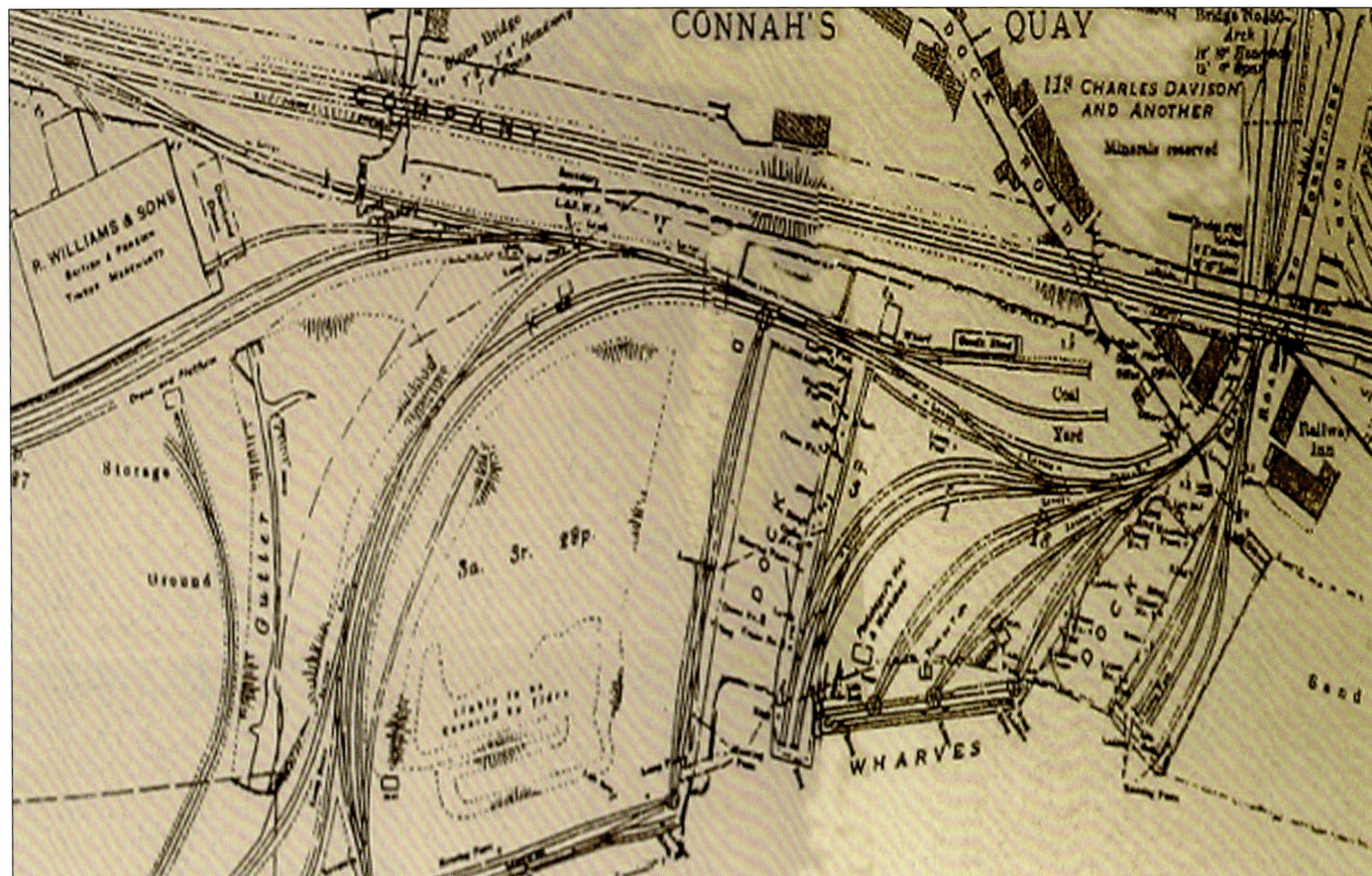

Fig 56: Connah's Quay railways c 1880.

Fig 57: Sail and steam vessels in Top Dock, Connah's Quay, 1911.

onto the L&NWR Chester to Denbigh line for access Mold. However, although a south to west rail link was constructed, parliament refused through-running powers (see **Fig 52** and **Fig 58** maps).

The rail link to the Chester-Denbigh line was primarily for freight traffic in an exchange of wagons between WM&CQR and L&NWR systems. For passengers, two Hope Exchange stations were created; Hope Exchange High Level was on the WM&CQR and Hope Exchange Low Level on the L&NWR so by changing trains, stations and operating companies, passengers could reach Mold from Wrexham via the WM&CQR. (see **Fig 58**).

As I mentioned earlier, I was inspired to research the WM&CQR because of its intriguing name and that it apparently linked a number of places and industries I was exploring in NE Wales. However, the links were sometimes tenuous – like Mold which the railway never reached – and I soon discovered that several other railway companies, like GWR and Manchester

Sheffield & Liverpool Railway (MS&LR), were also interested in the mineral riches which the Buckley Railway and the WM&CQR were built to exploit.

The Directors of the WM&CQR were ambitious but the management of the growing railway was sometimes careless and ineffectual. For instance, a Company Rule Book– which was a Board of Trade requirement – was compiled in 1865, before opening, but by 1867 it was still unprinted so some Hoylake Railway Rule Books were obtained to circulate to WM&CQR staff. Hoylake Railway, also opened in 1866, was only five miles long between the small fishing village of Hoylake and Wallasey Bridge Road near Birkenhead Docks. Traffic was small and debts considerable, so the *Morning Advertiser* of 22 September 1869 carried a Notice stating: 'Sale of a Railway: in pursuance of a Chancery decree . . .'

The problems faced by the Hoylake Railway should have been a warning to the WM&CQR Directors for their mounting debts were considerable too. By 1868,

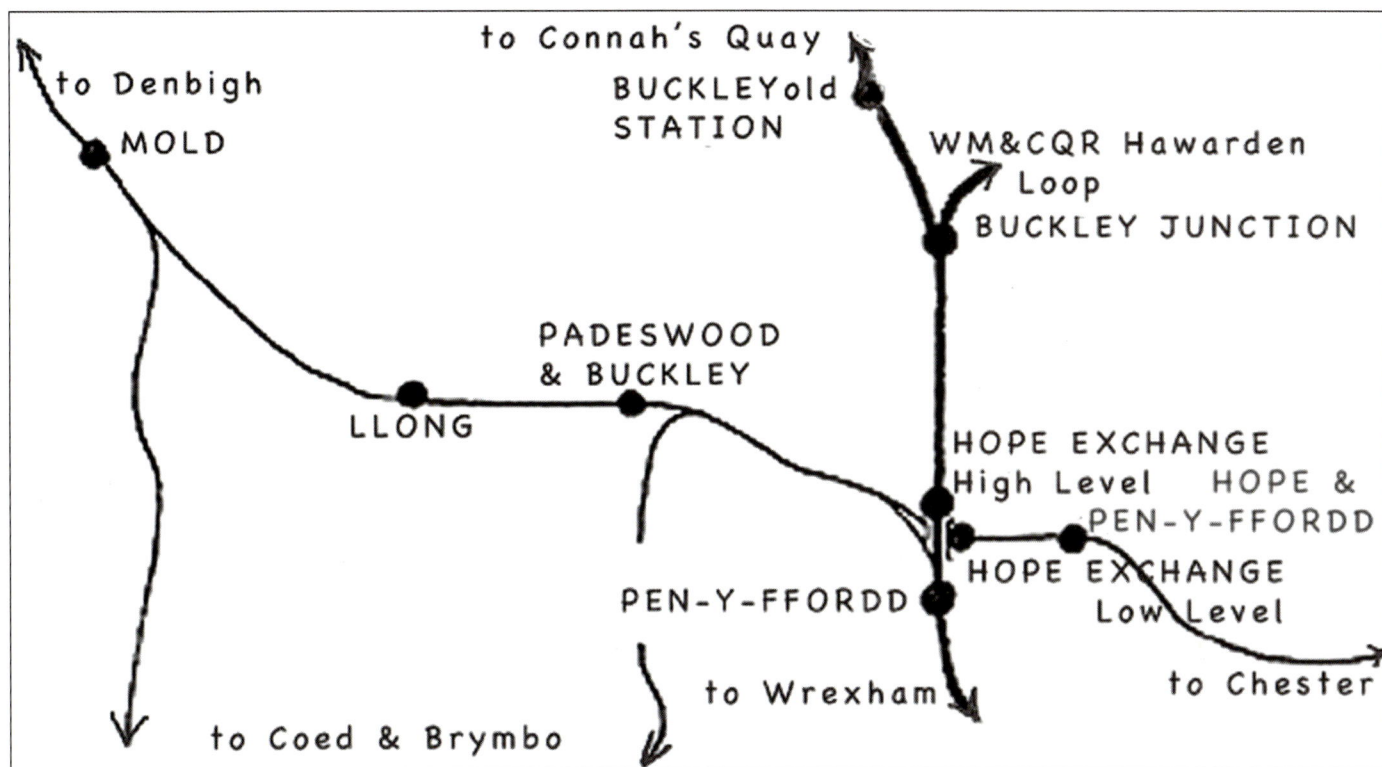

Fig 58: Sketch map explaining the complexity of WM&CQR stations to provide passenger access to the L&NWR Chester-Denbigh line and to justify the use of 'Mold' in the WM&CQR Company name. (*Author*)

negotiations were in hand with the L&NWR for that railway to work the WM&CQR for 50 per cent of the gross traffic receipts but no agreement was made. In the same year, and to save Company administrative costs, it was agreed that the posts of Secretary, General Manager and Accountant should be combined for a salary not exceeding £350pa which would also cover the costs of a clerk.

Perhaps not surprisingly the WM&CQR was described by some competitors as 'a ramshackle railway' but it took pride in the livery of its locomotives as shown in **Fig 59**.

Fig 59: 2-6-0T locomotive No 3 after rebuilding at WM&CQ works at Rhosddu in 1899. (*Jeff Howard*)

The railway struggled on and was helped by the increasing output from the Flintshire collieries. In 1877 the posts of Secretary and General Manager were separated again, and Thomas Cartwright was appointed to the latter post on 31 July. Cartwright, trained on the L&NWR, moved to WM&CQR from his managerial role on the Ruthin & Corwen Railway where he had earned a reputation as a very competent railway officer. In 1882 Benjamin Piercy began to work on railway projects again with Henry Robertson; by the end of the 1880s he owned sufficient WM&CQR shares to give him a controlling interest in its management and policy.

In particular, and because Piercy was a respected and experienced promoter to parliament of railway projects, he obtained Acts for the construction of extensions previously authorised but discontinued because they were never completed. They were:

- From Wrexham Exchange to a new station which was nearer to the middle of the town than Wrexham Exchange so became Wrexham Central. Substantial goods facilities were built to the west of Wrexham Central and subsequently goods facilities nearer to the station including a large brick-built goods shed, sidings, a cattle dock, livestock pens and a 2-ton crane.
- A 3.5 mile extension to Brymbo via Plas Power
- A mineral branch to Ffrwd Iron Works
- A mineral branch to Vron Colliery
- Hawarden Loop, initially from Buckley Junction to Hawarden and then extended to Shotton and a junction with the L&NWR's Chester to Holyhead Railway

Hawarden Loop is a useful segue in the story of WM&CQR and its takeover by the Manchester, Sheffield & Lincolnshire Railway (MS&LR) which was shortly to become the Great Central Railway (GCR). As is often the case in such developments, it is powerful and well-placed people who are the engines of change. Benjamin Piercy was keen to promote through-working with other powerful railways – especially those in which he had a financial interest – that were, or could be, near neighbours of the WM&CQR. He envisaged a link with L&NWR via Hope Junction and Connah's Quay, where the Chester to Holyhead Railway had been absorbed by the L&NWR in 1859 and via Hawarden Swing Bridge

which the MS&LR completed over the Dee to Shotton in 1889.

However, powerful men who are engines of change can be derailed by events beyond their control. In 1866 the banking firm of Overend, Gurney & Co collapsed; their principal business was buying and selling discounted bills of exchange. It was a well respected banking company and had substantial investments in a number of railway developments. The ensuing crisis was a turning point in British financial history. The next serious financial disruption that really affected the country was in the London money market in 2007-8 when Lehman Brothers, a real estate-hedge fund disguised as an investment bank, were bankrupted. Piercy, also facing possible bankruptcy, had to hand over his assets – mainly shares including a large holding in the WM&CQR – to trustees. And on 22 March 1888 Henry Robertson died as did Benjamin Piercy, two days later.

In what today looks like a game of falling dominos, Robertson and Piercy had fallen so Sir Edward Watkin, another powerful railway promoter, seized his chance, Watkin was the son of Absalom Watkin, a wealthy Manchester cotton merchant and, for a time, Edward worked for his father but moved into railway promotion, speculation and management in 1845. He is part of our story because in 1853 he became General Manager of the MS&LR and began possible joint working relationships with the Great Northern Railway, the Midland Railway and the L&NWR to ensure the survival, and growth, of his own company. It is a measure of his contacts and the growing respect for his expertise that in 1861, at the request of the Colonial Secretary, he was asked to visit Canada. He was to investigate means of confederating the five British provinces into the Dominion of Canada, and of transferring the Hudson Bay territory from the Hudson Bay Company to the control of the Canadian Government. He was also engaged in planning railways to Quebec and became President of the Grand Trunk Railway of Canada.

Watkins returned to Britain and became Chairman of the MS&L in 1863, a post he held until 1894. In addition, and for a short time in 1866, he was a Director of the GWR and, in 1867, of the GER. In the Wirral area he was keen to gain access to Liverpool for the MS&LR. He was a great believer in partnerships and joint working arrangements between railway companies, especially if his company – MS&LR – was leading the arrangement and benefitting itself. The close working together of MS&LR and Great Northern Railway (GNR) enabled them to evolve the Cheshire Lines Committee (CLC) and break the L&NWR's near monopoly in Southern Lancashire and Northern Cheshire.

The CLC worked in an area which included major cities like Manchester, Liverpool and the developing Lancashire coal fields but, not yet, across the Dee to the NE Wales coalfield. But, and it is a measure of Watkin's skills as a business man, CLC owned no locomotives, declared no dividends and held no shareholders' meeting. As **Fig 60** suggests, CLC counted the pennies and ensured by order that there was nothing for those who had not already bought a ticket!

A Watkin's initiative to cross the Dee and connect with the WM&CQR and thence, he anticipated, access to NE Wales, was engendered by the MS&LR promoting an 1884 Parliamentary Act for the Chester & Connah's

Quay Railway. The intention was a route from Chester to Wrexham via the WM&CQR's Hawarden Loop and to Birkenhead (for Liverpool) in conjunction with the North Wales & Liverpool Railway (NW&LR), MS&LR and WM&CQR. The junction between the railways was at Hawarden Bridge and involved the construction of the Hawarden Swing Bridge. (illustrated in **Fig 61**). The bridge was a major example of British engineering with a swing span 287ft long weighing 843 tons – then the longest and heaviest ever made. Contractor John Cochrane & Sons submitted a tender in February 1888 – which was accepted – at £55,802 for the steel structure and £6,850 for the hydraulic machinery to turn the swing span; approximately £63,000 which in 2020 would be £67M. This sum was apportioned between the three railways.

The Hawarden Swing Bridge opened for traffic on 3 August 1889 and both the Hawarden Loop of the WM&CQR and the Chester & Connah's Quay Railway

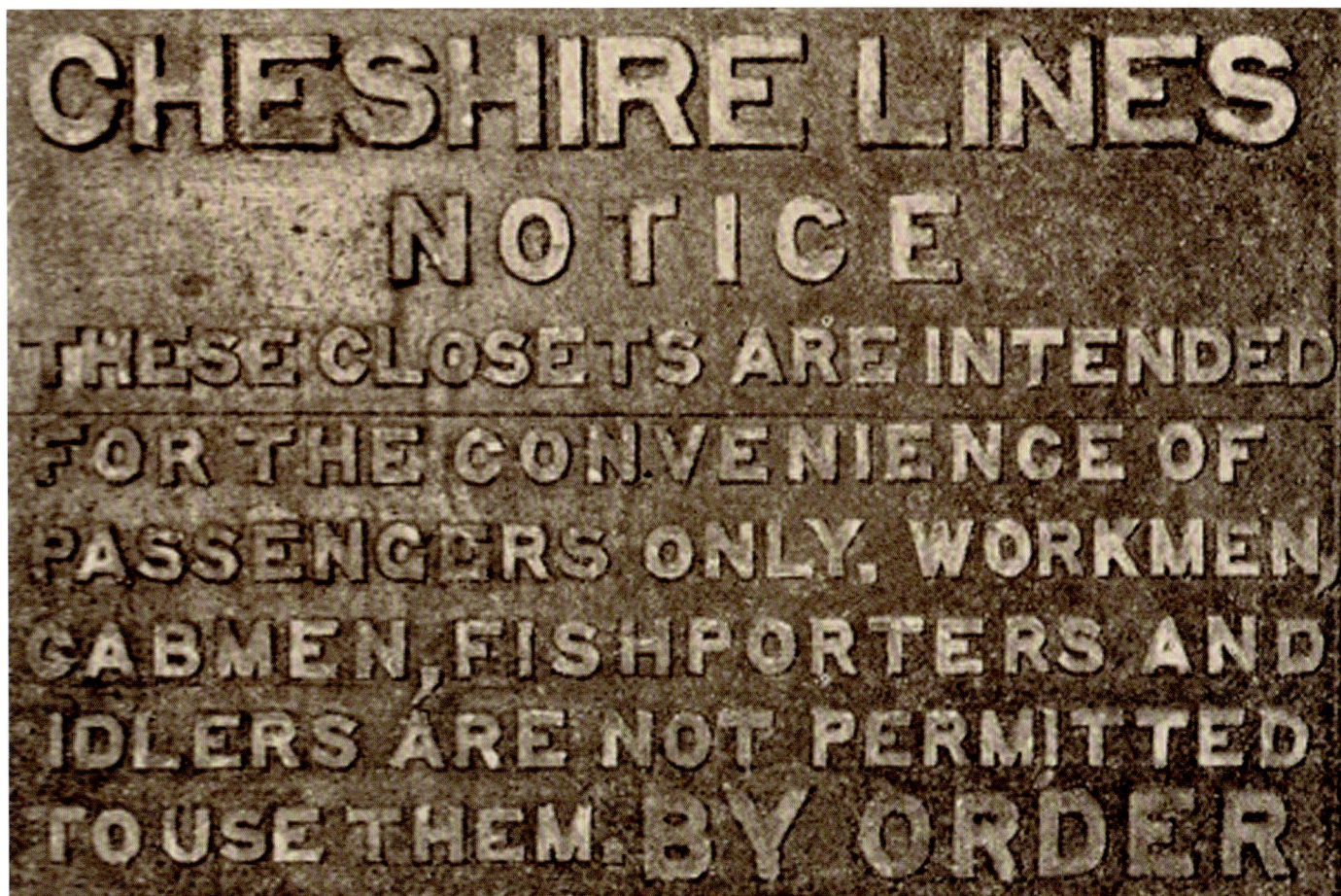

Fig 60: Cast iron Cheshire Lines notice illustrating the company's thrift in ensuring that only passengers who had paid for a ticket could use Cheshire Lines closets at their convenience.

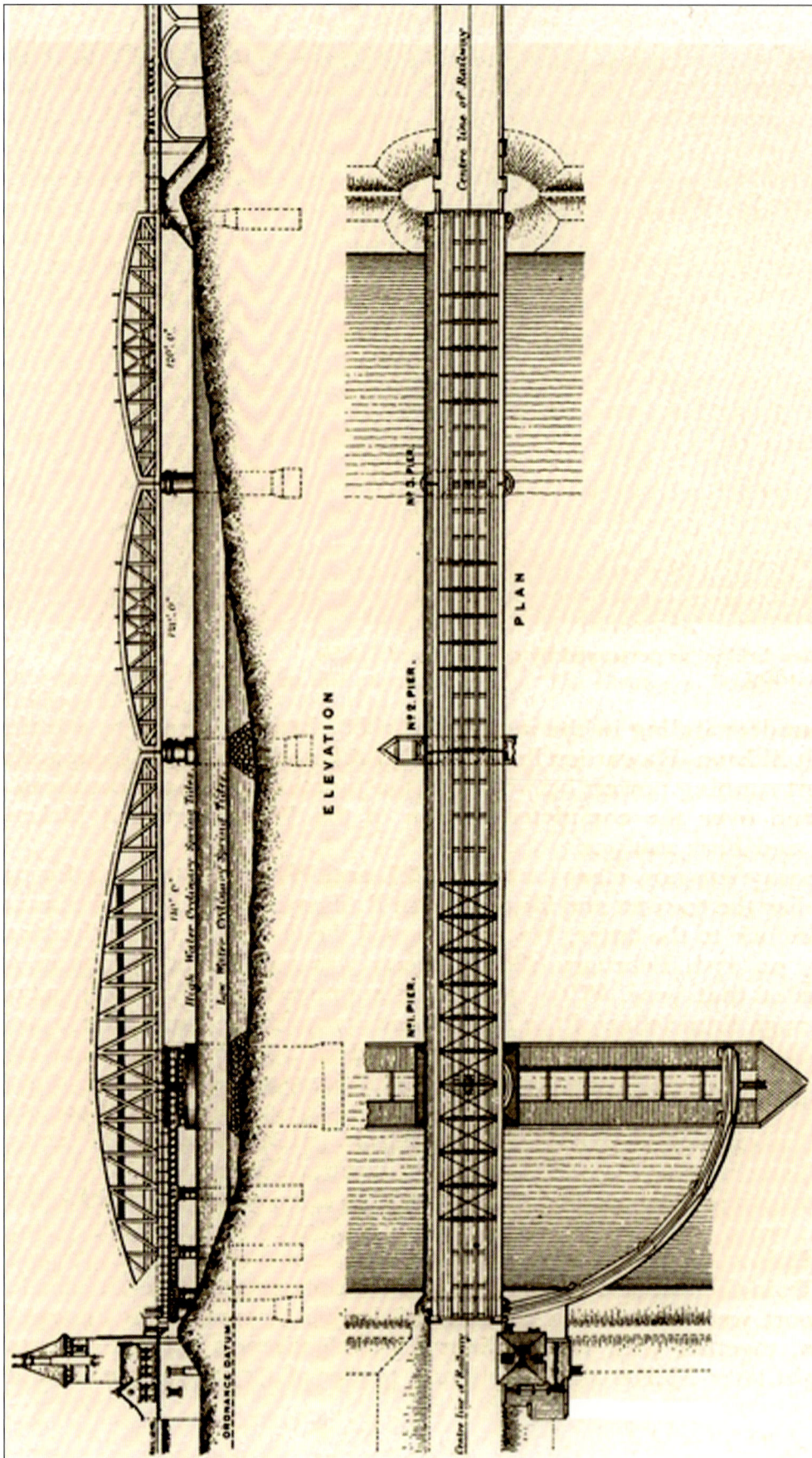

Fig 61: Engineering contractor's elevation and plan (not to scale) for the Hawarden Swing Bridge.

opened on 31 March 1890. The MS&LR worked the four weekday through trains between Chester Northgate and Wrexham Central so Watkin's company already had a wheel (or several wheels) along the metals of the WM&CQR. Soon there was more because the MS&L General Manager, Colonel Sir William Pollitt, had been negotiating with the late Benjamin Piercy's Trustees. By August 1890 he acquired for the MS&L Piercy's holding of £339,807 of WM&CQ Ordinary Stock and with it control of the railway. Two WM&CQR Directors resigned immediately so Pollitt and the MS&L Secretary, Edward Ross, took their places on 15 August; on 30 August Pollitt was formally installed as Chairman of the Board. In October, another resignation enabled Herbert Gladstone MP to join him – and to strengthen his political contacts.

Watkin's dreams were almost fulfilled by 1892 and in that year the MS&L Board decided to start building the Hawarden to Bidston line and informed the WM&CQR Board that they would have to start paying 10 per cent interest on their share of the estimated construction cost of £300,000. This the WM&CQR was unable to do but MS&L continued to build – increasing the WM&CQR's indebtedness and by May 1896 the new railway – now called North Wales & Liverpool Railway – was open for goods and passenger traffic.

In the late 1897 the MS&L – which was now the Great Central Railway – decided to protect its interests by obtaining an Order for appointment as the Receiver for the WM&CQR; Frank Williams, the GCR Accountant had oversight of the WM&CQR' accounts from 31 October 1897. The debts Williams uncovered in these accounts were considerable as were the shortcomings in rolling stock, structures and track listed by the GCR Engineer. Apart from total closure – which, of course, would not answer Watkin's needs and ambitions – the only solution was to transfer WM&CQR holdings to its principal creditor, which happened to be GCR.

In the course of these machinations another domino in this elaborate 'game' fell when Sir Edward Watkin died on 13 April 1901. (**Fig 62**) He was a highly intellectual man who was imperious, very energetic in pursuing his interests, and doggedly ambitious. Watkin's ambition resulted in vast expenditure on unnecessary schemes, and his unbending, inconsiderate manner led to the resignation of the SER Chairman and the resignation and subsequent suicide of the

Fig 62: Sir Edward Watkin in 1891. (*Author*)

MS&L Locomotive Superintendent Charles Sacré. Nevertheless, he achieved much: he had recognised the value of Connah's Quay as a Deeside port (**Fig 63**); he was instrumental in the MS&L's London Extension to the new station of Marylebone; he was chairman of the MS&L/GCR, the Metropolitan Railway and the SER so had a vision for a railway from Manchester to Paris via the Channel Tunnel; and even his wildest scheme for the Watkin Tower (to rival the Eiffel Tower) in Wembley Park did provide the site for Wembley Stadium in 1923.

The Watkin domino fell but he was replaced by another career railwayman, Sir Sam Fay, who succeeded Pollitt as Chairman of the MS&L/GCR in 1902. He was less aggressively ambitious than Watkin but was a hard-working and knowledgeable man. He was knighted in 1912 and retired from GCR Chairmanship at railway grouping in 1923. He continued to be active with two Argentinian Railway directorships and ten years as Chairman of Beyer Peacock & Co Ltd. He intended to write his memoirs but only managed rough notes concluding, inter alia, with, 'Worldly success and the good things of life have been mine to the full; for these and other blessings I am grateful with all that in me lies.'

In NE Wales, and with the knowledge and support of Sam Fay, an Act was obtained on 22 July 1904 to vest the

WM&CQR, the Buckley Railway, and the Hawarden & Bidston Railway – now called the N Wales & Liverpool Railway – in the GCR with effect from 1 January 1895.

My story of the WM&CQR is complete and it illustrates the number of local industrial and land-owning promoters who were prepared to sink money and energy into railway development in NE Wales and Deeside. So more bits of the jigsaw fit together and make a coherent picture but others remain . . .

A principal jigsaw piece and route centre for the area was Wrexham which was well-placed for the industries of Flintshire and Denbighshire; the resources were there (illustrated in **Fig 64**) but in the early nineteenth century, land transport was only by unsurfaced tracks, turnpikes, canals and tramways. News was shared in Wales about Stockton & Darlington Railway disputes on the potential for horses, or steam locomotives or steam stationary engines so the *North Wales Gazette* carried an article about:

'Rail-Roads and Loco-Motive Engines:
'Hitherto, rail-roads have been used for very limited purposes . . . in connection with Coal Pits and Stone Quarries. [But they are now] to be applied for the purpose of conveying merchandise over very extended lines of country . . . By the Loco-Motive Engine fifty tons of goods may be conveyed by a ten horse power engine on a level road at the rate of six miles an hour, [and] carriages for the conveyance of passengers at the rate of twelve or fourteen miles an hour.' 2nd September 1824.

There was an interest in railway development in NE Wales from Coal Owners and Iron Masters but

CONNAH'S QUAY.—Port of Chester, on the North Coast of Wales, on the River Dee. This place is the terminus of the Wrexham, Mold and Connah's Quay Railway, which is connected with the other Railway systems.

☞ For Dimensions of Docks, &c., See Appendix.

IMPORTS: Minerals, Timber, Iron, Straw, Iron Ore, Manure, &c.

EXPORTS: Coals, Bricks, Iron, Manure, &c.

DEPTH OF WATER alongside the Wharves: Springs, 16 to 18 feet; Neaps, 10 to 14 feet. This does not apply to the River below. Vessels of from 12 to 14 feet only can get here on Spring Tides, without lightening; 8 to 9 feet on the Neaps.

HARBOUR DUES: 1s. per Vessel, and 4d. per reg. ton Foreign, and 2d. Coasting.

PILOTAGE: There is a Pilot Boat for outside work.

TOWAGE RATES: Foreign-going vessels, 6d. per ton reg.; Coasters, 3d. to 4d. per ton reg.

BALLAST RATE: 1s. 6d. per ton put on board; Discharging Ballast, 1s. 1½d. per reg. ton.

M. J. CULHANE, Superintendent H.M. Customs.
R. B. MILLER, Agent and Harbour Master.
H. E. TAYLOR, Pilot Master for the Port.

Fig 63: Ralph Turnbull & Son's *Guide to UK Dock & Port Charges* 1904.

the obstacles to that development were the physical geography of the area, the opposition from turnpike trustees and the exalted ideas of many landowners for compensation if a railway was to cross their estate. Curiously, for a story that is concentrating on Wales, it was the demands for a swift route for the Irish Mails that led to the Chester to Holyhead Railway (opened March 1850) taking its present course. Ireland was still a single country in the nineteenth century and as railways developed the government wished to send government papers as well as postal mail to the island as swiftly as possible. Entrepreneurs in NE Wales saw an opportunity for a railway to Holyhead and several alternative routes were considered but George Stephenson's Survey and Report of 1838 decided the matter by recommending the present coastal route. A perceived advantage for some industrial sites, like

Buckley, Holywell and Dyserth, was that branch lines could connect with the coastal line.

So, the railways were coming and the industries could supply traffic for them, and marketing opportunities for the industries – as illustrated in **Fig 64**.

'"About five and thirty years ago . . . a cry went through the North country that a great deal of money might be made by opening Wales, that is by mining Wales in the proper fashion. . . There have long been mines in Wales but they have always been worked in a poor, weak, languid manner . . ." An old Durham miner talking to George Borrow near Devil's Bridge, Ceredigion, Wales in 1854.'

George Borrow was an East Anglian author and traveller, educated at Norwich Grammar School, who

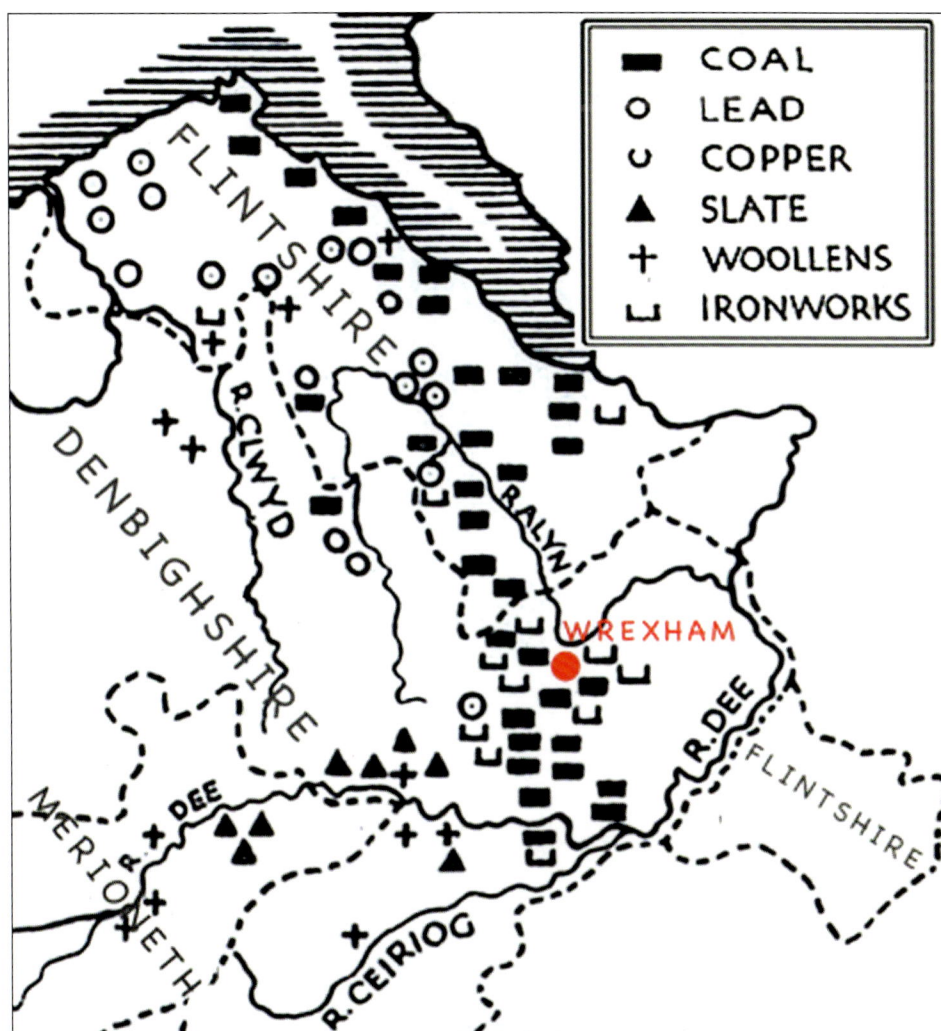

Fig 64: Developing industries in NE Wales and Deeside – 1760-1850. (*Author*)

developed language skills and a desire to travel. He was interested to find out how other peoples, and Romany travellers lived and talked. He enjoyed long walking tours in the UK and his visit to Wales provided material for *Wild Wales: Its People, Language & Scenery* first published in 1862. Borrow, in his book, and the Durham miner are supplying other parts for the jigsaw in this book. The resources implicit in the **Fig 64** map were known to wealthy English speculators such as Nathan Meyer Rothschild. English newspapers, like *Shrewsbury Chronicle* which circulated in the border areas of Wales, pointed out that North Wales offered rich opportunities for English capital and skills – like Durham and Cornish miners.

Wrexham area railways: I have added Wrexham to the **Fig 64** map because it is a large market town, route centre,

and now the administrative centre of Wrexham County Borough with a population of about 67,000. As a railway node it developed three railway stations, Wrexham Exchange, General and Central; all initially related to a particular railway company and best illustrated in the sketch map in **Fig 65**.

The fact that a relatively small town gained three separate stations is an indication of the potential wealth in passenger and goods traffic that the principal railway companies calculated they could develop. The WM&CQR/GCR demonstrated marketing skills in building a new station that really was more accessible to the town of Wrexham than Exchange or General, and calling it Wrexham Central – which it was!

But going back to the 1920s, illustrated in **Fig 66**, shows how the Wrexham area railways really did try to serve the industries to the NNW of the town.

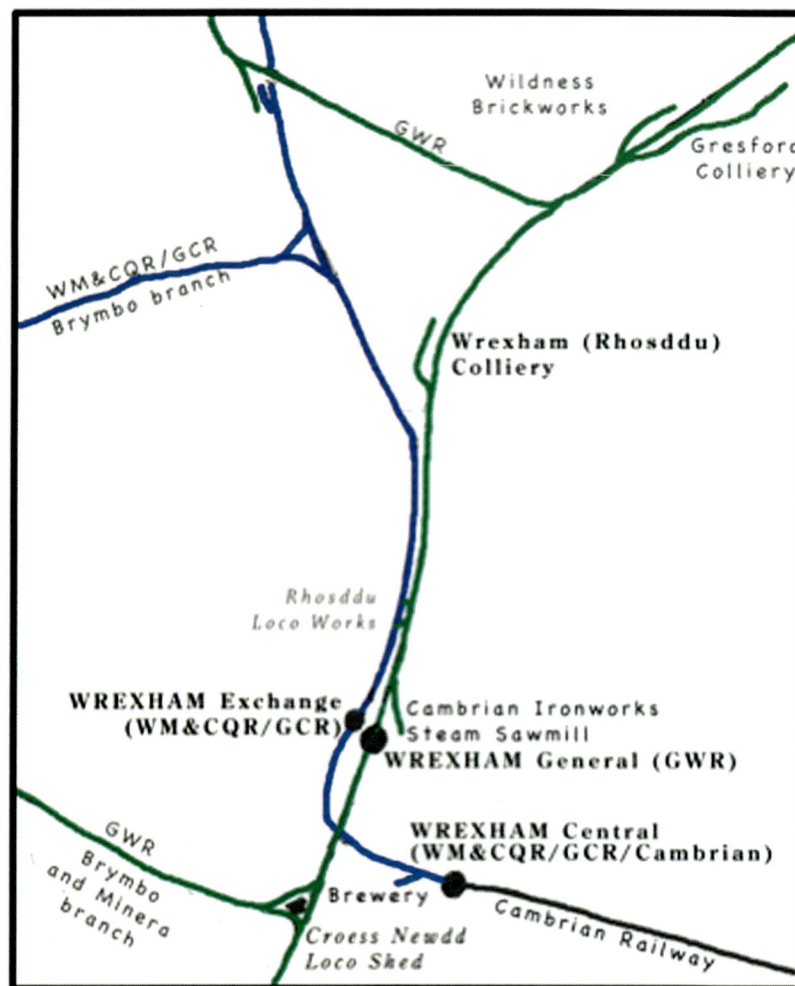

Fig 65: Sketch map (not to scale) illustrating the complexities of railways, and stations, at Wrexham c1946 – after the grouping but before British Railways was set up in 1948. (*Author*)

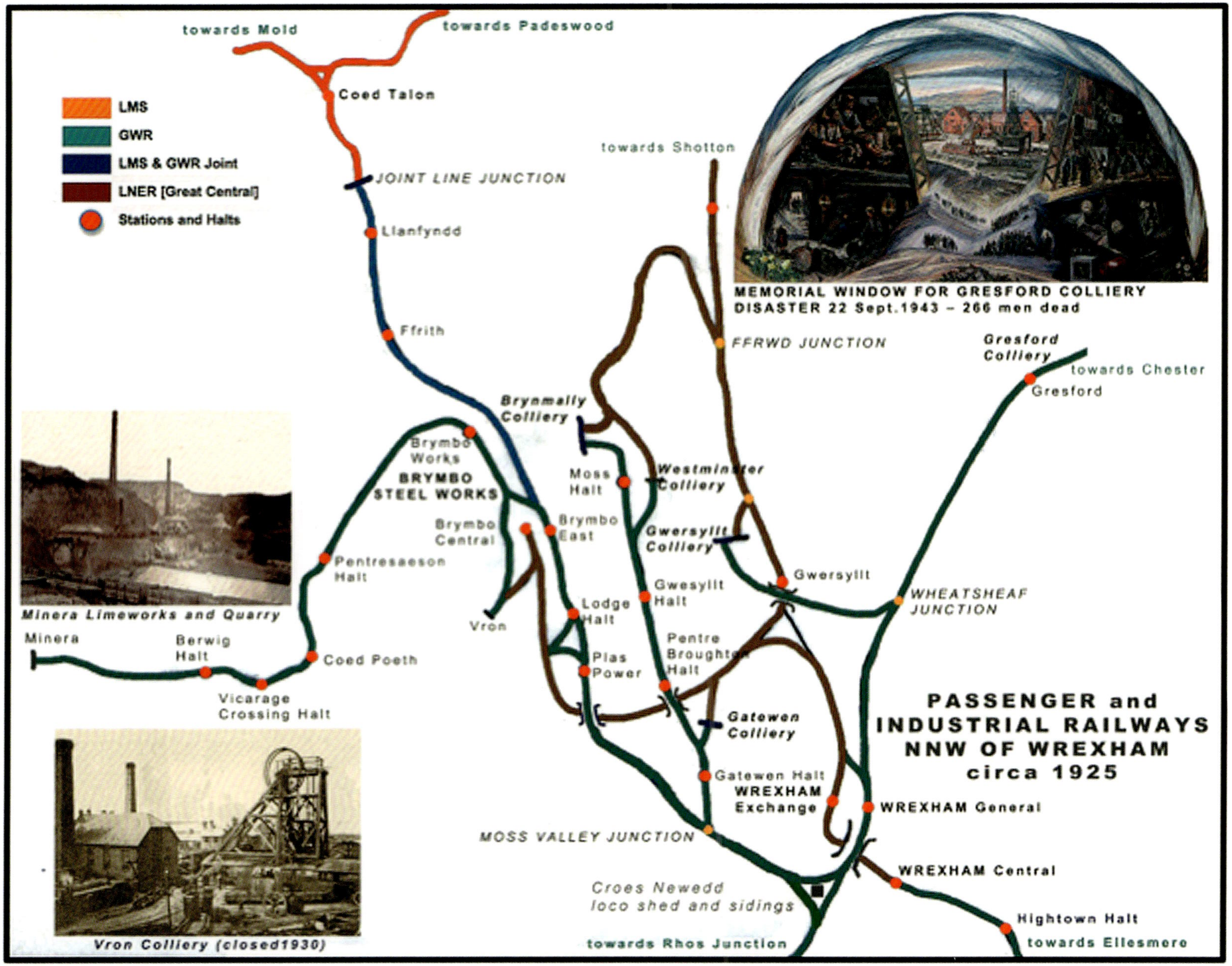

PASSENGER and INDUSTRIAL RAILWAYS NNW of WREXHAM circa 1925

MEMORIAL WINDOW FOR GRESFORD COLLIERY DISASTER 22 Sept.1943 – 266 men dead

towards Chester

Gresford

Gresford Colliery

FFRWD JUNCTION

WHEATSHEAF JUNCTION

Gwersyllt

WREXHAM General

WREXHAM Central

Hightown Halt

towards Ellesmere

Westminster Colliery

Gwersyllt Colliery

Gwersyllt Halt

Pentre Broughton Halt

Gatewen Colliery

Gatewen Halt

WREXHAM Exchange

Brymelly Colliery

Moss Halt

Brymbo East

Lodge Halt

Plas Power Halt

Vron

MOSS VALLEY JUNCTION

Croes Newedd loco shed and sidings

towards Rhos Junction

towards Shotton

towards Padeswood

towards Mold

Coed Talon

JOINT LINE JUNCTION

Llanfynydd

Ffrith

Brymbo Works

BRYMBO STEEL WORKS

Brymbo Central

Pentresaeson Halt

Coed Poeth

Vicarage Crossing Halt

Minera Limeworks and Quarry

Minera

Berwig Halt

Vron Colliery (closed 1930)

LMS
GWR
LMS & GWR Joint
LNER [Great Central]
Stations and Halts

Fig 66: The network of passenger and mineral railways which were developed to serve the iron works, collieries and brick works NNW of Wrexham. (*Author*)

I hope, with **Fig 66** as a visual guide, that the jigsaw to which I have referred before is shaping in the reader's mind as a nearly completed picture. Brymbo Steel Works

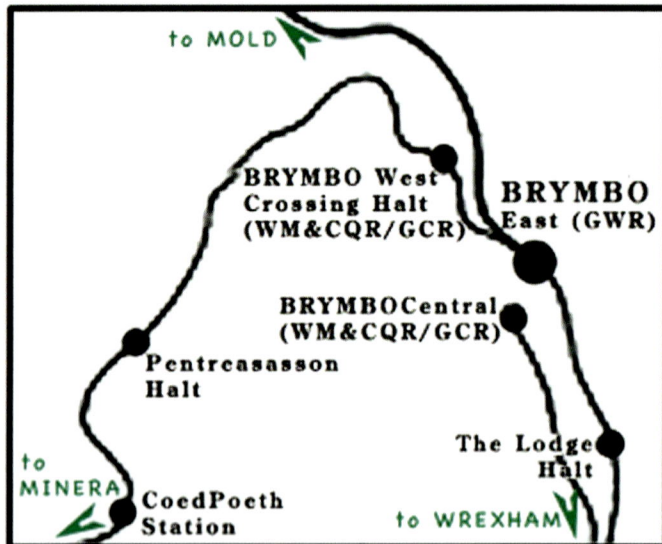

Fig 67: Sketch map (not to scale) of the two Brymbo stations and the railway companies working them. (*Author*)

is described more fully in the next chapter – & Iron and Steel making – but **Fig 66** shows that serving Brymbo was another example of competition between GWR at Brymbo East station and WM&CQR/GCR at Brymbo Central. Neither station was especially attractive and Brymbo Central was overlooked and dwarfed by Brymbo Steel Works which grew on its own levelled slag tips as subsequent pictures will show.

Fig 67 is a sketch map which shows the two principal railways providing a passenger service at Brymbo in the 1920s. The Great Western Railway (GWR) provide a joint service with the L&NWR from Brymbo East to Mold and a freight and passenger service westwards towards Minera where the were extensive lead and lime works.

Brymbo grew up around an early Iron Works which, as the next chapter explains, expanded to a large specialist Steel Works so the railway links were important for freight and for passengers.

The WM&CQR/GCR station was close to – hence the name Brymbo Central – and almost overwhelmed by

Fig 68: View over part of Brymbo Steel Works in 1890 showing railway links.

the Works (see **Fig 73**). It was not especially well-placed to where most people lived in the hilly valley along which Brymbo village had developed. Although GWR's Brymbo General station was in slightly more open country it, too, was not very convenient for passengers walking to the station.

Perhaps the most convenient was GWR's Brymbo West Crossing Halt (opened 1905) which was near the centre of the village where the Minera branch crossed the High Street, hence a level crossing (**Fig 69**). This station at less than 100ft above sea level was about 300ft lower than Brymbo General which was approached up Mount Hill Road.

But West Crossing Halt was only a Halt with timber platforms and no facilities for waiting passengers (see **Fig 69**). However, GWR General Station may have been worth the walk up Mount Hill because there were more trains, NW to Mold and SE to Wrexham. West Crossing Halt also served Wrexham, which was the nearest market town to Brymbo village, and Berwig Crossing Halt for Minera. (see GWR timetable 1922 in **Fig 70**)

Fig 69: Brymbo West Crossing Halt on the GWR Minera Branch c1910.

Fig 70: GWR Timetable by Bradshaw – July 1922. Brymbo West Crossing Halt is marked as a 'Halt'. Brymbo GWR General Station is also a booked stop and will be shown, too, in Table 475. Note the **H** and **K** references for some short workings which show that there is anticipated business to and from Brymbo West Crossing Halt.

Because freight traffic continued to Brymbo until the 1960s, several railway study and enthusiast specials were scheduled to visit Brymbo, usually from Wrexham to Brymbo Central station and sometimes onto the Minera branch. **Fig 74a** is the *Denbighsire Railtour* at Brymbo General Station in September 1952. The train travelled over several branches, including the Minera branch. It makes a useful comparison with **Fig 72** – photographed in 1960 – because the photographer is near the level crossing looking towards the station building. Perhaps the station sign was cleaned specially for the *Denbighsire Railtour*!

Fig 71: Brymbo General Station (GWR) c1910 looking towards the Minera branch and Mold.

Fig 72: Brymbo General Station (GWR) in 1960. The Station closed to passenger services in 1950 but freight traffic continued and the principal building shown in **Fig 71** remains, though somewhat derelict. However, the footbridge has gone.

Right: **Fig 73**: Brymbo Central Station (WM&CQR/GCR) 1935 looking north towards the buffer stops. The Station closed to passengers in 1917 but freight traffic continued until 1956 because it was a head-shunt for goods trains reversing into collieries and Brymbo Steel Works sidings.

Below: **Fig 74a**: A combined special train organised by SLS and the Manchester Locomotive Society (MLS) on 6th September 1952.

Location	Booked	Actual
Wrexham General	15.00	15.01
Rhos Jn	15 04	15.07
Rhos	15.16 ~ 15.31	15.15 ~ 15.27
Point 5m 30ch (1)	15.40 ~ 15.55	15.46 ~ 16.03
Rhos	16.04	16.22
Rhos Jn	16.15	16.33
Wrexham General	16.18 ~ 16.20	16.36 ~ 16.40
Croes Newydd North Fork	16.22	
Brymbo Station	16 32 ~ 16.47	16.52
Brymbo Jt. Jn	16.48 ~ 17.00	
Ffrith (2)	17.05 ~ 17.20	16.58 ~ 17.15
Brymbo Jt. Jn	17.25 ~ 17.27	15.20 ~ 15.27
Coed Poeth	17.37	17/36
Minera (3)	17.42 ~ 18.00	17.48 ~ 18.10
Coed Poeth	18.05	18.17 ~ 18.20
Brymbo Station	18.15	18.27
Croes Newydd North Fork	18.25	
Wrexham General	18.27	18.34

Fig 74b: The working timetable for the train illustrated in **Fig 74a**. The timetable details the route and has been edited from the timings recorded by Ian Clarke (SLS) with Stephen Bragg & Peter Greenough (MLS).

Fig 75 is another special visiting Brymbo, this time organised by the Railway Correspondence Transport Society in 1967, and relevant here because it shows

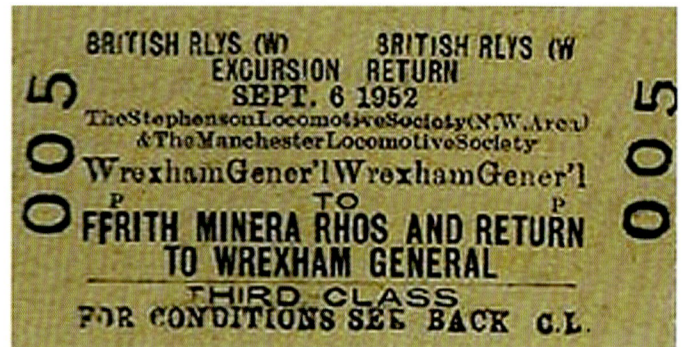

Fig 74c: Ticket for the SMS/MLS special train illustrated in Fig 47a.

a little of the rugged country in which Brymbo Steel Works was developed and that heavy trains and large locomotives could reach Brymbo. Although passenger traffic was generally handled by push-pull tank locomotives with an autocoach trailer, or with GWR steam railmotors, the mineral traffic – coal and iron ore inbound and steel products outbound – were hauled by larger locomotives – like BR WD-Austerity Class 8F 2-8-0s.

The GWR timetable for the Minera branch states that the trains were 'Motor Cars – one class only' which were the steam railmotors mentioned above. They were stabled and maintained at Croes Newydd Loco Shed but my researches have not uncovered a photograph of them at work on the Wrexham branches. However, Car 93 has survived as an autocoach trailer and without its steam bogie but the GWR Society, Didcot Railway Centre has now fully restored it as a steam railmotor so **Fig 76** shows it in steam again on the restored Llangollen

Fig 75: 7-coach R&CTS special leaving Brymbo General station on 29 April 1967 hauled tender-first (no turntables for large locos at Brymbo) by Class 8F 2-8-0.

Fig 76: Restored GWR steam railmotor No 93 on the Llangollen heritage railway in March 2011. Carrog is a station on the railway. (*Author*)

Railway in 2011. The restorers decided that the livery would be the GWR's crimson lake and lined in gold which was used from 1912 to 1922 so it may well have been seen in that livery on the Minera branch.

And finally, amongst the fascinations of the Wrexham area railways, the Minera branch wanders through the hilly country west of Brymbo and is traversed by steam railmotors like Car 93 in **Fig 76**. For passengers the branch journey ended at a rural Halt – Berwig level crossing halt in **Figs 77, 78** and **79**.

The sequence of Figs **77, 78** and **79** tell a story. The OS map, published in 1912, shows the details illustrated in

Above: **Fig 77**: Edited extract from OS 25in map of Denbighshire in 1912. The green arrow is the direction of the photograph in **Fig 79** albeit that was taken 48 years after the map was published! (*Author*)

Below: **Fig 78**: A view towards Berwig Level Crossing Halt in the early twentieth century.

Fig 78 and together they illustrate how GWR may keep their 'Halts' sparse and rather austere or may, though deep in the countryside, provide a Signal Box and a small shelter on the platform which, at Berwig, was the ticket office so therefore staffed although, with relatively infrequent trains (see timetable in **Fig 70**), the signalman may also have sold tickets. A touch of luxury may have come to Berwig as the GWR railmotor, like Car No 93 in **Fig 76,** hissed to a standstill and the driver changed ends for the return journey to Wrexham.

Fig 79: Site of Berwig Level Crossing Halt in 1960 when the line was still open for mineral traffic.

Fig 80: Gresford Colliery in the 1920s – rail connected as the sidings and wagons show.

Gresford Colliery: I have included Gresford on the **Fig 66** map of industrial rail links around Wrexham because one of the principal industries was coal-mining. Gresford Colliery, like may others such as Vron Colliery on **Fig 66**, was linked to the railway network. Gresford was an early twentieth century sinking – in 1907 – NE of Wrexham and alongside the railway from Wrexham to Chester. The coal owner was the Dennis family's United Westminster and Wrexham Collieries Ltd. They sank two deep shafts 50 yards apart as **Fig 80** shows. The downcast shaft – Dennis East – was 2,263ft deep and Martin – the upcast shaft – was 2,252ft deep and coal from three seams was raised by 1911. Production was principally house coal from the Crank seam, and steam and coke-making coal from the Brassey (named after the railway contractor Thomas Brassey) and Main seams; Main seam workings were very gassy. Production developed well and by 1934 – when Gresford suffered a major disaster – the pit employed 2,200 people, 1,850 miners below ground and 350 surface workers.

By the time large deep-mine collieries had been developed many of the smaller pits west of Wrexham were already worked out but it is instructive to learn a little of Simon Hughes, a nineteenth century lead miner born in 1892. Hughes' working life – and his picture – is briefly recorded on one of the interpretive panels at Minera Lead Mines Centre.

Fig 81: Simon Hughes in Speedwell Shaft Minera, c.1928.

'Simon Hughes, from New Brighton, Minera . . . was a skilled worker . . . repairing [and maintaining] all timber in the mine. He had to [sustain] . . . shoring and propping of loose ground, make and fix ladders, and lay rails for the tramways. [He also] helped to maintain the [steam] pumps, pipes and . . . [if required] worked on the ore crusher.

'Simon usually worked a 6-day week . . .with no paid holidays. [When he] finished at the mine in 1915 he was on 4/6d (about 22p) a day, though sometimes his wage was as low as 1/2d (about 6p) a day.

'He was surely a valued employee of the United Minera Mining Company . . . More importantly Simon survived his work in the lead mines – not everybody did.'

A perceptive reader might object that Simon Hughes was not a coal miner but his work underground and his working conditions were very similar to coal miners and he survived; many coal miners did not.

In 1934, Gresford Colliery experienced the worst disaster in British coal mining since the 1913 explosion at Universal Colliery, Senghenydd in Glamorganshire, killed 439 miners and one rescuer. At Gresford, at about 02.00 on Saturday 22 September, an explosion and a subsequent underground fire occurred in the Dennis section of the mine. Rescuers fought the underground fire, but it became apparent that they could not succeed and could not rescue the estimated 250 men in the Dennis section. It was agreed by the representatives of the owners, the men, and HMI Inspectors on site that the tops of both shafts should be sealed. There were further underground explosions and at 13.25 on Tuesday 25 September an explosion blew off the sealing on the Dennis shaft and the projected debris killed a surface worker.

Above: **Fig 82**: Gresford Colliery Disaster, September 1934. Huge crowds of men and women gathered on a colliery surface after a disaster awaiting news of family and friends. The wagons show the importance of rail connections for big collieries. (*Author*)

Left: **Fig 83**: Memorial to the Gresford disaster using one of the colliery's head wheels as a visible memory of a colliery, and an industry, that has gone. (*Author*)

Fig 82 shows the crowds waiting on the colliery surface for news – and the trainloads of coal awaiting despatch.

Only eleven bodies were recovered from the colliery and inquests recorded their cause of death as carbon monoxide poisoning. The Dennis section of the mine was never re-opened and the bodies of the 254 victims were sealed in the mine. An Enquiry opened on 25 October 1934 and highlighted management failures, lack of safety measures, bad working practices and poor ventilation in the pit.

Gresford Colliery re-opened six months after disaster with coal production resuming in January 1936. In 1937, court proceedings were started in Wrexham against the Pit Manager, the Under-Manager and the United and Westminster Collieries Limited, the owners of the mine. The court found the mine's management guilty only of inadequate record-keeping.

Gresford Colliery finally closed on economic grounds in November 1973 and the site was developed as an industrial estate.

I remember growing up in the 1940s and 1950s when house coal deliveries were a frequent event and domestic coal fires – often producing clouds of smoke from the house chimneys – were a welcome source of warmth in un-insulated and single-glazed houses. Gresford produced house coal from the Crank seam which was a relatively low-grade, gassy and smoky coal but when the coal man tipped several bags into the coal house it was much appreciated.

But we are very aware today that smoke from coal fires out of domestic chimneys or, on a larger scale, from steam engine boilers, works and mills are contributing to global warming and climate change. And we sometimes forget, now, that getting coal brought with it a human price:

> Close the coal house door, lad,
> There's blood inside,
> There's bones inside.
> There's bairns inside –
> So stay outside.

from *Close the Coal House Door*, Alan Plater. Methuen & Co Ltd. 1969 and dedicated to miners everywhere . . .

More NE Wales branch lines –

Holywell Branch: One of the perceived advantages of the Chester to Holyhead Railway was an opportunity for local entrepreneurs to build branch lines from inland industrial centres to the new 'main line.' Holywell branch was an interesting example of such a railway, not least because the standard gauge branch succeeded a late nineteenth century tramway built inland from a wharf at Greenfield on the Dee (see **Fig 84** map).

I have visited the Holywell branch – now a neatly tarmacked cycle and pedestrian track from a large car park off the A548 (OS Landranger 1:50,000 sheet 116 grid

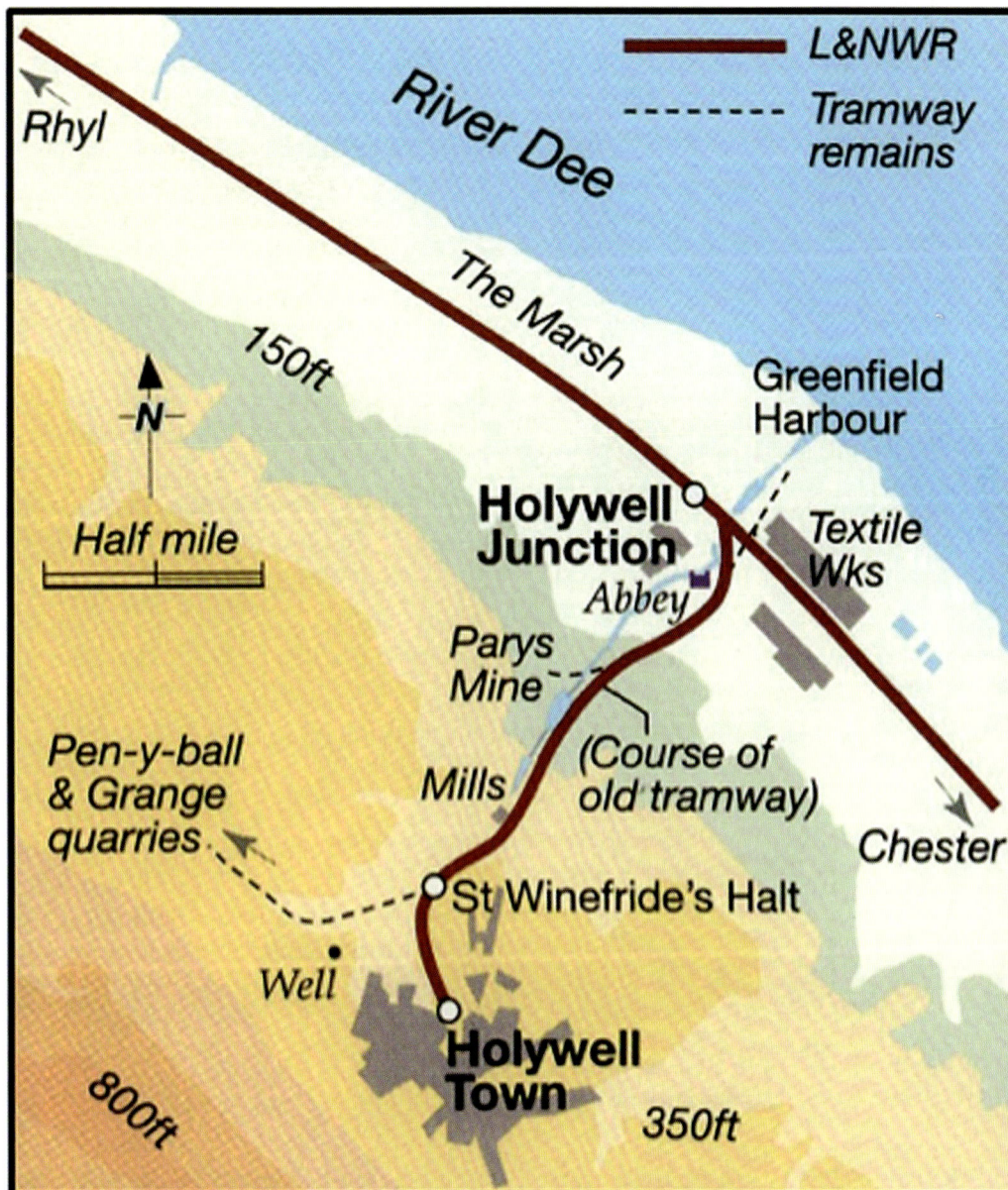

Fig 84: Holywell branch.

reference 196777) – and walked uphill to Holywell Town station site. I can testify to the 1 in 27 gradient which must have been taxing for horses on the tramway and posed some operating difficulties for the subsequent standard gauge railway. Fortunately for researchers a local historian, J.R. Thomas, living at Bagillt in 1995, has published *The Tramways and Railways to Holywell*. Another very useful source of contextual information is: *The Greenfield Valley – An introduction to the history and industrial archaeology of the Greenfield Valley, Holywell, North Wales*, K. Davies & C.J. Williams, Holywell Town Council, 1986.

Saint Winefride's Holy Well was reputed to supply water with curative properties and about 1131 Basingwerke Abbey was established. Its main function was to care for visitors on pilgrimage to the well but, like many abbeys, Basingweke set up water-powered corn mills, fulling mills and malt houses so helped Greenfield valley to prosper. Even the dissolution in 1536 did not undo the industries which the Abbey had fostered – or the importance of St. Winefride's well so Holywell came to be called 'the Lourdes of Wales'. Industries like lead miming, smelting, limestone quarrying, iron foundries, copper and wire works were progressively developed, and a cotton-spinning factory was established in 1777. Holywell became the largest town in Flintshire and the valley was prosperous; a railway seemed to be the key to further development and new markets.

In 1857 a narrow gauge horse-powered tramway – Crockford's Tramway – was built from a wharf at Greenfield inland to Parys Mine and Crescent Sidings near what became St Winefride's Halt, to serve the Pen-y-Ball and Grange limestone quarries. William Crockford was a London-born entrepreneur who made a fortune by gambling and unwisely 'invested' some of it with his sons and daughter in mining, quarrying and zinc manufacture in the Greenfield Valley where they owned land and quarrying businesses. Quite soon, however, the Crockford businesses were in Receivership and their tramway was no longer viable.

Another group of 'outside' speculators and entrepreneurs, including Lockington Dale Bunn – a railway contractor – saw opportunities for them and promoted the Holywell Railway Company which obtained its Act of Parliament in 1864. The plans deposited for a Parliamentary session in 1865 seemed

to be proposing and constructing another tramway with at least one steep incline which would have required a stationary steam engine and rope haulage. Eventually revised plans were agreed for a standard gauge railway, using much of the former tramway's route, with a ruling gradient of 1 in 27 which was just feasible for steam locomotive haulage.

Construction began in 1868, involving substantial civil engineering for the access to a Holywell Town station site which was to be in a cutting between 40ft and 50ft deep. 92,000 cubic yards of spoil had to be excavated and moved towards Greenfield wharf on contractor's track then tipped for embankments. Work continued slowly and a Notice in the *London Gazette* of 19 October 1869 presaged problems:

> 'Lockington Dale Bunn . . . late of Holywell, in the county of Flint . . . Railway Contractor, having been adjudged bankrupt under a Petition for adjudication of Bankruptcy, filed in Her Majesty's Court of Bankruptcy, in London, on the 29th day of September, 1869, a public sitting, for the said bankrupt to pass his Last Examination, and make application for his Discharge, will be held before James Bacon. Esq., a Commissioner of the said Court, on the nineteenth day of November next . . at twelve o'clock at noon precisely, the day last aforesaid being the day limited for the said bankrupt to surrender.'

On 11 March 1870 the line opened to traffic but a report in the *Flintshire Observer* hints at problems to come:

> 'This line has been opened for goods traffic and several trucks of coal have been brought up to the Town. In a few days it is expected that the arrangements will be completed for carrying on an extensive traffic in coal, which we trust will soon lead to another accommodation and that some return for the line will immediately be forthcoming.'

But the line was not yet complete and the Railway Company was in serious financial difficulties. The contractor, Messrs Jardine and Son, left the line unfinished and announced in the *Flintshire Observer* an Auction Sale on 11 July 1871 at the Royal Hotel, Greenfield comprising:

'. . . 40 substantial earth-tip waggons [at] 4ft 8½ins. . . large quantity of permanent way and temporary rails varying from 30lbs to 40lbs per yard . . . large quantity various sized chains and ropes, blocks and falls . . . fish plate bolts and nuts, several lots of glazed Buckley pipes 6in and 9in, sleepers, oak mortice and fence posts, the buildings and contents of the Blacksmiths' shops. and Carpenters' shops.'

In order to take their traffic, the Holywell Lime Company (Pen-y-Ball & Grange Quarries) had to complete the permanent way themselves on the lower length of the line with narrow gauge tramway track from their quarries then mixed gauge down to Greenfield Wharf. Only the Lime Company used the line and only for their traffic of several thousand tons of limestone. The Company's Managing Director, Mr Cookson, is reported (and quoted here from T.J. Williams' book with thanks) as recalling in 1892 that:

'I have heard (regarding representations of the Railway Company) only from Mr Jardine and one or two others who [made the railway] but one ran away and the other, I believe, drank himself to death . . .'

Even the indefatigable researcher, T.J Williams, has not discovered how the mixed gauge section of the Tramway and Railway was worked but he acknowledges that the Lime Company had no interest in the section of the railway up to the Town station site. In the light of Jardine & Son's abandonment of their contract it may be that the rails were only light weight contractors' track. It is known from House of Lords Record Office that the evidence of Robert Peck, Secretary of the Lime Company, on an L&NWR Additional Powers Bill of 1892, confirms that the upper section to the Town station site had been 'disused for many years [but]. . . rails were still in position although the sleepers had rotted away'.

The mention of L&NWR is a useful segue to their part in this story. The Company was potentially interested in the route to Holywell Town if it could yield useful business but obtaining the route was not easy. In 1891 they were able to purchase the trackbed of the mixed gauge tramway / railway up to the Holywell Town station site and obtained most of the shares of the original undertaking so they considered themselves the owner of the former Holywell Railway Company. Their

Additional Powers Bill of 1892 included a clause to dissolve the Holywell Railway Company, to statutorily vest the undertaking in the L&NWR, and to make provision for compensation at par value for any shares which they had not yet acquired. However, the Lime Company and their Liquidator – for they too were by now bankrupt – petitioned against the Bill because 'they would be at the mercy of a powerful railway company who would charge high rates for facilities at present used freely. So if the Bill is carried into effect the Lime Company would not be able to sell the business except at greatly reduced prices'. The Lords Committee on the Bill decided in favour of the Lime Company so the whole of the vesting clause was struck out of the Bill.

Not to be outdone, L&NWR as the principal shareholder re-incarnated the old Holywell Railway Company and convened a Board Meeting in August 1892. Richard de Aquila Grosvenor, 1st Baron Stalbridge, was Chairman of the L&NWR so became Chairman of this new, paper, Company and other L&NWR officers became Secretary, Solicitor and General Manager. No business was transacted but Minutes were kept, and regular meetings continued until 1895. The principal reason for what seemed a charade was that L&NWR had to confirm their ownership of the former Tramway / Railway from A548 – Bagillt Road – to the Greenfield Wharf including the bridge over their Chester to Holyhead line and the connecting curve to join it.

L&NWR turned to parliament again with an Additional Powers Bill of 1893 to obtain powers for compulsory purchase for the land they needed but again there was opposition. Most of the land concerned was owned by the Crockford family and leased to the Lime Company which used it for their traffic. Finally, Crockfords sold their interest to J.P. Jones early in 1903 but L&NWR were trying to progress their interests too and Mr Williams is again a source worth quoting:

'[In June1903 Mr Jones] . . . found [his fences removed] and150 men laying a siding on part of his land. He returned the following day with 10 men and attempted to put fences back on [his] boundary but was stopped by a large number of navvies under the control of L&NWR Inspector John Clements. The navvies were all armed with crowbars, picks, iron piping and cudgels [and] crushed Jones against a fence, knocked him down and kicked him.

Fig 85: From 1905 a L&NWR Milnes-Daimler motor bus provided a passenger service from Holywell, on the Chester to Holyhead line, uphill along the Greenfield valley to Holywell town. The route board on the side of the bus, reading 'Holywell Station' was, perhaps, advertising for the planned branch line which did not open to Holywell Station until 1912. (*Author*)

Fig 86: Holywell Junction c1912 with a train for Holywell Town in the bay platform constructed for the branch. Because of the 1 in 27 gradient on the branch the trains were always propelled.

The main line railway company were still keen to build a branch to Holywell Town so decided in 1905 on a sampling experiment which should provide data on likely demand for such a service. A Foden overtype steam lorry was purchased and then a more up-to-date single-deck Milnes-Daimler motor bus with a 4cyl 24HP Mercedes-type petrol engine and seating for 21 passengers (**Fig 85**). The lorry and the bus worked between Holywell Station – to become Holywell Junction – and Holywell Town which meant a steep 1 in 9 climb up to Holywell Town which was some 50ft to 60ft above the railway station.

Mr Jones was understandably unwilling to sell his land to L&NWR but, perhaps with evidence of the demand proved by the bus operation, he finally surrendered in 1910. Construction began during February 1911 and a test train was successfully run over the whole branch in early June 1912. An official opening for goods and passengers, by Sir Gilbert Claughton, then Chairman of L&NWR, was on Monday 1 July 1912; Holywell on the main line was renamed Holywell Junction.

L&NWR built St. Winfried's Halt so that pilgrims visiting the healing well nearby could travel by train, but no shelter was provided on the single platform. Just before the Halt, on a level area, Crescent Sidings and a passing loop were constructed to house up to 35 wagons and serve several textile mills in the valley.

The terminus at Holywell Town Station was in a steep-sided cutting and the gradient here varied between level for the small goods yard and 1 in 260 along the platform – see **Fig 87** and **Fig 88**.

Once the railway was open on 1 July 1912, the motor bus service, and the steam lorry goods service, ceased. By the time of grouping in 1923 what was known to locals as 'Little Train' services offered nineteen up and down weekday passenger trains and two additional trains on Saturdays; after LMS succeeded the L&NWR the weekday numbers had grown to twenty-four. As **Fig 87** illustrates, the platform at Town Station was short, as at St Winfried's Halt, so passenger trains were never more than two coaches and sometimes only one auto-coach for the driver in uphill services. Goods trains of three loaded – or five empty – wagons needed a 20-ton brake van front and back to supplement braking on the downhill journeys.

The Holywell branch was expensive to operate and, particularly once motor transport developed, it did not generate much income from either passenger tickets or goods charges. After Nationalisation in 1948 the 'Little Train' weekday services were reduced to six and ceased entirely in September 1954 so a good example of a pre-Beeching closure. A goods service was maintained for three years on an 'as required' basis to the textile mills at Crescent Sidings but final closure was in August 1957. Holywell Junction Station closed on 14 February 1966 as did several other smaller stations of the N Wales coast line to Holyhead.

Fig 87: Postcard view c1912 of the new Holywell Town Station from the terminal buffer stop behind the photographer and the goods yard to the right. The change in gradient is apparent from the relative level of the Station layout downhill towards Holywell Junction 1.5 miles away.

Fig 88: A comparative 2019 view of **Fig 87** showing the Holywell Station site approached from Holywell Junction on foot. The former goods yard would have been on the left in this view and the platform beyond the bridge on the right. (*Author*)

Fig 89: Working the Holywell goods yard in 1951; No 41270 Ivatt Class 2 2-6-0T shunts a 20--ton brake van to pick up a short goods train for Holywell Junction.

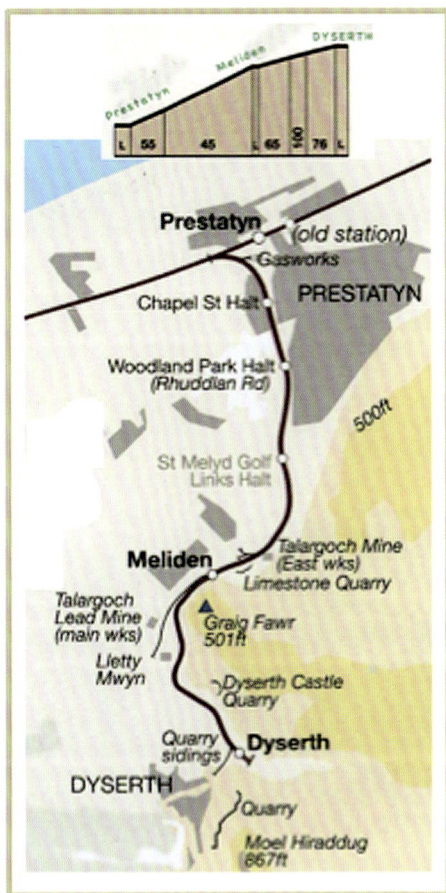

Fig 90: Edited map of the Dyserth branch.

Dyserth Branch: like the Holywell branch, the Dyserth branch benefitted from a connection with the North Wales coast railway at Prestatyn and extensive limestone, galena and haematite quarries en route to Dyserth which required, and provided, mineral traffic for the railway.

Unlike the complicated and troubled story of the Holywell branch, the Dyserth branch was more straightforward. As the **Fig 90** map shows there were industries needing railway transport to the L&NWR railway at Prestatyn so a case for parliamentary approval could be argued.

The principal landowner in the area was Lord Mostyn whose estate included most of Flintshire and his seat was Mostyn Hall near Mostyn on Deeside. He petitioned parliament after a public meeting at Prestatyn in November 1860 which supported the proposed railway with evidence of outbound traffic – 40,000 tons of limestone per year – and agricultural produce. It was also suggested that inbound traffic would be coal for steam pumping engines at the mines and general supplies for industries in the area.

However, there was still some doubt about haematite and lead traffic but L&NWR were interested and proposed a Dyserth Branch in their New Lines Bill in 1865, There was no opposition, so the Bill became an Act and construction began in May 1868. As the gradient profile above the map shows this branch, like the Holywell branch, climbed steadily from just above sea-level in Prestatyn to 258ft at Dyserth but the steepest gradient was 1 in 45 so much less steep than the 1 in 27 climb to Holywell Town Station.

The branch opened for goods traffic on 1 September 1869 and a passenger service was not offered until L&NWR succumbed to public pressure in August 1905, using a steam railmotor. Passenger traffic on the line meant some improvements and relaying with heavier rail which cost may well have deterred the L&NWR accountants! Halts were provided at Chapel Street (Prestatyn), Rhuddlan Road, St. Melyd Golf Links. and Meliden. A small L&NWR-style hut for a booking office with waiting room was built for the terminus at Dyserth. The 63ft-long platforms were cinder infills, edged by wooden sleeper copings, and completed by 8 July 1905. The whole of the branch track was relaid to passenger-carrying standards and a speed limit of 25mph was imposed in either direction.

Fortunately for the cautious accountants, the passenger receipts were encouraging on the eight weekday return workings; in September 1905 the daily average was between 400 and 500 passengers. Prestatyn was developing as a seaside resort so tourists seemed to like the novelty of a fifteen minute steam railmotor ride and Dyserth offered attractions too like hill views and waterfalls.

The mineral traffic must have been the mainstay for the railway for a number of years – over 50,000 tons of galena and zinc and over 28,000 tons of haematite outbound and coal inbound for mine pumping engines each year – until by 1875 many of the mines were worked out. The principal mineral traffic, however, was limestone for the blast furnaces of John Summers Steel works at Shotton and for Mostyn Iron Works. There was also a market for agricultural lime and, inbound, for agricultural machinery and general supplies.

The passenger services finished on 30 September 1930 principally because of falling demand on the railway,

W. L. HOBBS [Dyserth] Ltd.

LIMESTONE QUARRIES AND

LIME WORKS

The biggest employers in the district are the W. L. Hobbs (Dyserth) Ltd., Limestone Quarries and Lime Works, who provide employment for 50 persons. The quarries have been in existence for many centuries. Modern kilns and machinery have replaced stone kilns but the ruins of three are still to be seen. Thousands of tons of lime are transported yearly to Steel Works in both Lancashire and Flintshire and also to the Chemical Works of Monsanto at Ruabon and to Petrochemical at Carrington. The limestone is considered of high quality for such purposes as well as for road metal, and for use in the making of cement and for concrete work such as that used in connection with dock development in the Liverpool area

Fig 91: Twentieth century billboard advertising the output of one of the Dyserth limestone quarries which were rail-served by the Dyserth branch. (*Author*)

technical problems with the steam railmotors and the purchase by LMS of the local Crosville bus company. Transfer of passenger traffic to Crosville, which kept any profits within the LMS businesses, seemed sensible and it was argued that road-side bus stops were more accessible than the railway halts.

Parcels, general freight traffic, and the considerable output of the quarries around Dyserthm sustained the branch until September 1973 when limestone quarrying ceased, the branch closed and the track was lifted.

Although track was lifted soon after the branch finally closed, the track bed and most of the substantial bridges remained. I first encountered the Dyserth branch in 2006 when I was staying near Llanasa while helping

the Rhyl Miniature Railway to submit an HLF Bid for a new Central Station.

Each day, en route along narrow minor roads, I encountered the over-bridge in **Fig 93**, on a steep hill and at a blind corner. I was intrigued by what my hosts explained to me was a 'disused railway bridge' but I little thought that fourteen years later I would be writing about it.

While researching for this book in 2018 and 2019 I found the bridge again – Bridge 3 on the Dyserth branch – and was able to walk along much of the tarmacked track bed to Dyserth. It was fortunately less steep than the Holywell branch and some of the remaining bridges showed that L&NWR built stoutly and attractively even though the provision for passengers was rather more basic – **Fig 94**.

INSET

Above: **Fig 92**: Spur to limestone quarry at Dyserth showing the very the tight curve and BR Class 5 45156 Ayrshire Yeomanry at limit of shunt (September 1963) and inset – an outbound train of wagons loaded with limestone at Dyserth, September 1961.

Right: **Fig 93**: Bridge 3 on the Dyserth Branch near Meliden. (*Author*)

Fig 94: Bridge 7 on the Dyserth branch looking uphill towards Dyserth. This bridge illustrates the quality of the trackside structures built by L&NWR in the 1860s 150 years earlier than when the Author photographed it when walking uphill to Dyserth. (*Author*)

Fig 95: Ex-works L&NWR steam railmotor No 1 at Wolverton, where it was built in 1905.

I enjoyed the walk to Dyserth on a gloriously sunny day and with bridges like that in **Fig 94** as branch line reminders. But it would have been even better to stand beside the branch in the 1900s and watch a steam railmotor, packed with tourists from Prestatyn, pass me on the way top Dyserth – **Fig 95**!

THE FRIGHTFUL RAILWAY ACCIDENT NEAR ABERGELE
The *North Wales Chronicle*, Saturday 20 August 1868

It may seem curious to end a chapter on NE Wales and Deeside railways with a 'Frightful Accident' but we can learn from the mistakes of others and from the detailed accident reports of the BoT Inspectors. This accident was on the Chester to Holyhead line, a little west of Abergele and it involved the Down Irish Mail and, on the same Down line the shunting of a goods train. **Fig 96** is a map extract edited from 1:2,500 OS map published in 1873; in case the added text proves too small to read clearly, the double-track railway 'main line' from Chester to Holyhead 'main line' has a Down line towards Holyhead and an Up line towards Chester.

In the nineteenth century, a railway accident had to be reported to the Board of Trade Inspectorate who investigated all the circumstances – including taking witness statements from staff and members of the public involved – and published a Report. These reports, which are still available as matters of public record at The National Archives (TNA). TNA used to be called the Public Record Office (PRO) at Kew, where it still is, under its new name.

The Abergele Report is very detailed and available for fuller reference than here on the Web. It is worth quoting the opening paragraphs to set the scene and give a flavour of its style:

From:
Board of Trade (Railway Department)
Whitehall.
14th September 1868.
[A Report by F.H. Rich, Lieutenant-Colonel RE]

Sir, In compliance with the instructions contained in your minute of the twenty-first ultimo, I have the honour to report, for the information of the Lords of the Committee of Privy Council for Trade, the result of my inquiry into the circumstances which attended the collision that occurred on the twentieth August 1868, between Abergele and Llandulas stations, on the Chester and Holyhead section of the London & North-Western Railway.

31 passengers in the Irish down day mail train, 1 of the guards, and the fireman of the mail train were killed in this appalling accident.

[Another] train, commonly called the "Pick-up goods," left Crewe for Holyhead on the morning of the twentieth ultimo.

2 waggons, containing 50 casks – in all about 7 and three-quarters tons of paraffin oil (the igniting point of which was 137°F) – were attached to the train at the Flintshire Oil Works, at Saltney Wharf, which is about 3 miles to the west of Chester.

The trucks containing the oil were placed at the tail of the goods train, directly in front of the guard's van, which was the last vehicle of the train.

The Irish Mail L&NWR express train from London Euston was speeding north towards Chester and Holyhead; ahead of it was the pick-up goods also

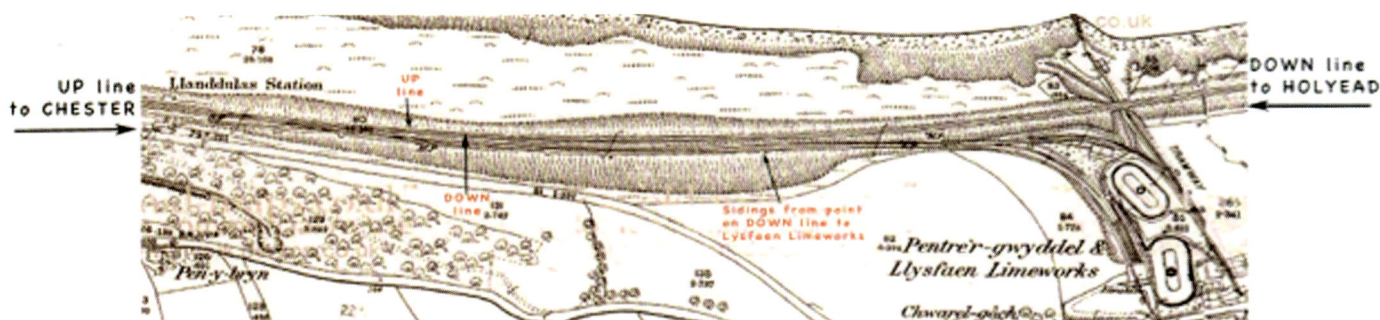

Fig 96: Extract from an edited OS 6in scale map showing the elements of the Abergele railway accident between the Down Irish Mail passenger express and some runaway goods trucks in 1868. (*Author*)

bound for Holyhead from Crewe. The goods called at the Flintshire Oil Works siding at Saltney and picked up two wagons containing 7.75 tons of paraffin oil in fifty casks; these two wagons were added to the rear of the train, in front of the brake van. The goods train now consisted of forty-three loose-coupled wagons of which twenty-six were empty and seventeen loaded. There were no continuous brakes in those days so the only brake for the whole train was on the locomotive at the front and on the brake van at the rear, screwed on by an upright brake-wheel inside the vehicle and controlled by the guard. At 12.24 this long train stopped at Llandulas station with the familiar clang, clang, clang sound of a loose-coupled train buffering-up towards the loco. The Llandulas Station Master was on his Down platform to greet the train because he knew the Mail was due to pass Llandulas at 12.39 so considered that the goods train should be shunted clear of the Down main line into the Lysfaen Limeworks sidings that were L&NWR sidings, under his control, and a short distance east of his station. The two sidings were parallel to the Down main line (see **Fig 95** map) but already held several wagons so could not contain the whole goods train without some additional shunting.

Llandulas Station Master's decision to carry out this shunting was a flagrant breach of L&NWR Rules: 'Goods trains, when likely to be overtaken by a passenger train, must not be shunted at stations where there are fixed signals at least 10 minutes before such a passenger train is due.' A re-reading of the arrival times at Llandulas – 12.24 for the goods and 12.39 for the Mail – would seem to have just given enough time for the shunt if the goods train could have immediately reversed into the Lysfaen sidings. But, and it was a fatal 'but', the Station Master must have anticipated that the necessary shunting had to be carried out on the main line as well as in the sidings and the main line between Llandulas and Abergele was on a continuously falling gradient varying from 1 in 147 to 1 in 100.

First the goods train was reversed so that the brake van and six wagons, including 7.75 tons of highly inflammable paraffin oil, were clear of the trailing lead into the Lysfaen sidings and were uncoupled from the rest of the train. The brake in the brake van was screwed hard down but no other wagon brakes were pinned down. The remainder of the goods train drew forward then reversed into the sidings and three wagons – a timber wagon in between two 'check' wagons to check the slightly over-hanging timber load from contact with other wagons – was coupled and drawn out onto the main line.

It should now be apparent to the reader that the fifteen minutes notionally 'in hand' before the Mail was due to pass must be nearly exhausted. But it is also apparent that the shunting had to continue in order to clear the Down line and in 1868 L&NWR was still reluctant to invest in signalling improvements between stations. The supposed safety inherent in 'time interval' train operation should have assured the driver of the Mail, who was already late and passing Abergele at 12.39, that he could continue towards Llandulas.

Meanwhile, at Llandulas the three timber wagons had been drawn out of the siding and onto the DOWN line and then 'fly shunted' – uncoupled and pushed by the remaining train to run free downhill – towards the stationary six wagons and brake van. A brakesman helping with the shunting ran beside the timber wagons to try to put down a wagon brake lever but failed and they cannoned into the stationary wagons which also began to roll downhill. We know from Lt-Colonel Rich's Report that the impact was sufficient to break off several teeth from the cast-iron cogs in the brake van's screw brake apparatus so the six wagons were now unchecked and moving away faster than the three timber wagons which followed them down the slope towards the on-coming Irish Mail express.

Driver Arthur Thompson on the Mail, climbing towards Llandulas at about 40mph, was looking ahead across the reverse curves in the cutting in front of his train and saw the oncoming wagons but believed at first they were running away on the Up line. When he realised they were on his Down line, he shouted to his fireman, 'For God's sake Joe, jump for it, we can do no more,' and he leapt off. and landed safely on the side of the cutting. The fireman did not jump and Thompson recalled for the Enquiry that, amidst the thunder of the collision which de-railed his loco, he recognized his fireman's voice in one despairing cry.

The de-railed loco spilt burning coals from its firebox and instantly ignited the paraffin from burst casks which engulfed the other wagons and the leading carriages of the Mail express. None of the thirty-two passengers in those carriages survived. 'They can only be described

Fig 97: L&NWR accident near Abergele when the Irish Mail was struck by some runaway wagons on the same track. The wagons contained casks of paraffin which burst. The released paraffin drenched the de-railed locomotive and was ignited instantly by coals from the loco firebox. This sketch was purportedly made about 90 minutes after the accident.

as charred pieces of flesh and bone,' wrote Lt-Col Rich. Fortunately, the rear of the Mail train was swiftly uncoupled so did not catch fire and its occupants were unharmed.

Lt-Colonel's Rich's Report strongly criticised the Station Master at Llandulas for initiating the shunting which was a breach of Company rules and caused the accident. However, and the Railway Inspectors' reports are generally much more valuable than simply naming offenders, Rich also criticised the L&NWR for timetabling an express with such a short interval after the preceding goods train. He also pointed out that L&NWR's Lysfaen Lime Works sidings had never been inspected by the BoT and added that, as elsewhere, provision should be made for goods trains to carry out any necessary shunting clear of the main line.

CHAPTER 7

IRON AND STEEL MAKING

Brymbo Iron and Steel Works John Summers & Sons Ltd – Shotton Steel Works

A principal user of railways in the NE Wales and Deeside area were iron and steel works of which there were a number but Brymbo and Shotton were sufficiently significant and, at Shotton so large, as to justify a separate chapter.

Chronologically, Brymbo – and Bersham Iron Works nearby – preceded Shotton and are associated with an entrepreneur and a remarkable man – John 'Iron Mad' Wilkinson. His developments at Brymbo were associated with the mineral exploitation of Brymbo Hall Estate and adjacent farms. In 1792, Wilkinson, ironmaster of Bersham, agricultural pioneer, would-be country gentleman, purchased the Brymbo Hall Estate of 500 acres, to safeguard resources for his Bersham Furnace, which had been in his family's possession since 1753. In 1769 he also secured rights to mine ironstone on the nearby Lodge Estate.

It is not necessary here to give too much space to Wilkinson because several published books will give a wider picture and context than Bersham and Brymbo alone. He developed a business empire stretching from Cumbria through North East Wales and the West Midlands to Cornwall, with links to the Continent. He manufactured iron, copper and lead, played a crucial role in the development of the steam engine, and had a distribution centre in London. And all that before telephones, IT-business, railways, motor traffic and aeroplanes. It is helpful to be reminded how much was achieved by some men, and women, in the so-called 'Dark Ages' before the growing Industrial Revolution in which Wilkinson played a part.

Isaac Wilkinson, John's father, a Midlands ironmaster, leased and developed Bersham Furnace in Flintshire which John took over from him in 1761. Isaac was very successful in making a number of cast iron products including canon and iron pipes.

John, as a good businessman, was concerned that all the iron ore and coal for Bersham had to be bought from others. In 1792, with a substantial loan from Boulton & Watt, he bought Brymbo Hall and Estate which included a number of coal and iron ore pits.

Fig 98: John Wilkinson – ironmaster and entrepreneur. (*Brymbo Heritage Trust*)

At Brymbo Works, Wilkinson built a blast furnace which was in-blast and producing pig iron by 1798. Known as 'Old Number One' this furnace, or perhaps a successor on the same site built in 1818 was in blast until 1894 and remains at Brymbo today.

Perhaps it will be helpful for readers not wholly familiar with the technology and terminology of iron and steel-making to refresh memories. *Encyclopaedia Britannica* explains that:

'A blast furnace is a vertical shaft furnace that produces molten iron by the reaction at a high temperature of air under pressure [the blast] blown up through the furnace charge of iron ore, carbon [from coal reduced to coke in a separate coke oven] and a limestone flux.

'The product of this reaction is molten iron which is heavier than the slag that floats above it at the bottom of the furnace. Periodically the furnace is tapped at the bottom, and re-charged at the top.'

The diagram in **Fig 99** is a more modern blast furnace than Wilkinson used at Brymbo but both Brymbo and Shotton – which is anyway much more recent – adopted improving blast furnace technology. The hot blast in the diagram which made the furnace more efficient and cost effective is an example of improved technology which would have appealed to Wilkinson.

John Wilkinson's ability as an Ironmaster can be briefly summarised from some of the materials lent me by Brymbo Heritage Centre for use in this book. (See Chapter 9 for further details of 2020s developments on the site of Brymbo Works).

Between 1700 and 1776 and later there was no thought of iron-working at Brymbo. All furnaces were blown by the power of water wheels and there is no river at Brymbo. The steam engine for blowing had not yet been invented. Brymbo was carrying on with agriculture and coal mining on a limited scale while Bersham, its neighbour, had a flourishing ironworks, with foundry and rolling mills. Coedpoeth and Minera had coal mines, lead mines and lead smelters.

Brymbo's star was rising, however, for in 1728 at Clifton, Cumberland, John Wilkinson was born. He was the man who really made Brymbo, and about whom many books and articles have been and are being written. A brief chronology explains Wilkinson's speculations, inventions, business and financial practices:

- 1754 Isaac Wilkinson took over the lease for Bersham Furnace.
- 1761 Isaac Wilkinson gave up Bersham Furnace so the lease was taken over by John Wilkinson and his brother William, forming the "New Bersham Company"
- 1773 Bersham Works flourished, and at this date, owing to a shortage of currency the Wilkinsons paid their workmen with "promissory Notes" printed on card or leather (Tradition says he issued leather money).

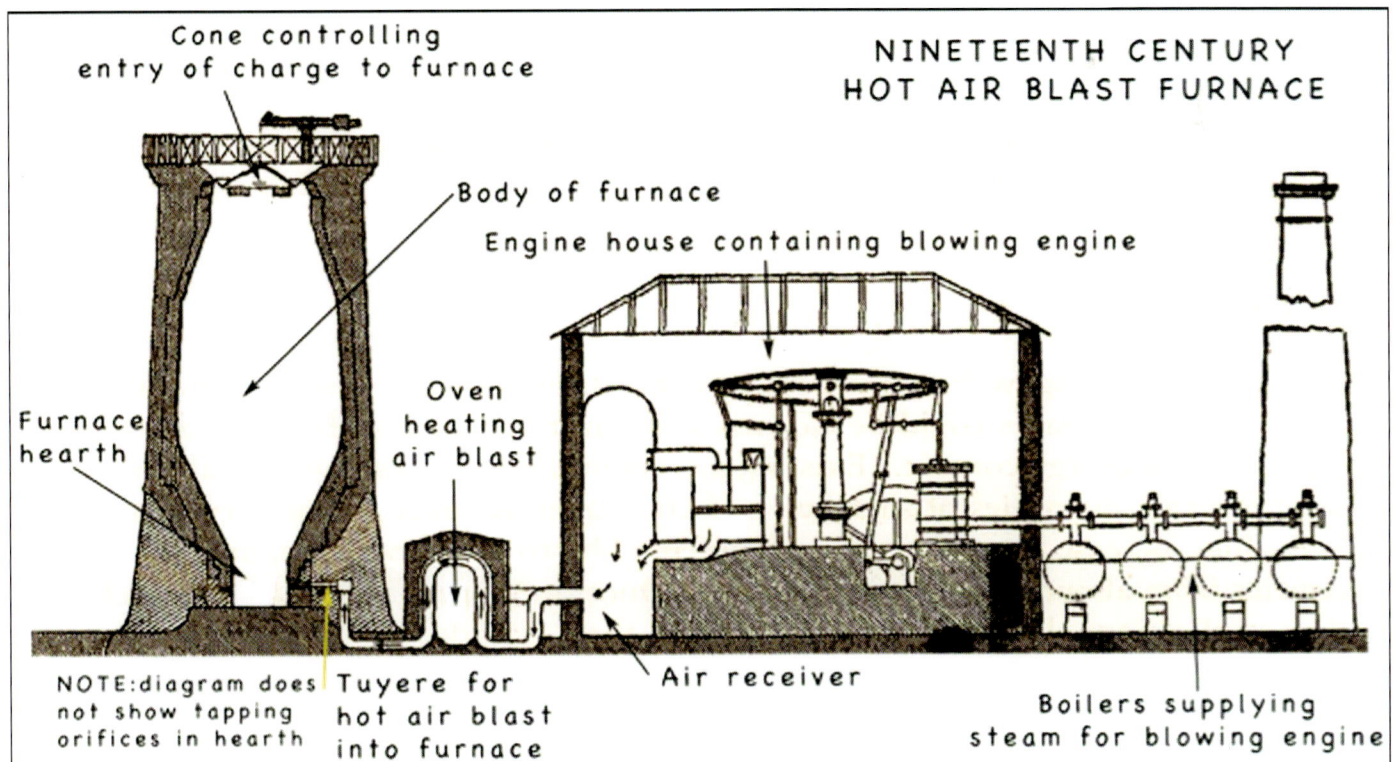

NINETEENTH CENTURY HOT AIR BLAST FURNACE

Cone controlling entry of charge to furnace

Body of furnace

Engine house containing blowing engine

Furnace hearth

Oven heating air blast

NOTE: diagram does not show tapping orifices in hearth

Tuyere for hot air blast into furnace

Air receiver

Boilers supplying steam for blowing engine

Fig 99: Diagram of a typical mid-nineteenth century hot air blast furnace. Pre-heating the blast air made furnace operation more efficient and cost-effective. (*Author*)

- 1775 The issue of "Promissory Notes" for less than 20/- was prohibited and the ban was not lifted until 1798.
- 1780 John Wilkinson extended his activities to France supplying and laying the Water Mains for Paris Waterworks. (He and his brother held shares, probably in part payment. England was at war with France at the time so Wilkinson was accused of supplying guns and munitions to France camouflaged as pipes.
- 1785 Paris Waterworks contract completed.
- About 1785 John Wilkinson started pirating the Boulton and Watt Patents and building steam engines on which no royalty was paid.

- 1792 Before June Wilkinson had purchased the Brymbo Estate and had to find £14,000 for the purchase price. Boulton and Watt helped him to the extent of a loan of £2,000. John did not take his brother William into partnership at Brymbo.
- Wilkinson was borrowing money on the strength of his expected payments from France which, however, did not materialise in his lifetime, owing to the troubled state of France.
- 1795 The Lease-holders put up Bersham Works for sale and sold to the highest bidder, John Wilkinson, who was now sole owner of Bersham and Brymbo.

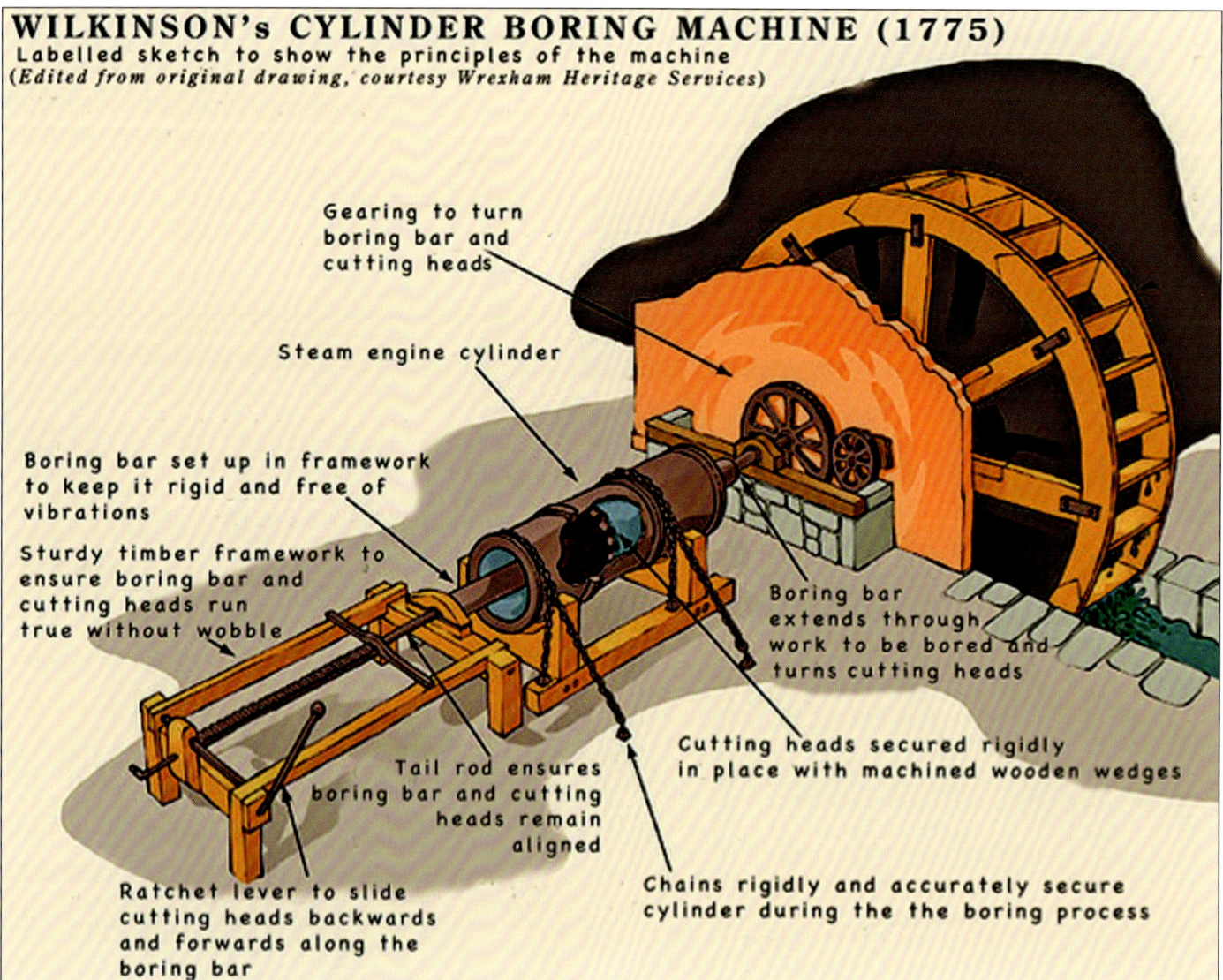

WILKINSON's CYLINDER BORING MACHINE (1775)
Labelled sketch to show the principles of the machine
(*Edited from original drawing, courtesy Wrexham Heritage Services*)

Gearing to turn boring bar and cutting heads

Steam engine cylinder

Boring bar set up in framework to keep it rigid and free of vibrations

Sturdy timber framework to ensure boring bar and cutting heads run true without wobble

Boring bar extends through work to be bored and turns cutting heads

Tail rod ensures boring bar and cutting heads remain aligned

Cutting heads secured rigidly in place with machined wooden wedges

Ratchet lever to slide cutting heads backwards and forwards along the boring bar

Chains rigidly and accurately secure cylinder during the the boring process

Fig 100: Wilkinson's cylinder boring machine was very successful because it was the first such machine which could bore cylinders for steam engines accurately, ensuring the internal diameter was sustained throughout the length so provide an even bore in which the piston precisely fitted. (*Author*)

- 1795 John Wilkinson devised a new mill for boring cannon and similar castings like cylinders for Boulton and Watt steam engines. (**Fig 100**)
- 1795 On July 27th Boulton and Watt stated they had erected only 3 or 4 stationary steam engines whose cylinders had not been made by Wilkinson; they had erected hundreds.

Despite some difficulties in both his personal and business lives Wilkinson was doing very well. He was living in Brymbo Hall and the 500 acre Brymbo Estate was soon enlarged to 872 acres by purchasing a number more farms. He was an agriculturalist as well as an ironmaster, improving his farmland by good tillage and manuring the poor clay soils with lime at the rate of 10 tons per acre – from his own limekilns. The cylinder boring machine he invented and patented brought him a lot of business from Boulton and Watt for their steam engines – and he could accurately bore canons and pipes too (**Fig 100**).

An early set-back for Wilkinson's transport arrangements to and from Brymbo was the foreshortening of a canal proposal. On 25 April 1792, he was one of a consortium of twelve who were each allocated £1,000 shares as the first promoters of a scheme for a canal which would link the rivers Severn, Dee and Mersey. It was to be the Ellesmere Canal and the section he favoured for Brymbo was from Pontcysyllte Aqueduct to Chester via Bersham, Wrexham, Gwersyllt and over the plain to Chester, with branches. The Ffrwd Canal branch was to have been to 'Brumbo' (sic). Alas, at a meeting of the proprietors on 13 June 1798, it was ordered that work be suspended on the Ffrwd Canal because it had been decided to abandon the main line of canal from Chester to Pontcysyllte.

Nevertheless, Wilkinson was pressing on with his plans for the enlargement of iron making at Brymbo Works. In a letter dated October 1799 he asserted that he intended to build two additional furnaces at Brymbo. Wilkinson's Brymbo Lead Smelter was already in production and earning money, not least because he owned the lead mines at Minera and had constructed a new road link from there, via Brymbo, to his market in Chester. He had limestone, too, as a flux for the furnace charges and a good water supply from the Estate catchment and water pumped from his coal and iron stone mines. The Black Bed Ironstone seam yielded an average of 2,900 tons each year. This output at four tons of ore per onr ton of iron gives an iron make of fourteen tons per week which agrees fairly closely with the sixteen tons given by the Excise Return for 1796. Records also show that some Cumberland iron ore was imported to Brymbo carried by a small fleet of coasting vessels carrying anything from 50 to 150 tons of ore. These vessels sailed up the Dee to Chester, trading and discharging at the small ports on the Flintshire coast such as Connah's Quay and Sandycroft; they were the nearest small ports to Brymbo.

Wilkinson was therefore in a position to build a new ironworks embodying the latest practice, with the experience gained from Bersham nearby (**Fig 101**) and three other plants in the Midlands. Archival evidence from Excise Returns show that Brymbo was making 884 tons of iron in 1796. For the whole year this output from

Fig 101: Bersham Furnace and Foundry 2019; surviving buildings include an octagonal canon foundry, an adjacent probable fettling shop and a boring mill later converted to a corn mill. The site is managed by Wrexham County Borough Museum & Archives Service but is currently closed to the public. (*Author*)

one furnace would be about sixteen tons per week, or three times as much as Bersham and similar furnaces. A sale catalogue of 1829 claimed that Brymbo could produce 40 tons per week per furnace and this figure had reached 56 tons per week in 1843.

Enlarging Brymbo Works in the early 1880s was quite a formidable undertaking, partly because the site is set into the hillside to improve charging access to the top of the new furnace. The new Works required a blowing engine and engine house, boilers, water service, coal storage space, a retaining wall against the hillside, stables, offices (albeit fairly basic at that time) and roadways on and to the site.

Research for the Brymbo Heritage Centre suggests that between 1792 and 1796 one furnace was built and blown in; the second, known as No 2, was subsequently built and worked intermittently until it was finally blown out on 2 February 2 1881. 'Old No 1' was in blast until 1884. The Blowing Engine was of the Boulton and Watt type (probably pirated). The steam cylinder was 51ins bore and the blowing cylinder 84ins with a stroke of possibly 8ft. The steam engine was single-acting; that is, there was no top cover on the cylinder so the steam below the piston raised the engine beam then was condensed in the cylinder so creating a vacuum and atmospheric pressure forced the piston down.

John Wilkinson died, a wealthy man, at Bradley Manor on his Staffordshire estate on 14 July 1808 and, typically of the man, his personal affairs were a little tangled. Because he considered himself a shrewd businessman, he attempted to ensure that his estate should be managed by those whom he chose and enumerated in his will His second wife had predeceased him, so he left some of his extensive property to his mistress, Ann Lewis, for her life 'as long as she remained unmarried'. She had borne him three children. The substantial rest was to be managed by his nominated trustees for twenty-one years 'to carry on his work at Brymbo and elsewhere'. Predictably what has been called 'The Battle for the Estate' started and continued until, by 1828, costly litigation had exhausted the estate's resources and a Chancery Decree ordered a sale to meet claims.

Brymbo Works was not sold but seems to have become semi-derelict and the blast furnaces were blown out. However, by 1836 the price of pig iron had risen significantly so perhaps that encouraged three more 'outsiders' (Wilkinson was an 'outsider' too) from Scotland who expressed interest. They came to Brymbo and operated the plant between 1838 and 1841 but could not raise sufficient money to purchase the Works. However, in 1841 another Scot, Robert Roy, a barrister, bought the Brymbo Estate out of Chancery and remained in active contact with the district for many years undertaking railway development, mining and operating Brymbo Works.

For a reader who has not yet lost interest in this long story, mention of 'railway development' and Scotsmen may be clues to the next significant insider who had a profound influence on the renewed development of Brymbo Works and the railways in NE Wales. Henry Robertson is one of the 'outsider' entrepreneurs who is described in Chapter 5. He became a Director of a new Company in September 1842 and the Deed of Constitution dated 29 September 1842 is a useful guide to the movers and shakers that are at the heart of this part of our story and their intentions:

'The Deed of Constitution of The Brymbo Mineral and Railway Company

Robert Roy, William Betts, William Mackenzie, James Leishman.

Alexander Mackenzie Ross – Civil Engineer of Brymbo

Henry Robertson – Civil Engineer of Glasgow

The Brymbo Mineral and Railway Company is formed to work the mines and collieries in and under the Freehold Estate called the "Brymbo Estate" (about 514 acres) to smelt and manufacture iron, and sell coal, etc., and for making a Railway from or near the said Estate to the River Dee with connecting or branch railways and wharves.'

Detailed history of Brymbo Works is out of place in a book concentrating on railways but the Brymbo Mineral and Railway Company had plans by 1842 for a railway from Brymbo to the Dee.

Progress on the proposed railway was frustrated by the physical geography of the Brymbo area and the land owners, and their tenants, who had several estates on the planned route. They would not consent to a railway being built through their lands. There followed three years of proposals, promoted Bills and some Acts which can be summarised thus:

- In 1844 an Act was obtained on 6 August 1844 but it only permitted a railway between Chester to Wrexham with no branch to the Mines and Ironworks.
- In 1845 the North Wales Mineral Railway Extension Act was passed for the branch to Brymbo and Minera and a railway from Wrexham to Cefn and Ruabon. Then a further Extension embraced the whole railway from Cefn to Shrewsbury to be called South of the Dee Railway.
- Finally, in a 27 July 1846 Act, South of the Dee Railway and North Wales Mineral Railway were amalgamated as the Shrewsbury and Chester Railway. This was the company that served Brymbo and the district until it was amalgamated with the Great Western on 8 May 1854.

The sketch map in **Fig 101** summarises possible solutions to the topographical problems which this first Brymbo branch had to overcome. Two short tunnels were necessary and two rope-hauled inclines, usually known as Brakes, were operational alternatives. Brakes were cheaper to construct but difficult, sometimes dangerous and slow, to work. The main line from Chester to Wrexham was opened on 2 November 1846, but the Brymbo branch, North Westward from Wheatsheaf Junction was not ready until 28 June 1847. An excursion was run from Brymbo to Chester to celebrate this opening but there is no account of how passengers fared in the tunnels or on the inclines – nor when horses or locomotives hauled the train.

Inclines – Brakes – (shown on **Fig 102**) were very much a feature of early railways and tramways. They could be rope-hauled stationary steam engine or counter-balanced so a few loaded wagons downhill could pull empties uphill with the haulage rope passing over a brake-wheel – hence the local name. The first, NW from Wheatsheaf Junction, was Wheatsheaf Incline which climbed the eastern slope of Gwersylt Hill to the eastern portal of Summerhill tunnel at a slope of 1 in 17. Moss incline was shorter and much steeper at 1 in 3.5 so a brake was very necessary. Both inclines and tunnels were abandoned in 1862 when a new Brymbo

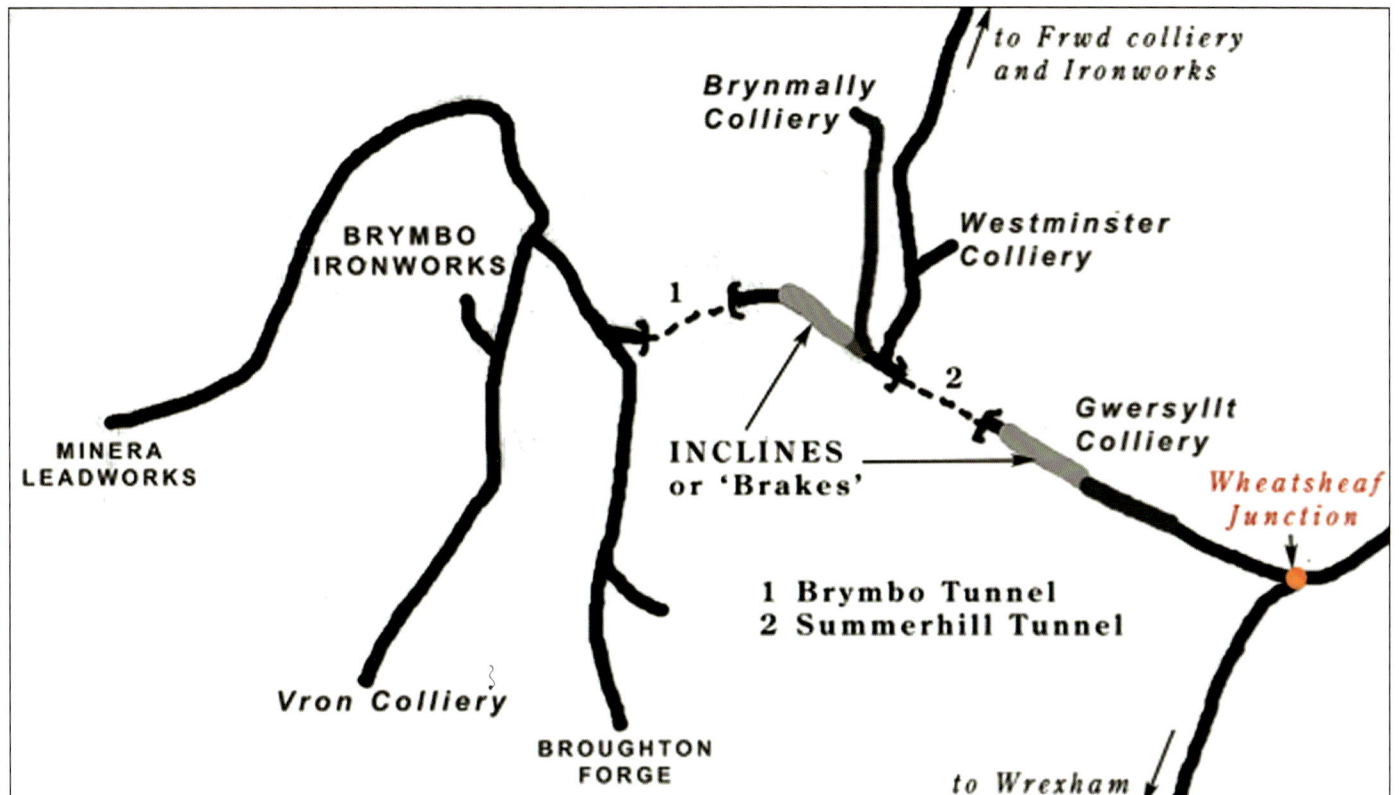

Fig 102: Sketch map of the railways to Brymbo, Minera and serving other Works and Collieries in the area after developments in 1846. (*Author*)

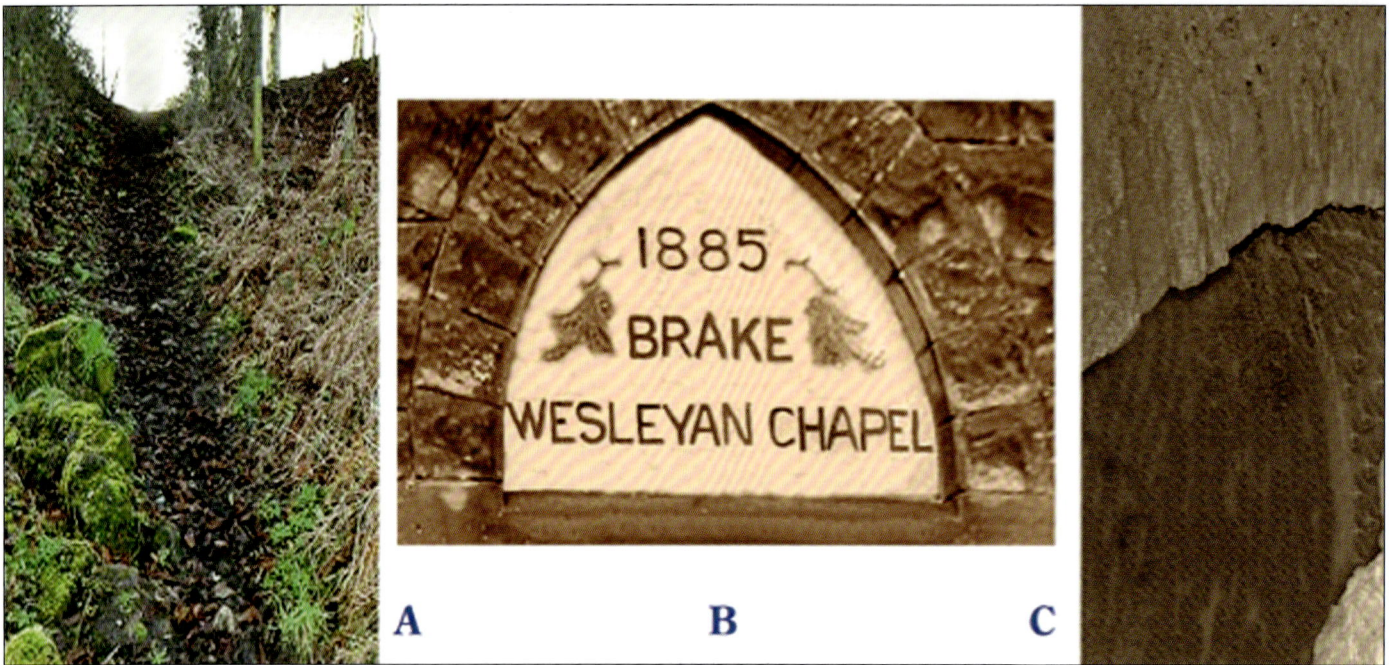

Fig 103: Twentieth century remains of 1847 railway link to Brymbo. A) Course of 1 in 3.5 Moss Incline or Brake. B) Door name plaque for Brake Methodist Chapel, built in 1885 on the 1847 railway trackbed near the entrance to Brymbo Tunnel. Chapel demolished in 2009. C) Arch entrance to Summerhill tunnel. (*Author*)

branch line was built from Croes Newydd taking a more circuitous route but with easier gradients (see **Fig 66**). A few remains of the 1847 line existed for a number of years (see **Fig 103**) but twentieth century housing developments finally obscured and covered them.

Once the 1847 rail link was in place and working, and Brymbo Works was growing, there was a need for steam locomotives. There are no records of them at Brymbo before 1858 when a new Beyer-Peacock 0-4-0T *Robertson* arrived. It was joined in 1869 by the third-hand 0-4-2ST *Python*, built by Kirtley & Co of Warrington in 1841. It was previously owned by a contractor who had worked in Spain and then by the Sheffield, Ashton-under-Lynn & Manchester Railway Co where it had been rebuilt as an 0-2-2 tender locomotive. The restricted spaces and tight curves at Brymbo Works necessitated its return as an 0-4-0ST. The records of Kirtley & Co are fragmentary, but the names recorded were of birds so perhaps the name *Python* came later and reflected a troublesome loco? The *Industrial Locomotives of North Wales* (V.J. Bradley [Compiler], Industrial Railway Society, 1992) records it as 'dumped in a siding at Chester' by 1865.

The new Brymbo branch line which opened via Croes Newydd in 1862 gave rail access to Brymbo without the steep inclines and narrow tunnels. The

Works progressively expanded, more railways were built, internally for Works traffic and externally for goods and, eventually, for passengers so can best be summarised in **Fig 104** and shown in detail from an OS 25in map in **Fig 105**.

By the beginning of the twentieth century, Brymbo Works' railways had multiplied. The Loco department, illustrated in **Fig 106**, from *Brymbo [Works] News*, had grown too and the picture reflects that growth and the pride the men took in their work. The locomotive behind them is believed to be *Bobs*, an 0-6-0ST built by Hunslet Engine Works in Leeds and delivered second-hand to Brymbo by 1898; *Bobs* worked at Brymbo until 1957 when officially scrapped.

Another loco at the Works was *Basic* which was an 0-4-0CT crane tank (**Fig 107**) built by Dübs of Glasgow and delivered new to Brymbo in 1884; it was rebuilt in the Brymbo workshops in 1937 and worked on until 1958. Crane tanks were useful tools in a site like Brymbo Works and the rebuilding after 53 years of work suggests the loco was worth maintaining for another twenty-one years.

A final loco story illustrates the thriftiness of Brymbo Works' management – **Fig 108**.

The Works periodically sold scrap to Isaac Watts Boulton's engineering works in Ashton-under-Lyne.

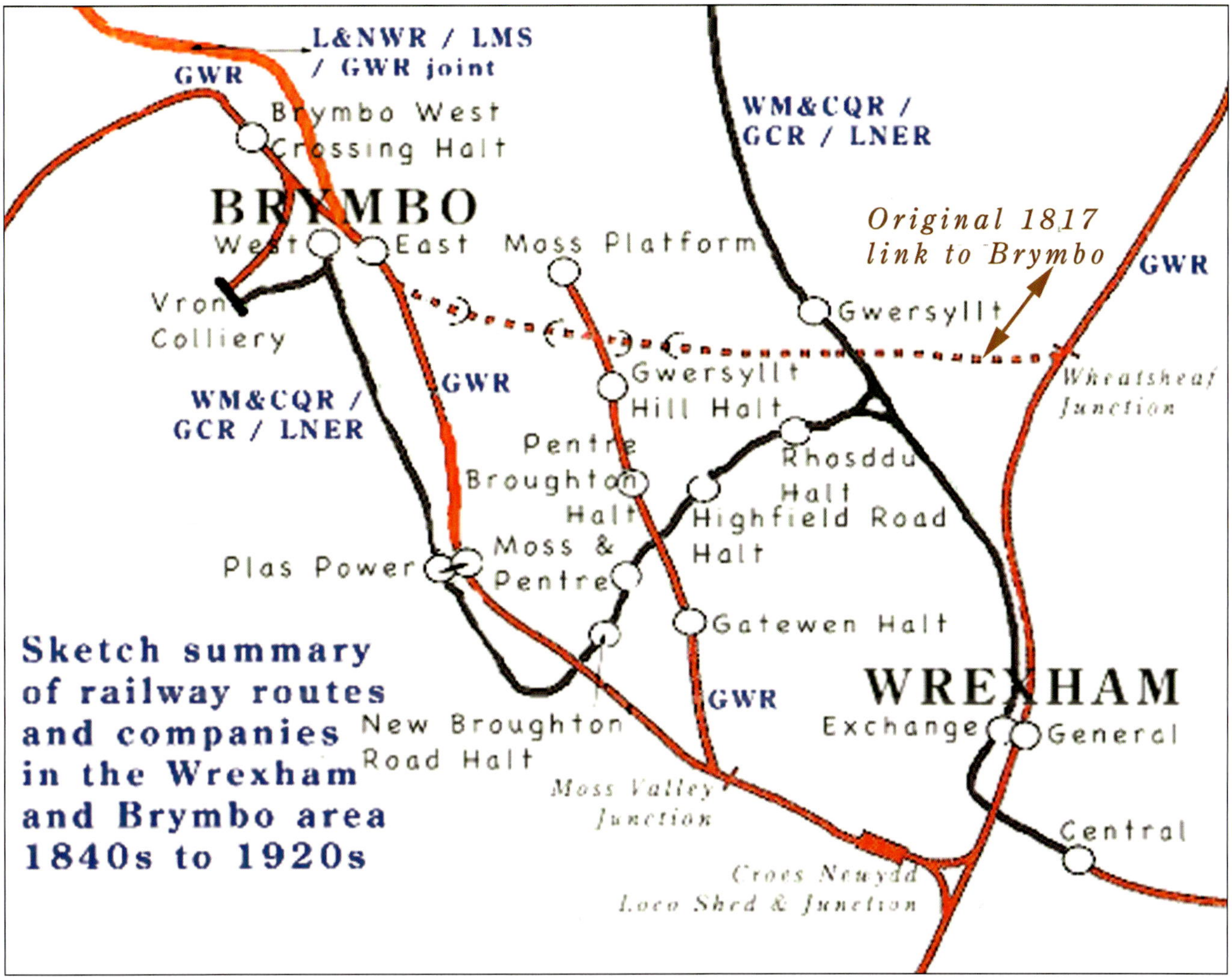

Fig 104: A sketch summary of the railway routes and operating companies serving Brymbo. (*Author*)

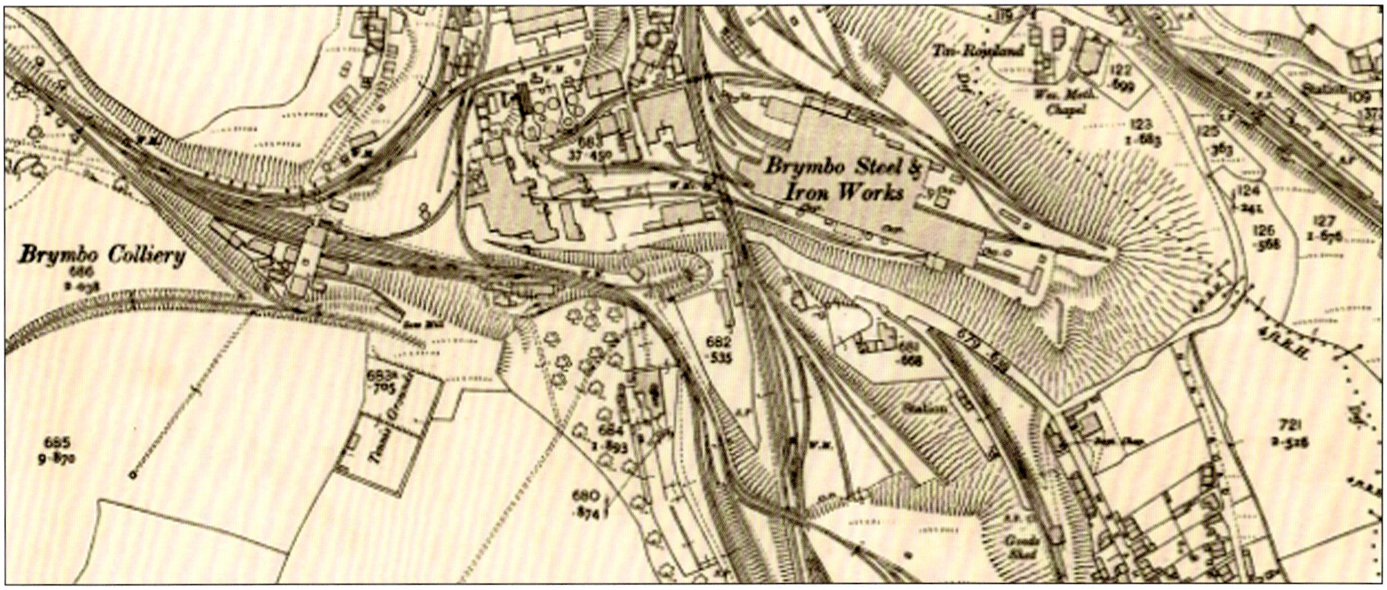

Fig 105: 1912 OS 25in map extract showing the network of railways in and around Brymbo Works.

Above: **Fig 106**: The Loco Department at Brymbo Works in 1904.

Left: **Fig 107**: Dübs, Glasgow 0-4-0CT crane tank which served Brymbo Works for 74 years.

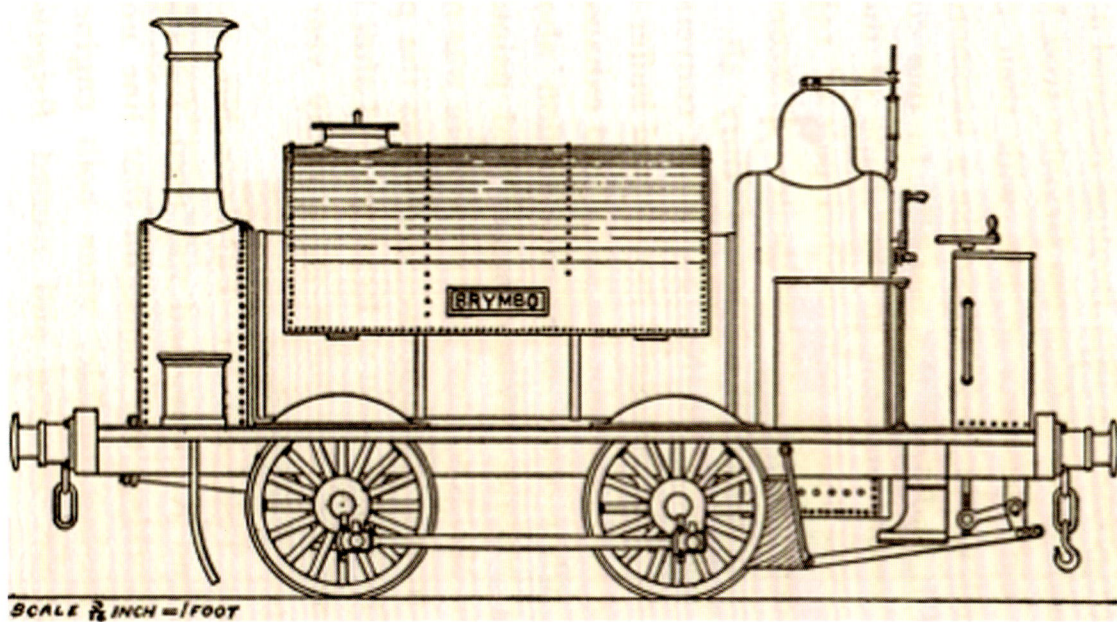

SCALE ⅛ INCH = I FOOT

Fig 108: *Brymbo* built from scrap supplied by Brymbo Works in 1900; purchase price £412.

Boulton bought 'scrap' main line locomotives and dismantled or rebuilt them for the use of contractors or branch line railways. In 1874 Boulton received two wagon loads of scrap from Brymbo Works which were old customers of his. The sale request was to 'kindly make a locomotive out of some of it and keep the rest'. In due course, a substantial result emerged in the shape of an 0-4-0 loco with a second-hand boiler, cylinders, 4ft-wheels, motion and buffer beams. But the steam and exhaust pipes were new. When lagged, painted and named *Brymbo,* the loco looked new. 0-4-0 *Brymbo* was delivered to the Works for £412, worked there for several years then once more reverted to scrap!

The train network in and around Brymbo served the people of the area for very many years. These local trains were personal, attractive, and interesting to the inhabitants of the Flintshire valleys. It was not unusual for a train to be held up waiting for a latecomer running onto the station platform; even for a driver to reverse his train into a station if someone had been left behind. And it was easy for train crews to see who had travelled on the train and whether his presence in the village served by its station was for the good or ill of residents. A story is still remembered of a lady living near the station who would warn her neighbourhood if the debt collector was on the train. If the station master warned her of his anticipated coming, she hung a red duster on her clothesline so all his intended victims could go 'missing' for the day.

However, eventually much of the rural and branch line railway network that Henry Robertson had worked to build was no longer required as public road transport developed and many folks could afford cars. The 1912 Ordnance Survey map in **Fig 104** tells of the changes at the Works – which is now called Brymbo Iron and Steel Works – and 'Steel' in the name illustrates another development which can be credited to Robertson. He was Chairman of the Works and in the1880s, after studying iron and steel making in several other Works, and in Russia, he resolved to set up a Steel Works at Brymbo and pioneered there, and in the UK, the Basic Open-Hearth Steel process.

In simple terms, steel, contains less carbon than blast furnace iron which was at first generally known as pig iron and was frequently re-melted to be made into cast iron objects. If the iron needed to be made into 'worked' objects – by a blacksmith for instance – it needed to be malleable, so the term wrought iron came into use. Cast iron may contain up to four per cent. carbon whereas wrought iron has a very low carbon content, so it is very strong, malleable, ductile, corrosion-resistant, and easily welded. Steel has an even lower percentage of carbon than wrought iron and, especially with the addition of alloys, can offer a variety of strengths and qualities. Ship building, bridge building, guns, armour plate, machinery of every sort, and steel building structures owe their development to modern steel. The two late nineteenth century names most associated

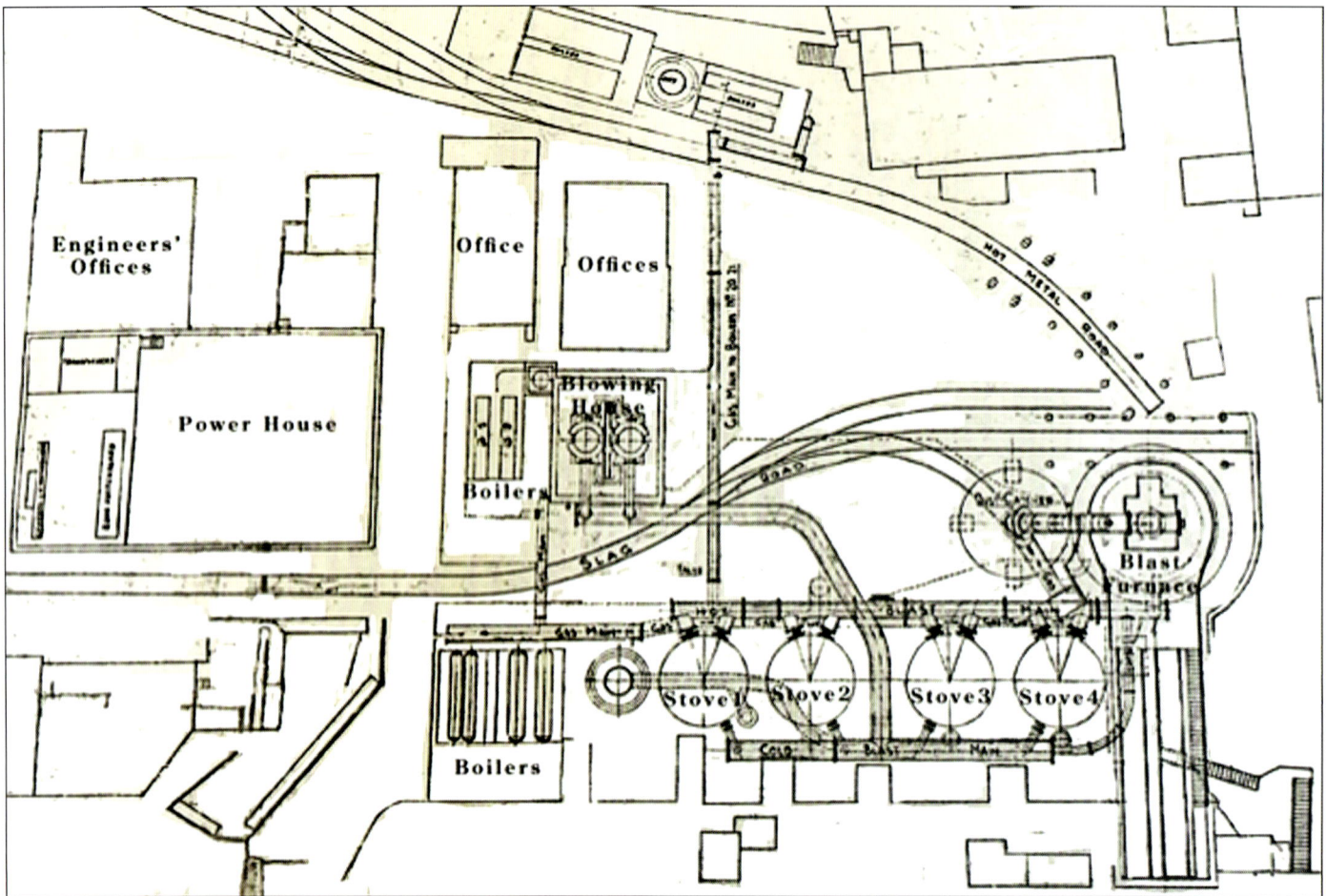

Above: **Fig 109**: Blast Furnace, steam-powered blowing engine providing the blast, hot blast stoves and the slag and molten metal railway tracks serving the Furnace. Original plan created in 1960s.

Left: **Fig 110**: Tapping a Cupola Furnace.

with the mass production of steel are Henry Bessemer – the converter – and William Siemens – the open hearth furnace. Brymbo, led by Henry Robertson, favoured the latter as shown in **Fig 115**.

It seems logical, in following the jigsaw pieces which make up the Brymbo story, and the progressive expansion of the Works in the nineteenth and twentieth centuries, to start with the Blast Furnace. This made the iron to feed the steel making process and is shown on the 1960s plan in **Fig 109**.

I have not discovered a picture of a Brymbo Blast Furnace Tap but, albeit on a smaller scale, **Fig 110** illustrates the tapping of a Cupola Furnace at Brymbo with molten iron flowing into a small ladle. The Cupola Furnace was for re-heating pig iron to lead it into a casting mould, for instance.

A blast furnace also discharged slag into a ladle which could be moved to the Basic Slag works on site to process it into an agricultural fertiliser which was a useful additional source of income for the Works.

Another use of slag at Brymbo was to increase the size of the plateau on which the Works had been developed and was now growing. **Figs 111, 112, 113** and **114** illustrate this process better than words.

After the Blast Furnace in the steel making process the next jigsaw piece was the Open Hearth Furnaces which are illustrated and labelled in the **Fig 115** 1960s plan.

Right: **Fig 111**: Slag tipping to extend the artificial plateau on which Brymbo Works grew.

Below: **Fig 112**: Tipping red-hot slag to extend the plateau on which Brymbo Works grew.

Above: **Fig 113**: Aerial view looking north over Brymbo Iron and Steel Works in 1975 – and see **Fig 114**.

Left: **Fig 114**: Slag tipping required a very nice judgement by the loco driver pushing this tipping ladle to the end of the track! See also **Fig 125**.

Opposite: **Fig 115**: Brymbo Iron and Steel Works plan of the Basic Open Hearth Furnace Shop and internal railways which served it. Note, too, the BR (ex GWR) Brymbo Station overshadowed by the Works.

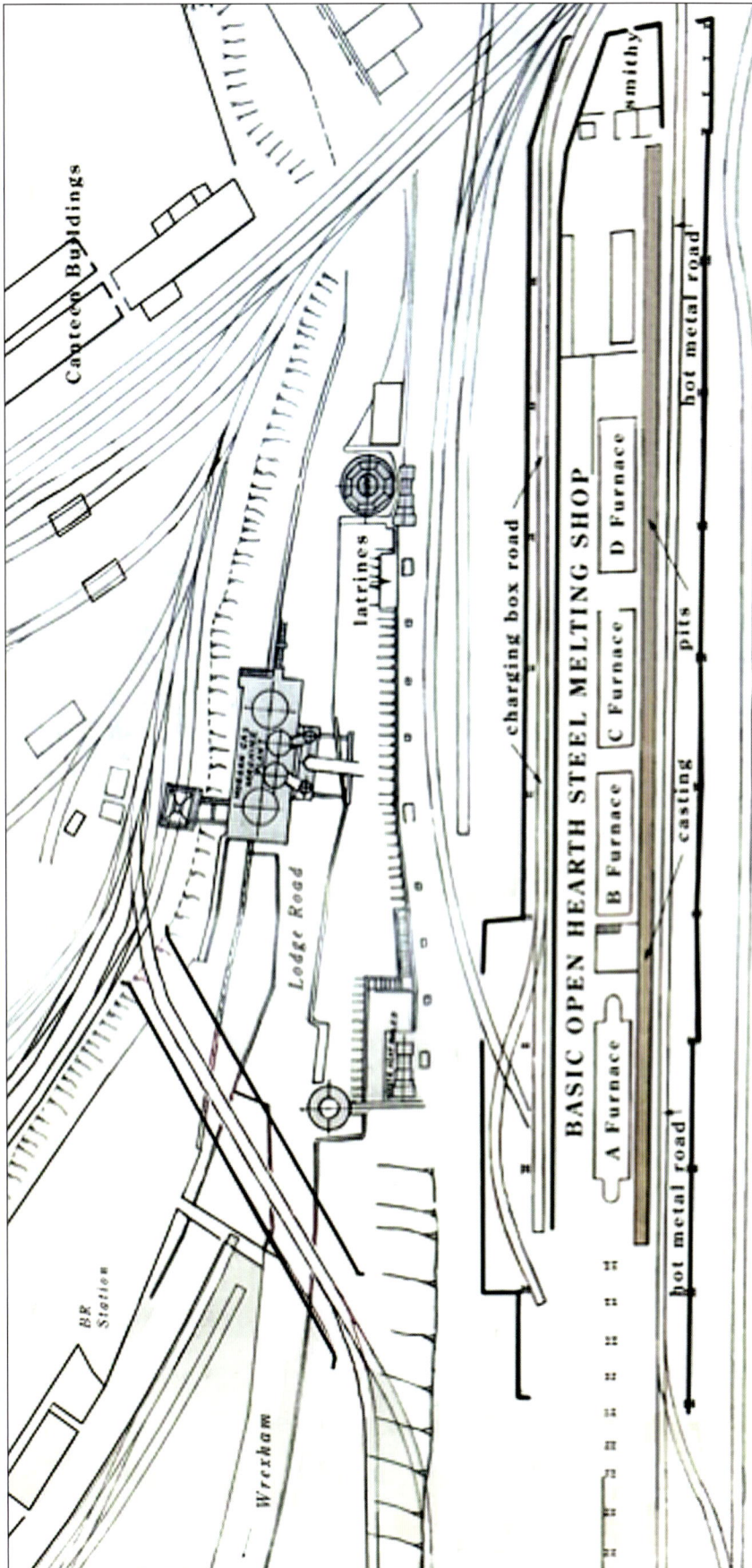

Canteen Buildings

Lodge Road

latrines

BR Station

Wrexham

charging box road

BASIC OPEN HEARTH STEEL MELTING SHOP

A Furnace

B Furnace

C Furnace

D Furnace

Smithy

hot metal road

casting pits

hot metal road

Above: **Fig 116**: Charging an open hearth furnace.

Left: **Fig 117**: Brymbo Works railways 50ton ladle bogie.

The slag tipping and open hearth furnace charging in **Figs 112**, **114**, **116** show the scale of the operations at Brymbo Works, the importance of the Works internal railways, the use of overhead cranes, and specialist railway wagons, like a 50ton ladle bogie in **Fig 117**.

Fig 113 shows the extent of Brymbo Works by 1975 and by then the open hearth steel making furnaces had been replaced by electric arc furnaces in two separate buildings – Electric Melting Shop 1, shown on the plan in **Fig 118** – and the much larger Electric Melting Shop 2 which replaced the Open Hearth Furnaces Shop and is the longest North-South building in the **Fig 113** aerial view.

The ingots (**Fig 119**) from the Electric Arc Furnaces had to be rolled to produce billets of various sizes, as customers required – (**Fig 120**) –and these billets left Brymbo by rail. Fig 121.

Brymbo Steel gained a reputation for quality and the Works specialized in steel alloys and special steels. Talks with Rolls Royce and the Air Ministry took place in 1939 and subsequently, because of its strategically isolated position, Brymbo was selected by the Air Ministry to supply them with aircraft steels. In 1948 Brymbo became part of the Guest Keen & Nettlefold Group (GKN Ltd.) of specialist steel makers which provided a steady market for the better grades of Brymbo steel.

In April 1959 Electric Melting Shop 2 (EMS2) was commissioned, replacing the old basic open hearth furnaces which had been in use at Brymbo for 74 years. Brymbo Works became one of the few all-electric steel works in the country. By 1963 quality control had reached the point where microscopical reports were made on all steel before it left the Works, and grain size control was rigidly practised. More and more time was being spent on the inspection and dressing of the steel to ensure that when it left the Works it would exactly meet customers' requirements. In 1969 the Works achieved some production records. In week ended 24 May 1969

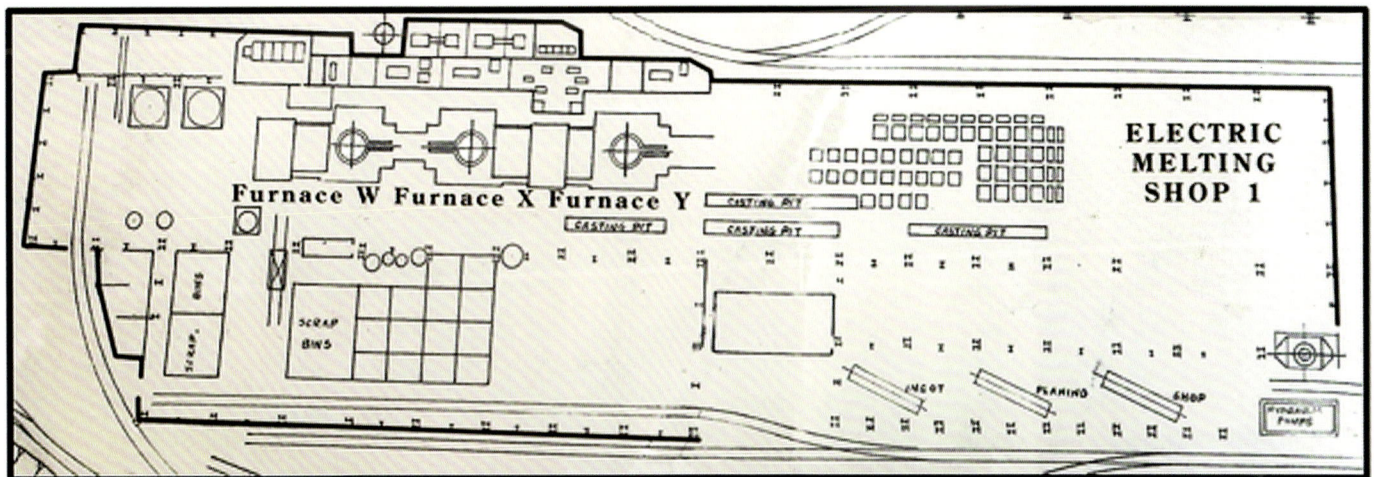

Above: **Fig 118**: Three Electric Arc Furnaces in Brymbo's Electric Melting Shop 1.

Right: **Fig 119**: Ingot from Electric Arc Furnace en route to rolling – see Fig 120.

Fig 120: Roller Mill controllers (left) in a cabin above the Roller Mill (right) reducing ingots to billets.)

EMS2. produced 6,192 tons which, together with the 1,892 tons from EMS1, gave a total ingot production in excess of 8,000 tons for the week – the first time this total figure had been obtained.

The Works was now part of the British Steel Corporation (BSC) which approved a £3.1M development which closed EMS1 replacement with a new 70-ton capacity electric-arc furnace in EMS2 (thus concentrating all the melting facilities under one roof). Other improvements were a new 100 ton capacity overhead crane, three new hot blast stoves and a new turbo-blower at the blast furnace to increase output there to up to 3,000 tons a week. To supplement the National Grid electricity supply, a new 6 MW turbo-alternator was added to the Works.

On 29 March 1970 BSC re-organised itself into Product Divisions. Brymbo Steel Works became a member of the Special Steels Division and was known simply as Brymbo Works. On 7 August 1973 BSC and GKN Ltd. announced that Brymbo Works was to be returned to GKN Ltd as part of a State hiving-off deal. This meant that the GKN Group were assuming ownership of Brymbo Works for the third time since 1948 when they bought it for development for their special needs, lost it in 1951 at nationalisation, re-acquired it for a second time on de-nationalisation in 1955, had it wrested from them again on re-nationalisation in 1969 and were now running the Works once more. The news was received with satisfaction by management and

unions alike. It confirmed GKN's faith in the integrity of the Works' products and the inherent skills of its Brymbo workers who were looking forward, together with GKN, to continued prosperity untrammelled by political upheaval.

GKN was awarded the Queen's Award to Industry for export achievements in 1976; Brymbo Works was acknowledged to have played a prominent part in that achievement and railways played a part too. British Rail began to operate what they called 'block trains' for steel traffic to the West Midlands. Thirteen trains ran every week-nights from steel-making centres like Brymbo direct to nine West Midlands railheads. Each train had the capacity to move up to 800 tons of steel for overnight delivery – **Fig 121**.

The Brymbo train departed from Croes Newydd at 20.45 for the West Midlands railhead at Wednesbury serving Wolverhampton and the Black Country. BR's guarantee of overnight delivery depended on strict observance of the rule that no traffic was forwarded which could not be accepted at the consignees' premises on the following day. The West Midlands railhead depot's working would be disrupted if inward traffic had to be stabled or stored because customers were refusing to take immediate delivery.

Full details of the type and quantity of the steel loaded on the train was ready at Brymbo by 16.30 on the day of despatch. This data was then tele-printed to the receiving depot so that deliveries were pre-planned, and the consignees were advised of approximate delivery

Fig 121: Train load of steel billets shunted at Brymbo Works for export.

times. BR gave this steel traffic an operational priority equal to that for perishable freight. The wagons were equipped to carry various types of traffic, such as tubes, billets and coil strip which travelled in sheeted cradles to ensure all-weather protection.

A much earlier programme of 'block trains' (though the term was not then in use) arrived at Brymbo from 1899 to 1946. They carried calcined ironstone, with the occasional wagon of raw ironstone, from Hook Norton quarries in Oxfordshire on Mondays, Wednesdays and Fridays of each week. Land was acquired in the Park Farm area and quarrying started in September 1899. Park Farm ironstone was siliceous and low in lime content, but other districts supplied different ironstones. Several calcining kilns were opened (**Fig 122**) and, by judicious mixing at Brymbo, 'self fluxing' charges were put into the Blast Furnace thus avoiding the need for additional slag formers. For many years, trains of fifteen to twenty wagons ran from Hook Norton to Brymbo on Mondays, Wednesdays and Fridays of each week.

At Hook Norton Brymbo Works developed a network of narrow gauge railways for transport to the quarries and to the nearby main line. Generally, the Works internal railways at Brymbo were all standard gauge and for many years steam locomotives were used. **Fig 106** shows

the men in the Works loco Department in 1904 and, characteristically, they were very fond of their 'steamers'.

The old 'steamers' were looked upon with a sort of affection and *Wrekin, Arenig, Sir Henry, Basic, Gwynedd, Anzac* and *Berwyn* became household names around the Works and at home with the men who drove and maintained them. Some of the steam locomotives came new to Brymbo, others were second or third hand, like *Arenig* which arrived in 1919, purchased from the National Shell Filling Factory in Banbury for £2,000. The youngest of the Brymbo Steamers was *Berwy*, an 0-6-0ST built by Peckett & Sons in 1950 and bought new for £5,094.

A progressive change to diesel locomotives began in the 1950s, partly because of the age of the steamers and perhaps, too, because elderly steam locos did not fit the publicised image of a modern and developing electric steel works. On 16 January 1956 *Esmond* arrived; it was a 200hp diesel-electric 0-6-0 built by Yorkshire Engine Co (YE) with a Rolls Royce 6-cylinder supercharged engine. Three more locos of this type came to Brymbo in 1957 called *Hope, Spencer* and *John* and all subsequent locos were ordered from YE.

To cope with increased rail loads at the Works two 440HP diesel-electric 0-6-0s arrived in March 1962, called *William* and *Emrys*, and this completed the take-over

Fig 122: Brymbo Works ironstone calcining kilns at Hook Norton Quarries, Oxfordshire

from steam although some more second-hand diesel-electric shunters were added to the Brymbo Works fleet – **Fig 123**.

A slight irony in this story of the main line and Works railways is reflected in **Fig 124** showing the delivery by road of the electric arc furnaces to the Brymbo site.

It is a useful reminder of the difficult terrain in the Brymbo area for the development of an iron and steel works and a segue to the next very large iron and steel works in this story – Shotton. So a final internal railway system picture for Brymbo is **Fig 125** looking down on the end of the built-up slag plateau on which the Works developed and another YE diesel-electric loco ready for more shunting.

John Summers & Sons Ltd – Shotton Steel Works: Brymbo was the brainchild of John Wilkinson; Shotton Steel Works owes its name and growth to John Summers and his sons – 'outsiders' again.

John Summers was born in Bolton. Lancashire, in 1822 and by the age of 20 was in business making clogs

for cotton workers in the Dukinfield and Stalybridge areas of North Cheshire. At the 1851 Great Exhibition in London, he paid £40 for a nail-making machine which he set up in an old engineering works in Stalybridge. He was a hard-working and ambitious man, so he purchased land near the Stalybridge works and built a new ironworks – Globe Works. There, in 1860, he installed sheet rolling mills to roll puddled iron into crude steel sheets for clog nails.

John Summers died on 10 April 1876. Three of his sons, James, John and Alfred, carried on the business, and they were joined by another brother, Henry Hall Summers – 'Harry' – who was as energetic and ambitious as his father had been. He suggested that they should import sheet bars from America and the Continent to make 'black' uncoated sheets. Six rolling mills, driven by a steam engine, were installed and for the first time in Britain, iron bars were being rolled into long sheet lengths. The next step was to set up zinc galvanising as the company's first move towards

Above: **Fig 123**: Yorkshire Engine Co's 0-6-0 diesel-electric 220hp shunters *Austin* and *Charles* at work at Brymbo Works (United Engineering Steels) in 1986.

Right: **Fig 124**: Pickford's low loader negotiates a narrow village street en route with an electric arc furnace for Brymbo Works.

Fig 125: The rounded end of the slag plateau on which Brymbo Works developed is a reminder of the complexity of the internal railway system, the precipitous end of the siding occupied by a YE diesel-electric shunter, and the way the Works overshadowed the settlements around it.

Fig 126: A YE diesel-electric shunter and an empty slag tipper like those used to build up the slag plateau on which Brymbo Works developed.

becoming the largest producers of galvanised steel sheets in the country.

Soon space for further expansion at the Globe Works was exhausted so in 1895 the company bought 40 acres of marshland close to Hawarden Bridge from the Manchester, Sheffield and Lincolnshire Railway (MS&LR) with an option on a further 50 acres. Because the area was marshland it was cheap and there was as much to be had as reclamation could win from the saltings. For the new works there was also plenty of water, coal and some iron ore nearby; the MSLR and the ports of Liverpool and Birkenhead were within easy reach.

The original Works – originally called Hawarden Bridge Steel Works – covered six acres and employed 250 men. In the next 40 years it expanded to 250 acres, with a labour force of 6,000 men. Then in 1938 came the most momentous step in the Company's history with the installation of a continuous hot strip mill. The capacity of the new strip mill, which came into operation just in time to play a valuable part in the Second World War

effort, exceeded that of the existing steelworks. As soon as the war ended, therefore, the Company decided to create a complete integrated iron and steel works with a much larger melting shop and a complete installation of blast furnaces and coke ovens.

By 1958 the Works employed 10,000 people and was making over one million tons of steel a year. To service the Works, twenty-two locomotives, eighty miles of railway track and twelve miles of roads were needed. **Fig 127** shows the sale and size of this operation.

In this story I am concerned with the scale and history of the Works and, particularly of the railway developments. The scale is often best illustrated by pictures, so **Fig 128** shows the size of cranes in the enlarged melting shop, and the railways on the shop floor and **Fig 129** some of the new internal railway.

Grant Lyon & Co, one of the contractors employed for enlargement of the Shotton Works in the 1950s, were specialists in track laying for congested industrial sites as in **Fig 129**. The increasing size of the Works required extensive alterations to the sidings, and these

Fig 127: Aerial view of Shotton Steel Works in the 1950s.

Left: **Fig 128**: Wellman ladle cranes installed in the melting shop at Shotton Steelworks in the 1950s.

Below: **Fig 129**: Advertisement for new internal railways at the Shotton Integrated Iron and Steel Works developed in the 1950s by John Summers & Sons Ltd.

were carried out entirely by the Works permanent way section. Some 36 miles of new tracks, including 280 sets of points and crossings, were laid. The rail used was the new 95lb Revised Bullhead Standard (RBS) for running lines and service sidings, 85lb RBS for standing sidings and, for routes where there were heavy axle loads, new 113lb flat bottom rail laid on base plates with plain sleepers and elastic spikes.

The work was supervised by an experienced railway PW inspector. Four gangs of twelve men, each in charge of a ganger, worked with three steam cranes, electric boring and screwing machines, mobile cabins (converted from railway box wagons), suitable bolster and drop-sided wagons, and a mobile water tank to supply the steam cranes. Readers familiar with railway PW practices will judge that the Shotton Steel Works gangs must have been as good – and perhaps sometimes better – than PW gangs on the Big Four and BR permanent way.

All ground was prepared to a uniform level of 18ins below rail level, which was afterwards ballasted 6ins deep, and then boxed up with ashes supplied from the Works' own arisings and by BR. The hot-ingot line on an embankment from the melting shop to the stripping bay 4ins of limestone ballast. Sleepers on this track, and on other lines where the axle loads were more than normal, were laid at 26 to the length of 60ft rail. Steel keys were used exclusively throughout. Where there was a possibility of spillage of hot metal and slag, the timber sleepers were covered to rail level by non-combustible ballast. Lengths of track, including points and crossings, were prefabricated and lifted by Works cranes to their final position.

Shotton Steel Works links with BR were via Dee Marsh Junction and controlled by the signal box there. **Fig 130** is a sketch plan of trackwork at the Junction and

Fig 131 is a visual from a John Summer's publication detailing the raw materials required for a week of steel-making at the Works.

Fig 132 illustrates the complex internal railway network which served Shotton Steelworks site in the 1960s and the main line links at Dee Marsh Junction. As early as 1910 a journalist likened the scene to 'a large railway junction' and described the Summers' loco shed as 'of such size that many small railway companies need not have been ashamed to own it'. The loco fleet

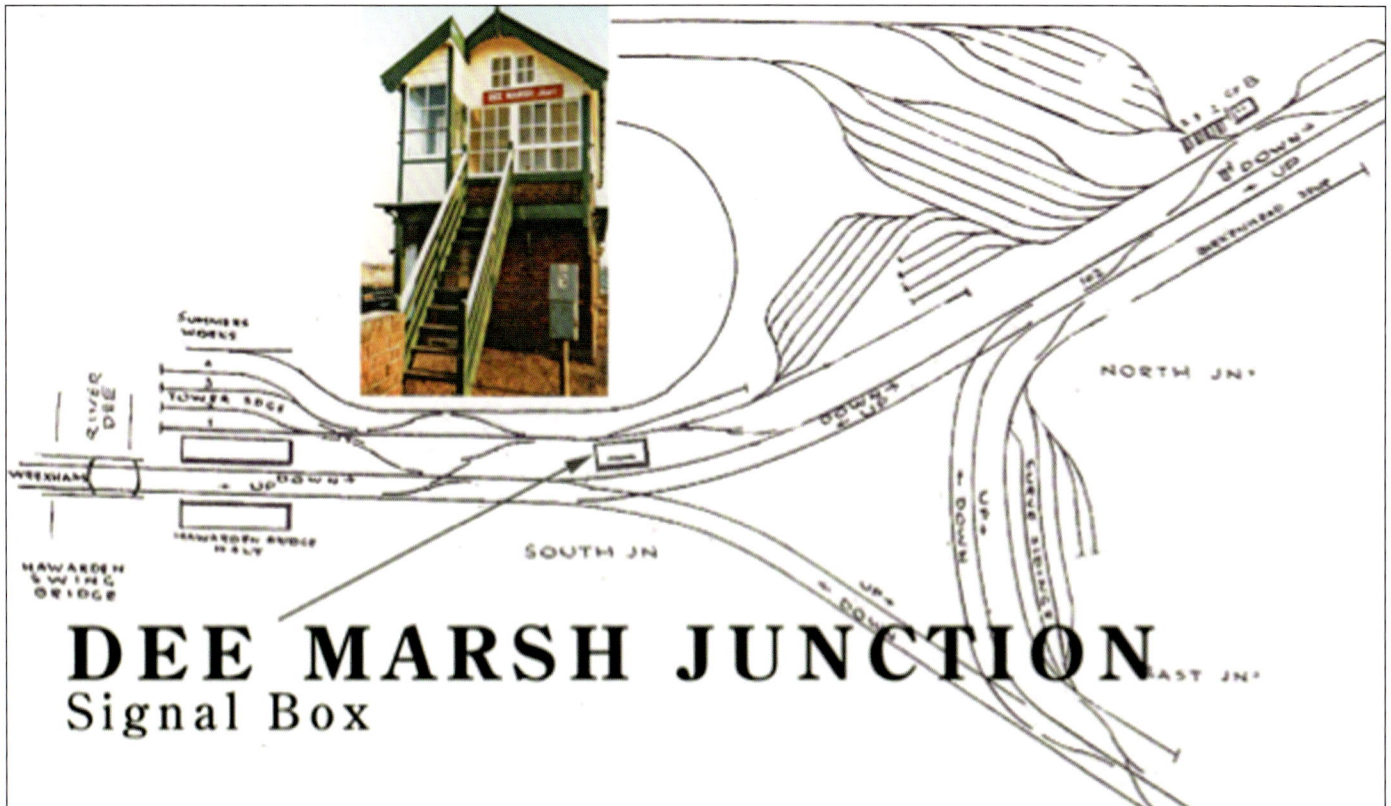

DEE MARSH JUNCTION
Signal Box

Above: **Fig 130** Sketch plan of Dee Marsh Junction and the turnouts into John Summers & Sons Shotton Steel Works and their reception and despatch sidings.

Right: **Fig 131** Raw materials required, and delivered by rail, for a week's steel-making at Shotton Steel Works.

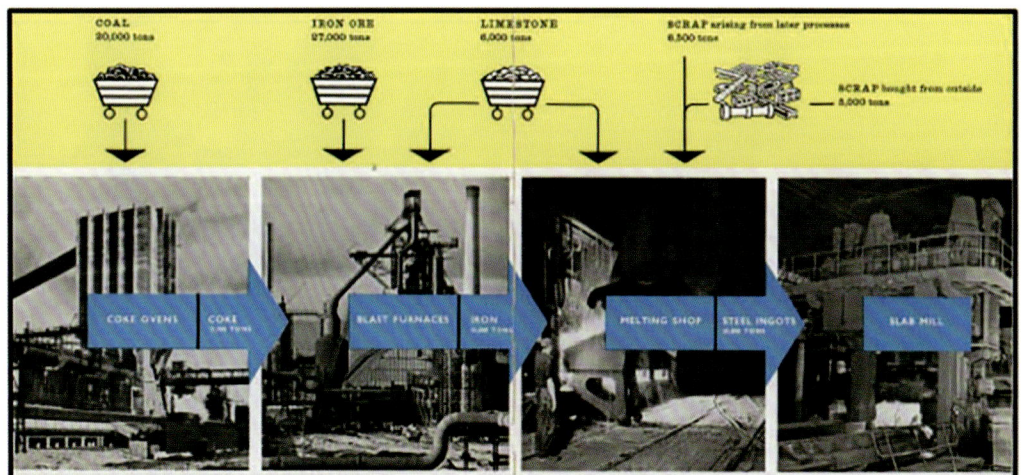

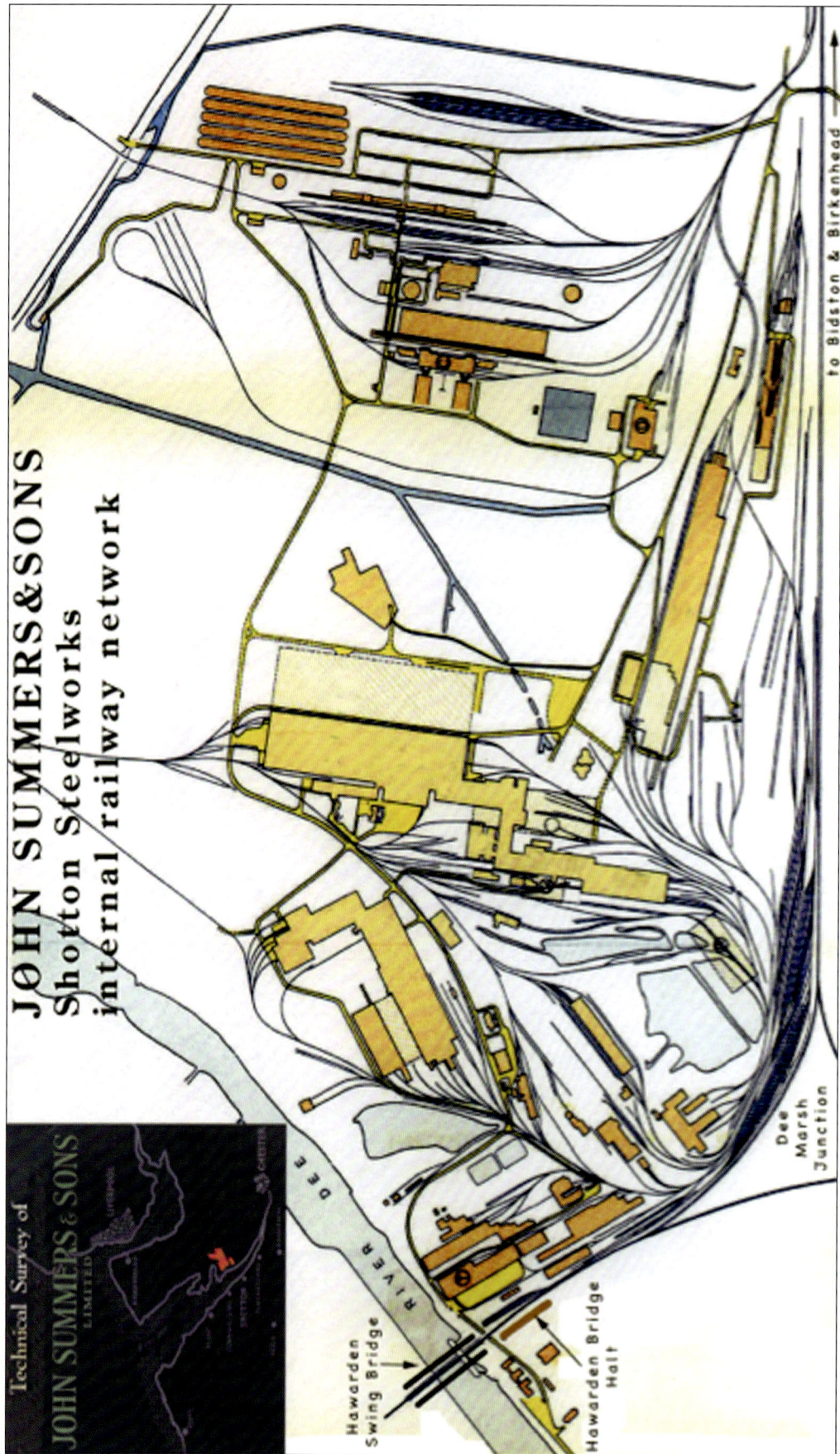

Fig 132: Shotton Steel Works internal rail network and links to BR at Dee Marsh Junction.

Fig 133: Hudswell Clarke 0-4-0 saddle tank shunter *Jupiter* delivered new to Shotton Steel Works in 1910. The crew, left to right, are: W. Hargreaves (driver), C. Jones (fireman), W. Evans, E. Griffiths (shunters).

numbered eight in 1910, all 0-4-0STs built by Hudswell Clarke of Leeds. **Fig 133**, of *Jupiter* from that first batch, also shows the named driver and fireman and two named shunters who were very important members of the Works team. There were no automatic couplers then so shunters, with their poles shown in **Fig 133,** skilfully coupled and uncoupled wagons, and the locos, often using their poles as levers over the top of the buffers to lift heavy 3-link chain couplings.

As the Works was enlarged, the steam loco fleet was increased to service two open hearth steel plants as well as rolling mills and galvanising departments; by 1948, the Works had 46 miles of track and the internal locos were handling 5,000 wagons of main line traffic a week. In the early 1950s as full integration of the plant was completed, a new marshalling and holding yard, known as Shotwick Sidings was brought into use adjacent to the incoming exchange sidings at Dee Marsh junction. Two more powerful steam locos *Titan* and *Thor* were added to the fleet, to move steel ingots from the new No.3 melting shop to the slab mill.

The first 0-6-0 diesel-mechanical shunters, built by Hunslet Engine Works in Leeds and 'named' 1 and 2, came to the Works in 1947. Subsequently, Summers bought diesel-electric and diesel-hydraulic shunters from several manufacturers as well as Hunslet. At first most were 0-4-0 204HP locos but, as the Works expanded and work for the railways became heavier, 500hp 0-6-0s were purchased.

Fig 134: *Vesta* new to the Works in 1916 and presented to NT by the Summers family for display at Penrhyn Castle.

The last steam locos were taken out of service in 1958. The Summers family marked the end of steam traction at the Works by presenting 0-6-0T *Vesta*, (**Fig 134**) new to the Works in August 1916 to the NT rail museum at Penrhyn Castle near Bangor where it can still be seen.

At the height of iron and steelmaking, up to the closure of the 'Heavy End' of the Works in 1972 and the end of iron and steel making, twenty-six diesel locos were in operation on site. They moved iron ore, molten iron, steel ingots, raw materials, steel coils, scrap, molten liquid slag and numerous other loads on 70 miles of internal track (**Fig 135**).

The internal track was all standard gauge except for a 2ft 6in gauge system installed in 1971 as part of a £1.5M British Steel Corporation (BSC) project to transfer semi-finished hot-rolled coil from the Hot Strip Mill to the Cold Strip Mill, Annealing and Finishing Bays. The narrow gauge railway system was operated by four 0-6-0DH Hudswell Clarke Badger-type locos (**Fig 136**). They were based on a flameproof underground design for the NCB with tall cabs for a driver and an entrance from the left-hand side only. For safe working they were fitted with a warning klaxon, and 'emergency services' type revolving lights because they worked inside the various Bays where workers were on foot.

Sharp-eyed readers will have spotted a reference to BSC in the previous paragraph, so it is helpful to summarise the changing ownership of Shotton Steel Works:

- John Summers and Sons Limited (1896-1967)
- British Steel Corporation (1967-1988)
- British Steel PLC (1988-1999)
- Corus PLC (1999-2007)
- Tata Steel Group since 2007.

I have Tata Steel's Shotton Records Centre to thank for much of the information and the pictures in this part of the story (**Fig137**).

Shotton Records Centre started life in 1972 as British Steel's archiving store for the North West, one of five regional archiving hubs across the UK. In 1989, operations were relocated to a larger, purpose-built

Fig 135: A diesel-hauled train of iron ore in Summers' Private Owner ore wagons.

storage facility on the Shotton Steelworks site. As other regional hubs closed and re-allocated their archives, the Shotton Records Centre became the sole records management site for British Steel. TNA records the Centre as holding 122 files of historic records for iron and steel businesses.

The centre consists of a purpose-built facility, providing a full and comprehensive archiving service for the collection, storage, referral, and confidential disposal of an array of company documents, including commercial, financial, historical, legal, medical and other sensitive records. It is one of the largest records management facilities within the UK.

The main warehouse has a storage capacity of over 180,000 cubic feet, accommodating a wide variety of archive material. With a state-of-the-art fire protection system, high level security and regulated temperature controls, documents are afforded the best records

Above: **Fig 136:** Hudswell Clarke 'Badger'-type diesel hydraulic loco for the 2ft 6in gauge internal railway system installed at Shotton Steel Works in 1971. Note driver entrance is only on the left-hand side of the cab.

Right: **Fig 137:** A website glimpse of a small part of Shotton Records Centre – which has contributed significantly to this book.

management service available, and a fully trained and experienced staff help with any enquiries.

To return to the John Summers & Sons steel-making story, and its internal railways. When the Works became a fully integrated iron and steel making plant it required thousands of tons of iron ore for the blast furnaces on a weekly basis. The ore could no longer be supplied from NE Wales or the UK, so most ore came from abroad, via the docks at Birkenhead and then by rail to the Works.

To carry this traffic Summers ordered a fleet of privately owned bogie hopper wagons from Charles Roberts & Sons of Wakefield. Each wagon weighed 24 tons and carried 65 tons of ore. Livery was a medium grey with 'SUMMERS' in large black lettering; to emphasise the quality of Summer's brand the wheel rims were picked out in white. For main line railway practice the wagons were labelled 'NON POOL'.

To accommodate them, and an increase in other inward and outward rail traffic, an extensive marshalling yard, known as 'Shotwick Sidings', was constructed near the existing rail entrance to the Works. These exchange sidings with the Wrexham to Bidston/Birkenhead line are still in place today (2020) and Dee Marsh signal box continues to signal them when required.

The ore wagons were not fitted with vacuum brakes so mainline drivers and guards had to apply great skill in working the heavy trains in order to bring them safely into the Works before the Works' diesel shunters took them via the internal railway system for discharge into the iron ore stockyard.

Initially these 900 to 1,000 ton trains were hauled on the main line by ex-LMS 8F 2-8-0s, usually in rakes of nine or ten wagons plus a brake van. Subsequently these trains were handled by Standard 9F 2-10-0s, and **Fig 138** shows Sir Richard Summers on the footplate of BR 9F 2-10-0 No 92233.

BSC had been progressively changing Shotton and in 1990 it became the first Works in Europe capable of coating one million tonnes of steel strip each year. Four lines were applying either zinc or zinc alloy coatings by either hot-dipping or electro-plating and two lines were applying a range of organic paints. The metallic coatings protected the steel strip from corrosion and paint gave a colourful finish and extended life.

BSC, and Corus after 1999, continued to change the configuration and layout of Shotton Steel Works. In 2001 rolling operations at Shotton finished after 105 years. The pickle line, five-stand cold reduction mill, No 2 electro-galvanising line and annealing/tempering facilities in Shotton's Cold Strip Mill all closed.

Fig 138: Sir Richard Summers on the footplate of BR Class 9F 2-10-0 loco with a train of iron ore bound for Shotton Steel Works in Summers' private owner bogie hopper wagons. Sir Richard was a long-time railway enthusiast and for a time was Chairman of the LMS company.

Fig 139: EWS Class 66 loco on the remaining main line access rail in the Tata Steels Shotton Works.

Fig 140: John Summers & Sons' General Office for their Shotton Steel Works. It was designed by Manchester architect James France who was one of the 'Manchester School' of architects who favoured the terracotta and redbrick style of which this listed building is a good example.

From 1990 demise of the internal loco fleet began and the myriad lines, points and crossings of the internal railway system gradually disappeared. However, in 2005 a new railhead warehouse opened on site as part of an £11M 'Future Shotton' project to hold 16,000 tonnes of cold reduced strip for metallic coating and 1,500 tonnes of finished products. A sole remnant of the internal railways network was re-laid and upgraded to connect with the warehouse and, depending on market conditions, some 800,000 tonnes of steel coil are brought in annually by rail on purpose-built wagons from Port Talbot, South Wales.

Main line locos are able to enter the Tata Steels Shotton site, as in **Fig 139,** but internal movement is now by two ex-British Rail Class 08 0-6-0 diesel shunters owned and driven by a firm of outside contractors.

This story now moves on from Shotton Steel Works but, unlike Brymbo Steel Works, Tata Steel remains on part of the original site. One of the early buildings – the Company Offices – is now Listed and is an impressive indication of the John Summers & Sons' pride in the Works they created (**Fig 140**). The Office building was constructed in terracotta and red brick in 1907 and designed by Manchester architect James France. It has a particularly fine Art Nouveau interior which includes a flying imperial staircase, numerous crests and shields bearing the motif, 'JS&S', and fine stained glass windows with verses from Charles Kingsley's poem *O Mary, call the cattle home across the sands O'Dee.*

A memory, from the Company's records, of the numbers they employed at the Works is in **Fig 141** showing change-of-shift business in the 1950s at Hawarden Bridge Halt (as it was once called) on the Wrexham to Bidston railway.

Fig 141: Hawarden Bridge Halt in the 1950s, thronged with men at Shotton Steel Works change-of-shift.

CHAPTER 8

MID-TWENTIETH CENTURY DECLINE AND FALL

Industries and Railways Close

It seems important to me in telling this story that I record the 'downs' as well as the 'ups' in the fortunes of the Works and railways in the previous chapters. I have looked for phrases to embrace and reasons to explain this decline and fall of a very prosperous area and I suggest:

- exhausted resources of lead, zinc, iron ore and coal
- increasing working costs for mines, quarries, mineral and passenger railway branches which are themselves generating less income
- change of product
- nationalisation and internationalisation as companies combined, were bought up by other larger, and richer, companies, became Groups and reviewed the value-for money contribution to the whole combine from individual business entities within a Group
- Government policies which may favour, or seem to disadvantage, businesses or regions
- Unexpected crises like the Covid-19 pandemic which is having a world-wide impact and, albeit in the twenty-first century, is very much in my mind because I am fortunately surviving and finding the extended lock-downs good for completing this book!

The mineral resources of the area were gradually worked out. The huge Minera Limestone Quarry and Lime Works was once the largest lime producer in North Wales. Full output continued until 1993 which was longer than Dyserth Quarries that closed in 1983. **Fig 142** at Dyserth Quarries in 1984 shows modern technology – a Liebherr mobile hydraulic crane with an extended lattice jib – removing the remains of the nineteenth century rock crusher high on the quarry side.

Coal, too, in North Wales was worked out. In 1918, sixty pits in Denbighshire and Flintshire were all working and much of the coal they produced travelled away by train, so the North Wales railways were busy too. Some of the bigger, deeper, pits had employed up to 1,000 men working three shifts throughout the day. Smaller pits might employ only 200 but coal was still an important product at the beginning of the twentieth century.

Many pits became worked out, or too expensive to operate as shafts went deeper and more water needed to be pumped away. The oil industry too, and natural gas, offered competition so by the late 1970s only Point of Ayr near Mostyn, Bersham and Gresford near Wrexham collieries were left. Point of Ayr closed in 1996, Bersham in 1986 and Gresford in 1973.

I have already mentioned that Brymbo Works ceased trading in 1990 then was progressively demolished and the site cleared. For the men, and many women in the offices, the closure was a very sad business and the demolition even more moving to watch. Sone men had worked there for years and it was a bitter blow to see their place of work disappear – like the blast furnace in **Fig 143**.

Shotton Steel Works survived but in different hands – the Tata Group – and with a different product so that story continues in the next chapter.

Industrial closures, competition from buses and the ownership of private cars precipitated closure of most of the railways described in Chapter 6 and it seemed neatest to me to illustrate the changes with a map, in **Fig 144**. This can directly be compared with **Fig 66** map on page 63 which showed the railways and their ownership before BR.

Several of the lines shown in **Fig 144** continued as mineral branches for a number of years after passenger services ceased, A summary of some station closures relating to **Fig 144** map are:

- Minera Branch (GWR) – Berwig Crossing Halt:
  Closed to Passengers 1 January 1931
  Closed to Goods 1 January 1972
- Brymbo East (GWR): Closed to Passengers
  27 March 1950
  Closed to Goods 2 November 1964

- Brymbo West (GCR / LNER): Closed to Passengers 1 March 1917
  Closed to Goods April 1956
- Coed Talon Station (WM&CQR / L&NWR): Closed to Passengers 27 March 1950
  Closed to Goods 22 July 1963

For potential passengers the different closure dates may have been difficult to recall as the sounds of a working

Above: **Fig 142**: Modern technology demolishes nineteenth century technology; the final end of Dyserth Quarries.

Left: **Fig 143**: The end of Brymbo Blast Furnace.

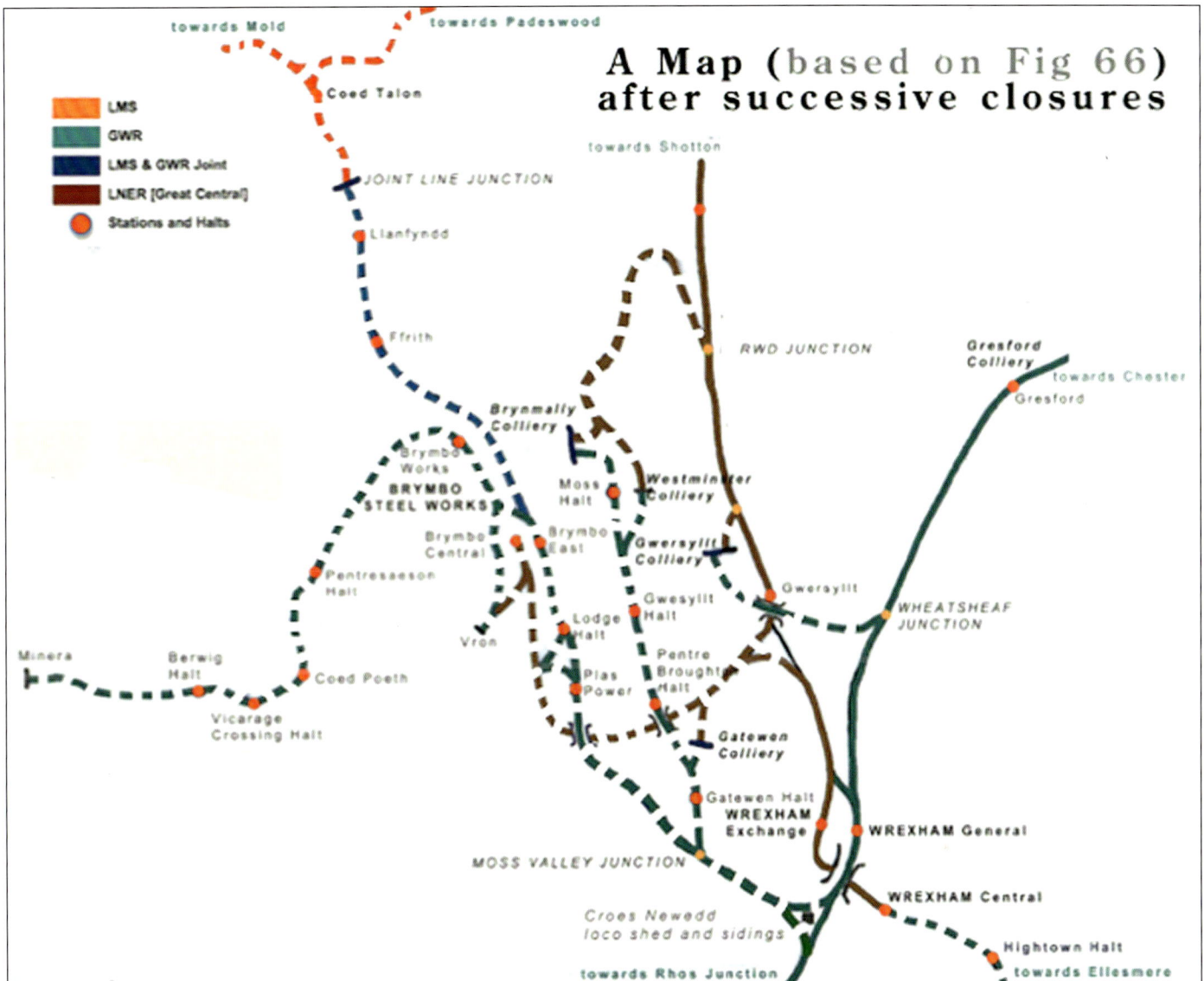

Fig 144: **Fig 66** showed the railways in the Wrexham and Brymbo areas and their ownership before BR. This is the same base map but only two open routes now remain – Shrewsbury to Wrexham via Rhos Junction and thence to Shotton or to Chester. (*Author*)

railway continued at Brymbo, for instance, for a number of years – as in **Fig 145.**

Other railways detailed in Chapter 6 were also progressively closed as passenger traffic demand diminished and mineral traffic ceased. For example, the Holywell branch, from Holywell Junction to Holywell Town. Passenger services to Holywell Town station ceased on 4 September 1954 but goods traffic on the eastern part of the branch continued until 1957. Holywell Junction station on the main Chester to Holyhead line had a bay platform for Holywell Town passenger trains; the whole station closed to passenger traffic on 14 February 1966. It was an architecturally impressive

station designed by Francis Thompson, now Grade II* Listed and described by Gordon Biddle (*Britain's Historic Railway Buildings*, OUP, 2000) as resembling 'an elegant brick Italianate villa with similar front and platform elevations . . . Rose motifs adorn a broad frieze'. **Fig 146** illustrates this 'Italianate villa' beside the Chester to Holyhead railway but no longer serving any railway purposes. The Holywell Town bay platform is now choked with bushes and the one-time island platform survives but without any furniture and surrendering to bushes and weeds.

The branch from Prestatyn to Dyserth also closed, in 1973. It was promoted as a branch serving Dyserth

Fig 145: BR/Sulzer Class 25 Bo-Bo diesel-electric loco 25165 leaves Brymbo with a train of steel billets from Brymbo Steel Works on 27th September 1977.

limestone quarries and was opened by L&NWR in 1905. It was principally a mineral branch but offering tourist passenger services for folk to enjoy the hills and waterfalls around Dyserth. However, passenger traffic was never very remunerative so ceased in 1930 but regular limestone trains operated until 1973.

The *Branch Line News-sheet* 100, 28 February 1968, reported on the working of the Dyserth branch and this report suggests that even mineral traffic was no longer generating much income. The branch was worked on Mondays to Fridays by locos shedded at Rhyl. On 15 December 1967, BR/Sulzer Class 24 Bo-Bo diesel electric loco D5084 left Rhyl at 10.10. The loco and a brake van, picked up empty wagons from the sidings at Prestatyn and propelled the train up the steep single-line branch. The branch was worked as a siding from Prestatyn so the train crew operated the level crossing about ½ a mile from the junction.

The only traffic was limestone, although a coal merchant still used part of the station yard at Dyserth. At Dyserth, a loading bank had been provided on the site of the old station which enabled lorries to tip directly into the wagons. There was also a siding into the quarry and wagons were loaded there with crushed limestone. The BR loco was not permitted to work into the quarry so wagons there were shunted by a rubber-tyred tractor.

After shunting and making up a train it returned to Rhyl about 11.30 with an average load of about eight wagons of limestone. The same loco worked this traffic forward from Rhyl during the afternoon.

So, from the middle of twentieth century, many of the works and railways that have been the principal subjects of this book were closing but, as Chapter 9 reveals, many things changed and NE Wales is still a bustling area with much to offer residents and visitors.

Fig 146: Holywell Junction Station on the Chester to Holywell Station but no longer serving any railway purposes. It is in the style of an 'Italianate villa' and to the left of the building is the bush-choked bay platform which was used by Holywell Town branch trains until 1930.

Fig 147: End of the line to Minera near the former Brymbo West (GWR) Station.

CHAPTER 9

LATE-TWENTIETH AND EARLY TWENTY-FIRST CENTURY RESURGENCE

Landscape re-modelling and heritage tourism, railway preservation or re-use: Tata Steel Brymbo Heritage Centre, Airbus Factory at Hawarden/Broughton

It seemed appropriate to start this chapter with 'landscape re-modelling' because, from mid- to late-twentieth century, a number of the areas covered in earlier chapters have been physically altered to facilitate new developments. Brymbo, in **Fig 148**, has been profoundly changed after Brymbo Steel Works ceased to work and the whole site, save for a small area where the original Foundry and Iron Works stood, was cleared.

At Dyserth and Holywell Town, the removal of the branch lines has opened up their trackbeds for hard-surfaced cycling and walking routes. At Minera, the former Limestone Quarries have been transformed to an extensive nature reserve in the care of the North Wales Wildlife Trust (NWWT) – **Fig 149**. The Trust's website eulogises the attractions of the site:

'Woodland has [been] established in the oldest parts of the quarry [and] bare rock still remains in the most recently worked [areas offering habitats for] nesting ravens and raptors. In summer, the lime-rich soils [support colourful] grassland [areas with] . . . many species of orchids [and] , , , rare and threatened plant species such as moonwort and pale toadflax. . . [Visitors may hear] spotted flycatchers, redstarts and blackcaps , , , and, in the evening , , , tawny owls can be heard.

A RADAR key [gives] access to disabled parking [for exploring] the reserve by following a wheelchair and pushchair accessible path.'

Lafarge/Tarmac were the last company to work the Minera Quarries so Minera Quarry Trust (MQT) was established in 2005 with the explicit aim of conserving the site for the benefit of the public. MQT, in partnership NWWT and political endorsement from Wrexham County Borough Council, negotiated with Lafarge about the future of the site. NWWT was able to purchase the Minera Quarry for £1 from Lafarge/Tarmac, who also donated £100,000 for work to make the site safe for public access.

Minera Nature Reserve (**Fig 149**) is a good exemplar for re-use of transport and industrial sites. Flintshire County Council and Wrexham Borough Council have done good work in enhancing and providing interpretation for some of the important heritage sites in their care.

Holywell Branch line used to link Holywell Town with Greenfield Docks on the Dee and the railway is now a metalled walk and cycleway from an extensive carpark beside the bridge where the branch line railway crosses the A548 (**Fig 150**) to Holywell Town. The Holywell Town station site has been landscaped and is illustrated earlier in the book in **Fig 88** where the fences bordering the path leading down to the site echoes the sloping pedestrian access to the original station from the town. The former branch is now a stimulating walk with views across the Greenfield Valley of the former industrial and pilgrimage sites which the railway served.

The branch reached the Dee at Greenfield Dock which is still accessible by car but no longer along the

Site of
Brymbo
Steel Works

remains of
blast furnace

Original Brymbo
Foundry – now
Heritage Centre

from GOOGLE EARTH – 2018

Fig 148: Changing the landscape at Brymbo – an edited Google Earth view of the site of Brymbo Steel Works in 2018 and inset, a reduced version of **Fig 113** showing the twentieth century growth of Brymbo Works on a plateau of tipped slag. (*Author*)

Fig 149: Site of Minera Limestone Quarry re-invigorated by the North Wales Wildlife Trust as a managed nature reserve, open to the public with disabled and push-chair access for walkers and family groups.

former railway. The Dock is now somewhat derelict, but a bilingual interpretation panel (**Fig 151**) explains and illustrates the one-time importance of this little dock.

The Dyserth branch railway, from Prestatyn on the coast, is another stimulating walk (or cycle ride) but, at a continuously rising gradient of 1 in 27, is a little testing as well! It is no longer possible to complete the walk to Prestatyn at the northern end of the railway, but it is encouraging to find the original Prestatyn Station and Goods Shed have survived and been converted to a furniture showroom for David Jones' business – **Fig 152**.

At the Dyserth end of the Prestatyn to Dyserth branch line, little has survived on the Dyserth Station site except for a bridge (**Fig 87**) and the crane from the Goods Shed re-erected behind a stone-backed bench illustrated in **Fig 153**. The crane is a reflection of the physical work necessary for goods handling on a railway. The crane is listed in the Railway Clearing House 1904 *Handbook of Railway Stations* with a capacity of 1ton 10cwt and was operated manually by a continuous loop of rope round the large wheel in **Fig 153**.

Although there are no surviving Heritage Railways in the immediate area of this book, the Llangollen Railway is nearby in the upper Dee valley between Llangollen and Corwen. Another railway just out of the book's area is the narrow gauge Glynn Valley Tramway (GVT). It ran from its own adjoining platform at Chirk standard-gauge station to Glyn Ceiriog and the quarries above that village. GVT was another mineral railway which was a roadside tramway and ran passenger trains. Two separate preservation societies are now seeking to re-create this railway, working from either end and, fortunately, now agreeing that both should adopt the unusual GVT gauge of 2ft 4ins.

The only heritage railway surviving and still operating in the book's area is the 15ins gauge Rhyl Miniature Railway (RMT) at the west end of Rhyl's seafront. It opened 1 May 1911 on an almost mile-long loop around the man-made Marine Lake. It is unique in several ways and particularly as an extended fairground ride. Rhyl, sometimes described as 'another Blackpool', once attracted great numbers of visitors

Fig 150: The substantial brick and stone bridge by which the Holywell branch crossed the A548. The extensive car-park beside the road is convenient for walkers taking the railway track bed to Holywell Town. (*Author*)

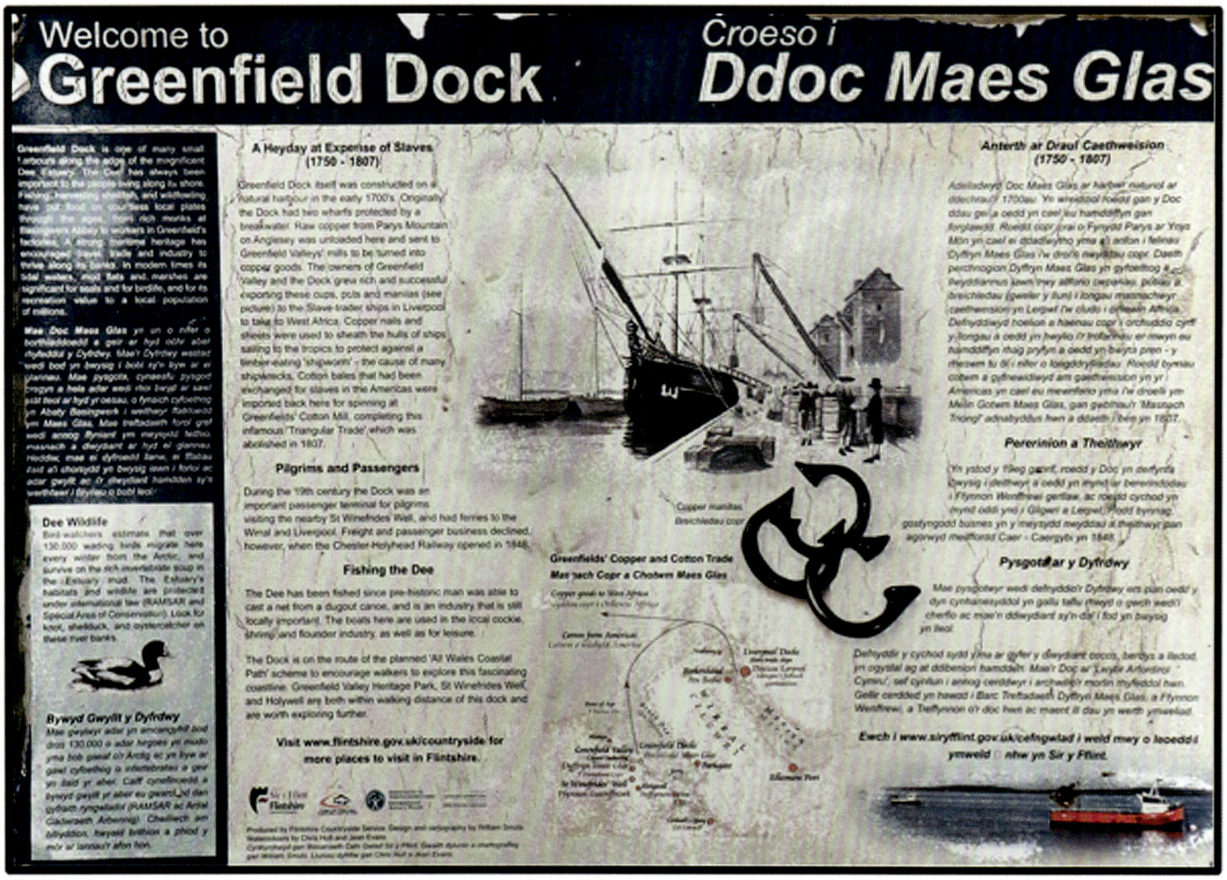

Fig 151: A bilingual interpretation panel at Greenfield Dock, once the Deeside terminus of the Holywell branch railway. Fortunately, the sign has not been spoiled by graffiti, but it is beginning to decay round the edges so is a reminder that such signs must be maintained. (*Author*)

Fig 152: Original station and Goods Shed at Prestatyn and the mainline junction for the Dyserth branch line. The buildings, supplanted by station larger facilities as the Chester to Holyhead line became busier, were derelict for a number of years but are now carefully restored and a furniture showroom for David Jones' business. (*Author*)

from north-western industrial towns and the Marine Lake and two huge adjoining fair grounds were one of Rhyl's attractions. RMT had its Central Station in the more landward of the fairgrounds and the ride looped from there round the Lake.

The railway is now operated by the Rhyl Steam Preservation Trust. I have included them in this book because I was able to work with them in 2008 creating a new Central Station and interpreting a little of the railway's history for visitors. I have already explained that I have visited, photographed, and walked along several NE Wales railways but, even better as **Fig 154** shows, I was able to drive one of the RMT steam locomotives. *Joan*, numbered 101 on the RMT, is a 4-4-2 tender locomotive built in 1920 by Rhyl engineers Albert Barnes & Co; Mr Barnes was the owner of Rhyl Amusements Ltd.

The largest operator of private railways – about 70 miles of track – in this book's area was John Summers &

Sons Ltd at the Hawarden Bridge/Shotton Steel Works and the site of that enormous Works has been materially altered by landscape changes and creation of new industrial opportunities as Summers passed to BSC, then to Corus and finally to the Tata Steel Group.

Fig 155 is a visual reminder of the size of Summers' original Works and **Fig 156** is the current site plan which Tata makes available for booked visitors to their Records Centre on a small part of their site. As steel-making, and employment, on the Hawarden/Shotton Steel Works site declined in the 1970s, the development of a new industrial park for Deeside was announced in 1976. Peter J. Summers, great grandson of John Summers, was appointed Industry Co-ordinator, Shotton, with BSC Industry Limited which was the job-creating subsidiary of BSC.

BSC Industry Limited was initially granted planning permission by the Welsh Development Agency for the development of an industrial park covering 375 acres

Left: **Fig 153**: Dyserth – 1ton 10cwt hand-operated crane rescued from Dyserth Station Goods Shed and installed behind a stone-backed bench alongside the Dyserth walk- and cycle-way along the former railway trackbed. (*Author*)

Below: **Fig 154**: Author Rob Shorland-Ball driving Rhyl Miniature Railway steam loco *Joan* in 2008.

adjacent to the Steel Works. Some 2M tonnes of sand were pumped in to prepare land for factories on the new park. This £1M operation raised some 300 acres of low lying-land by over three feet to give correct fall for drains and sewers.

By 1979 nearly all the seventeen advance factories had been let and nearly 1,000 new jobs were expected to be provided during the next three years. Deeside Enterprise Trust Limited, a private company, was set up in 1982 to continue the works of BSC Industry in the area. It had the backing of regional and local government, BSC Industry, private enterprise and trades unions. By 1986 some 3,000 people were working for forty companies located on the new park.

Continuing a policy of landscape re-modelling, BSC made additional land sales between 1976 and 1983: 5,040 acres to RSPB; 30 acres to Deeside Titanium; 156 acres – the former blast furnace site – for Shotton Paper Mill; and 467 acres – the remainder of the Steel Works 'heavy end' site – to Flintshire County Council – **Fig 156**.

Fig 155: An early impression of Hawarden Bridge Steel Works site from a nineteenth century letterhead.

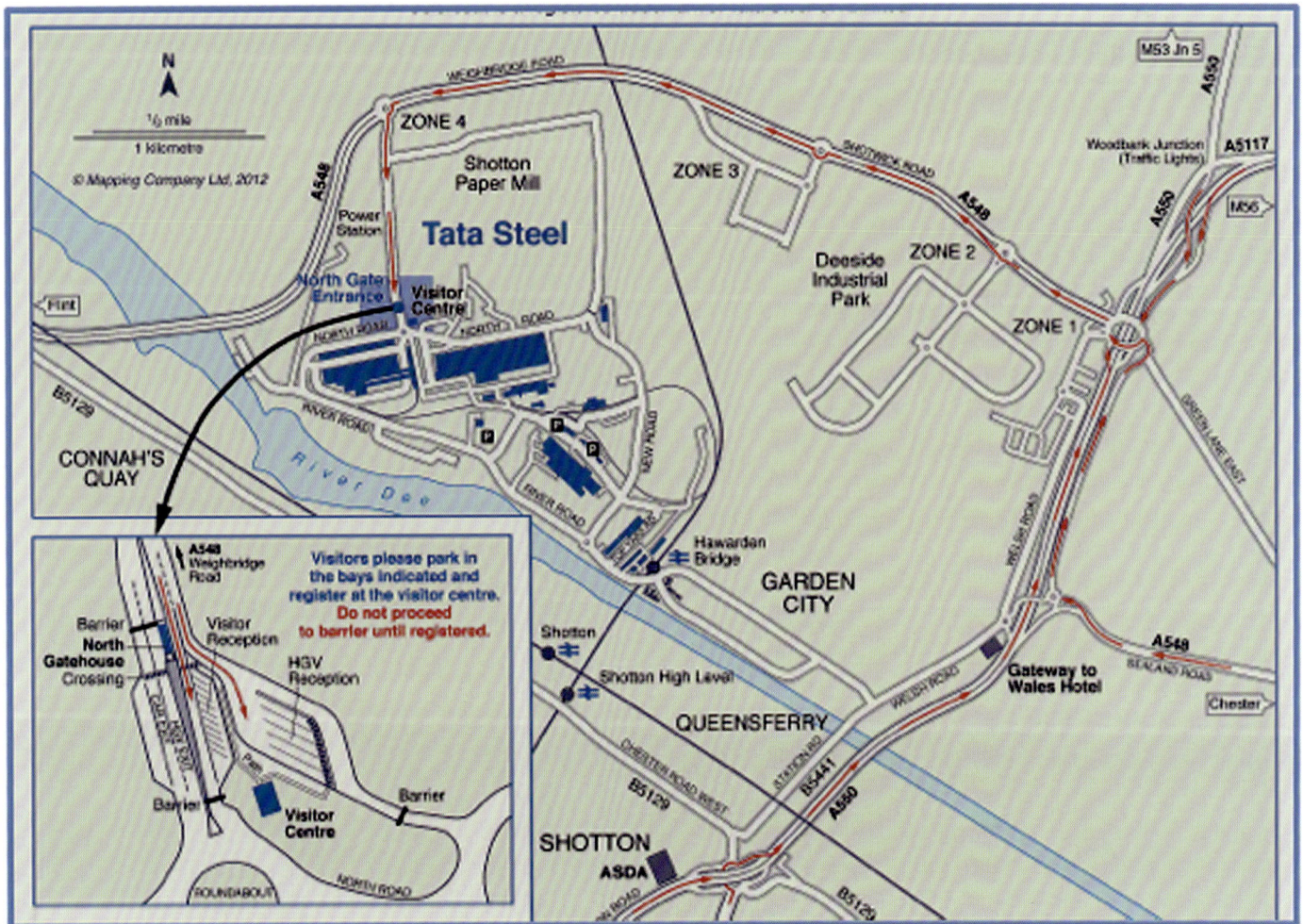

Fig 156: Map issued in 2018 to booked visitors for the Tata Steel Records Centre. Compare the view over Hawarden Bridge northwards in **Fig 155** with the site layout on this map.

I can best conclude the first section of this chapter by quoting from a small visitor information leaflet I was given when I visited the Tata Steel Records Centre whilst researching for this book:

Tata Steel at Shotton

'The Works has 700 employees and is currently producing 500,000 tonnes of galvanised and pre-finished (painted) strip, of which 40 per cent is exported. Product manufacturing plant comprises 2 galvanising lines, 2 *Colorcoat* lines, 10 profiling lines, 2 composite panel lines, and 6 further processing lines including blanking and multi-strand slitting.

'The primary markets are the construction industry and consumer products sector. Among major construction clients for products [such as] insulated panels, built-up systems, facades, structural roof and floor decking profiles are Jaguar Land Rover, IKEA, Travis Perkins, Wickes and Airbus. Painted steel is supplied to Mitsubishi, Indesit and Thorn. For domestic consumer product applications including kitchen appliances, interiors and lighting.

'13 new products have been developed at the Works in the past 5 years and differentiated products make up more than 75 per cent, of the Works' order book.'

Brymbo Steel Works site has, until recently, been less fortunate than the Tata Steel site in re-development but the recent award by National Lottery Heritage Fund of a £4.1M grant to the Brymbo Heritage Trust (BHT) is very encouraging.

BHT has been one of my inspirations for this book. I first visited the site in 2018 on the R&CHS AGM Weekend based in Wrexham. A guided tour of the original Brymbo Iron Works site was led by Colin Davies, former Brymbo Steel Works Rolling Mill Manager, whose knowledge and enthusiasm captivated me. Subsequently I have met Colin again, Gary Brown, the BHT Manager, and Lynze Rogers, Education Officer. They have loaned me a number of pictures and text documents – which I was pleased to digitize for BHT – so I am very grateful for their contributions to this book.

I was given a copy of the BHT Big Plan Summary and two of the pictures in that document – **Fig 158** and **Fig 159** – illustrate the ambitions of BHT. They were recently summed-up by Nick Aymes, Chair of the Trust:

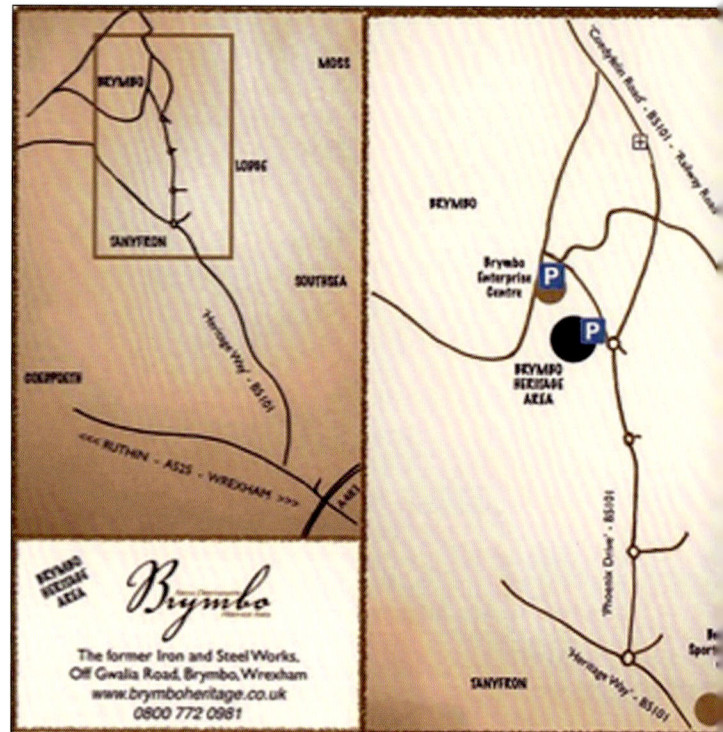

Fig 157: BHT have identified a 'Heritage Area' around the remains of John Wilkinson's Iron Works site. Appropriately the BHT office and archive is at present in the new Brymbo Enterprise Centre above and just north of the Works site.

'Brymbo's coal was medal winning, its iron fuelled the expansion of steam [power] and the railways, and its steel was at the heart of Britain's engineering prowess. It's a place that should feel proud [of itself]. Yet our community lives in the shadow of the loss of its industry in 1990.

'Following the site's closure 30 years ago, its historic core stood empty for many years. Since 2014 the BHT has been delivering a range of temporary activities at the still derelict site, building awareness, enthusiasm and momentum, and countering the vandalism, arson and anti-social behaviour that had started to set in.

'We've been successful in attracting investment already, but most of it has been dependent on securing this final piece of major funding. This massive boost from National Lottery players will enable us to give this former major industrial site a new lease of life; we will use Brymbo to help build a new sense of pride, hope and co-operation for the local community, while helping put Wrexham ever more firmly on the map for visitors to North Wales.'

Fig 158: Brymbo Ironworks site derelict in the 1990s. On the right of the picture are the remains of an early blast furnace, perhaps in blast when 'Iron Mad' John Wilkinson owned the site. Compare this view with BHT proposals for the site in the 2020s in Fig 159.

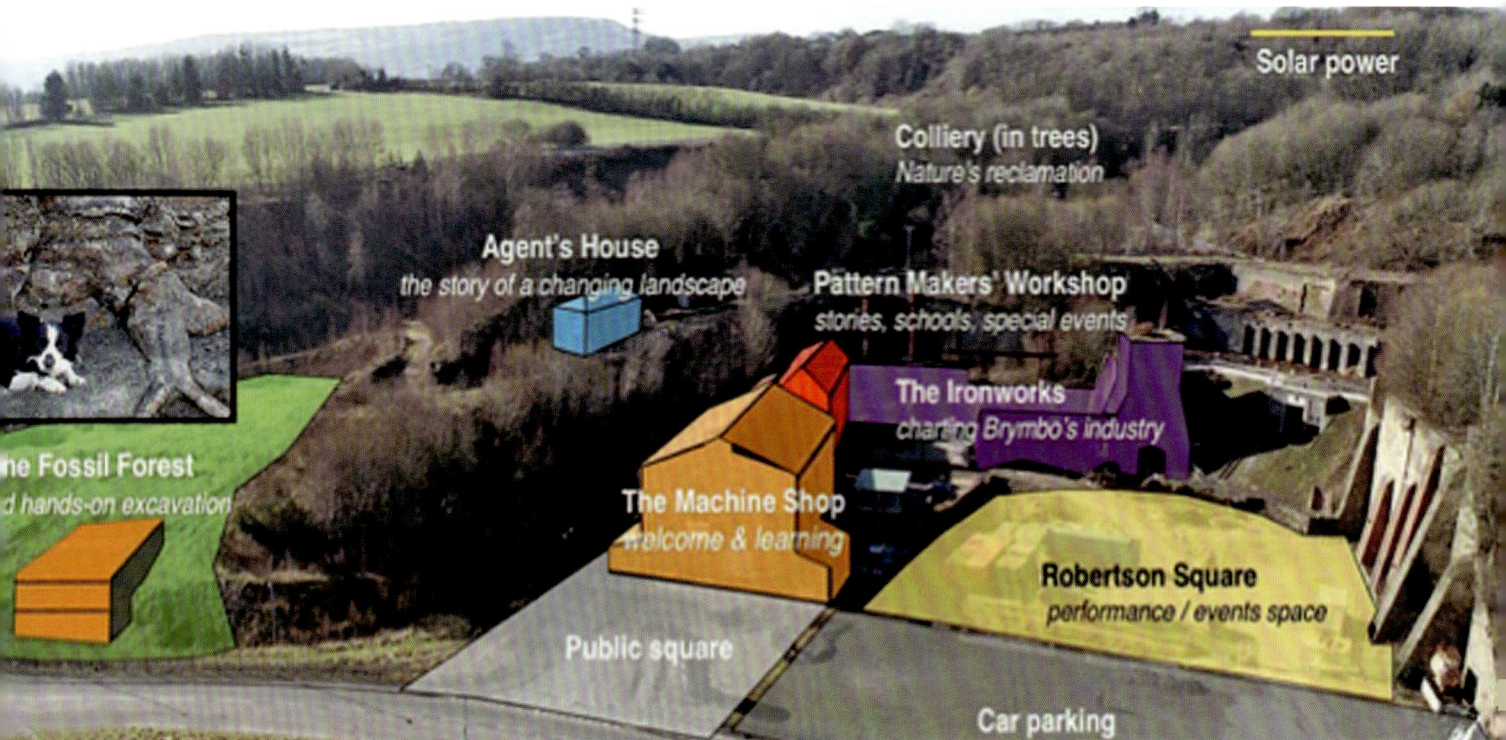

Fig 159: BHT proposals for the Brymbo Ironworks site which have secured a National Lottery Heritage Fund grant of £4.7M. Inset is an exposed part of the Fossil Forest (and a living dog for scale) which enhances the Brymbo story from trees to coal, iron and steel.

An exciting addition to the 'Brymbo Story' has been the discovery of a Fossil Forest which has proved to be the best Coal Measure Forest in the world, showing plants in growth position and the coal seams that they formed. The associated coal mine within the site is an added bonus. The fossil interest has been recognised by the Countryside Council for Wales as being nationally important, so it is proposed to protect it as a Site of Special Scientific Interest.

And, as a tribute to Brymbo's resurgence, here is a poem by a Brymbo Steel worker looking back at what had been – and what will be recalled and remembered for residents and visitors in the near future:

Brymbo, an end of an era
Orange dust no longer rising,
The sheds are cold and still,
The rolls have all stopped turning,
Way up upon the hill.
The Ladles are all empty now,
The furnaces burn no more,
Shouts of men, no longer heard,
Across an empty floor.
Rolling mills stand hushed and wasted,
The days of use are gone,
Gone are weeks of breaking records,
Where men worked hard and long.
Shouts of "Shears to roller",
Or "Halt it – cogging mill",
Would echo from the 'tannoy',
To the workers on the hill.
Cranes rusting, still and silent,
Pits empty, dusty, bare,
No sounds of hot saws whirring,
In the dark gloom of despair.
It's just a sad reminder,
Of days that have gone by,
Where they'd make and roll the billets,
And stack them to the sky.
The men who pushed the barrows,
Are still alive today,
I bet they never even thought,
They'd see it out this way.
'Twas the ending of an era,
When Brymbo tapped the last,
But better steel you'll never see,
Nor pride, nor work, nor cast.

There's just a ghostly silence,
That remains upon the hill;
Sons of sons have worked there,
Alas, no more they will.
　　Keith 'Wallis' Williams – Brymbo Steel 28in mill (1967-74)

Keith Williams was at Brymbo from 1967 on the 28in Mill so he would have recognised the process in **Fig 160**, and the weights involved. I hope that BHT will include some pictures and references to the importance of railways in the story they plan to tell visitors. **Figs 114, 117** and **121** illustrate the Brymbo railway connections at work; the railway enthusiasts' special train **in Fig 75** was arranged by the Merseyside Branch of the Railway Correspondence Travel Society (RCTS) in 1967 to celebrate the centenary of the Wrexham, Mold & Connah's Quay Railway. Its length, and the size of the loco hauling it shows that Brymbo West – and Brymbo Steel Works – was accessible to and could be serviced by heavy trains.

It is a nice irony that the story of industries and railways I have been telling in this book ends with a huge out-of-gauge aeroplane wing on a lorry – **Fig 161** – but that is a piece of this jigsaw which brings my story to the present in 2020. It is an Airbus wing for the A380 super-jet manufactured in a specialist factory at what used to be Hawarden Aerodrome and was originally RAF Hawarden, established on 1 September 1939 as one of the main RAF airfields during the 'Battle of Britain'.

Its detailed history is outside the scope of this book but makes an interesting story. Airbus's West Factory was opened in 2003 and named Broughton after the nearest village. It was the largest factory that had been built in the UK for a number of years and fits into this resurgence chapter though, alas, no railways have any part in the Airbus wings story. The factory can accommodate 1,200 staff over a huge floorspace - equivalent to twelve full-size football pitches. The Broughton site assembles wings for the 555-seater A380 aeroplane which are transported by road, barge and ship to Toulouse in France for final assembly.

The *Chester Chronicle* reported in February 2020 that Airbus 380 wing assembly was to cease at Broughton and summarised the complex journey each 35 tonne wing had to make.

Fig 160: A red hot and heavy ingot on the Brymbo Rolling Mill – the Steel works needed railway connections.

Fig 161: An Airbus 380 wing, built at Broughton factory on Hawarden Aerodrome, Flintshire, NE Wales and en route for Queensferry wharf on its road, barge and ship journey to Airbus final assembly line at Blagnac, near Toulouse, in France.

- specialist road transporter from Broughton to a specially created wharf at Queensferry on the river Dee
- transfer to *Afon Dyfrdwy* barge for a 21.5 miles journey to the Dee estuary port at Mostyn
- transfer to Ro-Ro (roll=on/roll-off) sea-going ship, *Ciudad de Cadiz*, for a voyage to Pauillac on the Gironde estuary in France.
- transfer to a floating pontoon with two barges, *Le Breuil* and *Le Brion*, for a 59 mile journey up the river Garonne to a wharf in Langon.

- specialist road transporter from the river wharf at Langon to the Airbus final assembly line at Blagnac, a suburb of Toulouse.

The final 150 miles road journey in France is over two nights at between 5 to 15mph. During the intervening day the convoy waits a on specially made parking area.

The last Airbus 380 wings were completed and shipped out of the Broughton West Factory in February 2020 and manufacture of the A380 aircraft is to cease.

In July 2020 Airbus confirmed the significant impact the COVID-19 pandemic has had on the UK's commercial aircraft manufacturing activities which are concentrated in Broughton. The Company announced that 1,435 jobs will be cut from the Broughton plant. West Factory is obliged to remain operational until the last A380 aircraft has been fully built in case any wing repair work is needed before delivery of the aircraft to the client airline.

However, the factory's future beyond summer 2021 is uncertain.

I am sorry to end my story on this sad note but it is important that the book, and the story, should be as up-to-date as possible. I am signing-off, therefore, with **Fig 162** and a railway-related analogy; I hope that by the time this book is published we can see a light at the end of the tunnel!

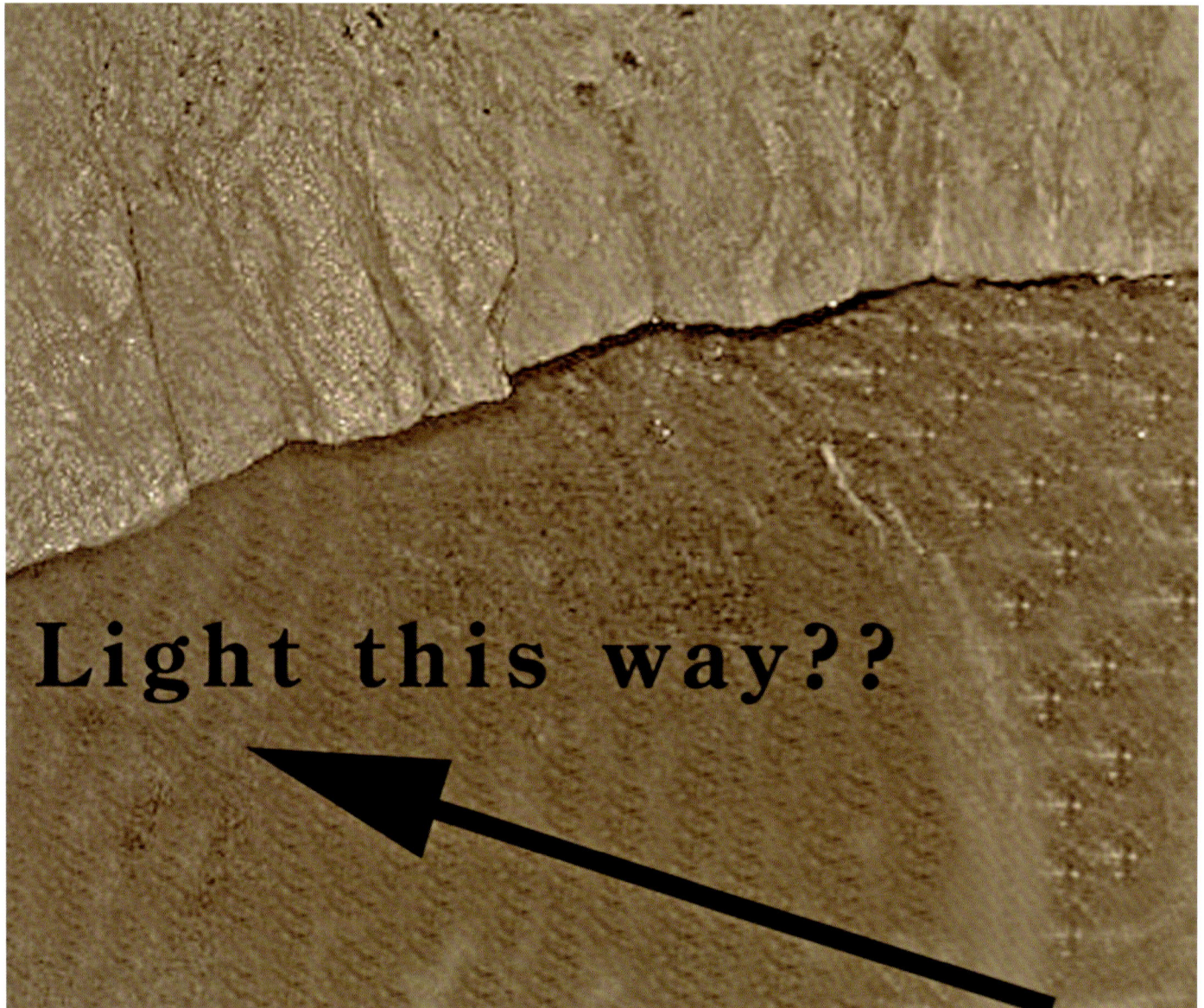

Fig 162: Summerhill Tunnel in the Moss Valley and leading to Brymbo. Hope for the future! (*Author*)

LIST OF ILLUSTRATIONS

Illustrations are from the author's collection (RSB) or, with their permission to him, from those who are acknowledged and thanked here including: Buckley Society and its publications (BS) Brymbo Heritage Centre (BHT), Gordon Biddle (GB), Cadw (Cadw), Clwyd-Powys Archaeological Trust (C-PAT), Glyn Davies (GD), Gordon Edgar (GE), Editor *BackTrack* (MB), Huw Edwards (HE), Michael Fell (MF), Jeff Howard (JH), Industrial Railway Society (IRS), Ralph Potter (RP), John Scott-Morgan (JS-M), Tata Steel Records Centre (TSRC), Pam Thomas (PT), Wrexham County Borough Council (WCBC).

The author, a long-time keen photographer, has accumulated his extensive photographic collection from: working on BR in the 1950s and 1960s, teaching Geography at a Grammar then Comprehensive School in Harrogate, time at museums in Yorkshire, Suffolk and National Railway Museum (1987-1994); as an active member of the Railway & Canal Historical Society and a former member of the Railway Study Association.

He always tries to contact all possible copyright holders and checks any unacknowledged illustrations with forensic image search engines. He can be contacted at <robsb@wfmyork.co.uk>

Acronyms in the Provenance column relate to the names acknowledged in the first paragraph above.

Fig No	Caption	Provenance
1	View along the GWR branch to Brymbo passing a Mile Post. Brymbo East signal box is ahead which originally was Brymbo Station box, The Station closed to passengers in 1943 but freight services to Brymbo Steel Works were maintained until 1980; the branch is now closed and the signal box disused.	HE
2	Part of NE Wales and Deeside showing topography, principal railways, industrial centres in this book – and the approximate boundaries of interest.	©RSB
3	Sketch map showing the current local government administration for the area containing the railways and industries in the context of this book.	©RSB
4	[edited from Transport for Wales summary route map]. WM&CQR enters from the left-hand side of the N Wales Coastline Railway and joins it North of the site of Connah's Quay Station opened by the L&NWR on 01st September 1870. Shotton Station was opened on 01st October 1891 by the WM&CQR as Connah's Quay & Shotton and became Shotton High Level. Here was an end-on junction with the MS&LR's line from Chester Northgate via Hawarden Bridge.	RSB
5	Another summary map and a suitable conclusion for this Chapter because it illustrates the reasons why the WM&CQR was built and why it offered great minerals potential to LNWR and GCR – who failed to secure it – and GCR / L&NER which owned it from 1904 to 1923.	©RSB
6	From Railway Clearing House *Official Railway Map of England & Wales 1921*	RSB
7	Sketch map showing Carboniferous limestone – in solid colour – and the Flintshire extent of the NE Wales coalfield – oblique shaded. The coalfield was extensively worked in the nineteenth and twewntieth centuries, for industries which developed in this area and for export. The coalfield extended eastwards into England where there were more deep-shaft collieries.	©RSB
8	Rail connection to Bersham Colliery near Rhostyllen (just visible on **Fig 06**), Wrexham, opened in 1864 and closed in 1986. Steam engine near entrance is Peckett 0-4-0ST *Hornet*.	GE

Fig No	Caption	Provenance
9	Provisional Patent Specification No 7329 AD 1902 for a Ponkey – "Floating Signal to Discover Sunken Ships."	©HMSO
10	Diagram edited from the Ponkey Patent Specification.	RSB & ©HMSO
11	Extract from 1st edition 6" OS © map of 1869 (published 1871). Hancock's Exchange sidings.	BS
12	Buckley Station was the passenger terminus for the Buckley Railway so the tracks onward to Connah's Quay were goods only. The sidings off to the right are where the narrow gauge Hancock's Tramway goods traffic was exchanged to the standard gauge WM&CQ railway. The photographer is looking towards Connah's Quay.	BS / RSB
13	Buckley Railway standard gauge shipping wagon designed for 6 shipping boxes. (Drawn by J Bentley)	BS; C-PAT; Cadw
14	Sketch map (not to scale) showing the collieries and other industries in and around Ponkey.	RSB
15	Railway viaduct parallel to canal aqueduct across the River Ceiriog valley, Chirk.	anon
16	The extensive limestone quarries, lime kilns and brick works at Minera c1905.	*courtesy* GD
17	The first standard gauge shunting tank engine purchased for work at the Minera Quarry. Built in 1868 by Beyer Peacock (Manchester), noted for their larger locomotives but their high engineering reputation was sustained and enhanced by some smaller locomotives like MINERA.	*courtesy* IRS
18	Part of advertisement for W L Hobbs' Dyserth Quarry.	RSB
19	Extract from OS © Map (reduced from 1:2,500 Dyserth & Meliden 1910 – *courtesy Alan Godfrey Maps*) illustrating the problems with loading limestone traffic from the Quarry's narrow gauge railway system and counter-balanced incline to the standard gauge spur north of Dyserth Station	RSB
20	**Main picture**: Stanier 2-6-0 'Black 5' 45156 *Ayrshire Yeomanry* easing empty trucks round the sharp curve of the Quarry spur at Dyserth almost to the loco's LIMIT OF SHUNT. *courtesy* Trefor Thompson **Inset**: loaded trucks shunted to form a train to Prestatyn. September 1963.	JS-M; RSB
21	Meliden Road bridge in 2019 looking south towards Dyserth; note the sturdy structure of the bridge and the steep gradient.	©RSB
22	Underside of a Minera lead ingot mould.	©RSB
23	Lead mines and railways in the Minera area (*edited from 1907 plans courtesy of Glyn Davies 1964 et seq*)	RSB; *courtesy* GD
24	Sketch map edited from *Atlas of the GWR as at 1947*	RSB
25	Minera Goods Station & Junction looking towards Wrexham; the New Brighton Branch curves in from the right. The passenger train is an SLS Wrexham & District Rail Tour in 1959.	BS; RSB
26	Grandpa remembers his coal field in 1945 *courtesy* Peggy M Hart. *The Magic of Coal*. Penguin Books. 1947	RSB
27	N Wales coalfield, centred around Wrexham.	©RSB
28	A typical deep shaft colliery, like Llay Main and Gresford.	RSB
29	Bodfari Iron Mine headgear. The timber headgear is powered by a horse whim and is a useful comparison with the deep-shaft colliery headgear in **Fig 28**. (*Courtesy* Clyn Davis)	C-PAT

Fig No	Caption	Provenance
30	Fig 30: extract from 6" scale OS © map, 1914. Note the number of 'Old Collieries' and 'Shafts' marked.	RSB; BS
31	Coed Talon station – *courtesy* of the Signalling Record Society	*courtesy* RP
32	extracts from 6"scale 1914 OS © map showing clay industries N and S of Coed Talon station	RSB; BS
33	Clay quarries and brickworks north of Buckley served by sidings off the WM&CQR.	BS; C-PAT
34	Advertisement from *Flintshire News*, 24th December 1912	RSB
35	Archaeological sites of Buckley Potteries and railways serving the area from C-PAT Report 1246: *The Buckley Potteries. An assessment and survival and potential.* 2014. Railways, branch lines and private sidings have been added to the OS base map by C-PAT. Most have now gone	*courtesy* C-PAT
36	Header from the *North Wales Chronicle*	RSB
37	Henry Dennis's Red Works, Ruabon	RSB
38	Victorian decorative faience – glazed tiles – at Worcester Shrub Hill Station (GWR 1865)	*courtesy* GB
39	An engraving of Henry Robertson (1816 - 1888) copied with thanks from *Henry Robertson, Pioneer of Railways into Wales*. George L Lerry. 1949.	*courtesy* George Lerry
40	A sketch map illustrating Henry Roberson's railway projects edited with thanks from *Henry Robertson, Pioneer of Railways into Wales*. George L Lerry. 1949. **Note:** sketch is South orientated	*courtesy* George Lerry
41	Palé Hall from *The Architect*, July 5, 1875: "The mansion at Palé, Merionethshire, has recently been erected for Mr H Robertson MP from designs and under the superintendence of Mr S. Pountney Smith, Architect, of Shrewsbury".	RSB
42	The late Mr G.H. Whalley MP, edited from a portrait presented by the citizens of Peterborough and placed in Peterborough Museum.	RSB
43	Henry Dennis, civil engineer specialising in railway, mining and quarrying industries	*courtesy* George Lerry
44	Hafod Brickworks Quarry, near Ruabon and managed by Henry Dennis	RSB
45	Thomas Savin, railway, mining and quarrying contractor, speculator, Mayor of Oswestry and bankrupt in 1866 with £2,000,000 debts.	RSB
46	An extract from a brochure advertising George Frederick Wynne's Exposure Meter	RSB
47	*Henrietta* standard gauge 0-6-0ST with inside cylinders and probably built by Manning Wardle in 1861. The loco was owned by the United Minera Mining Company so could shunt the quarry lines, which were all privately owned, and work up to and sometimes a little along the GWR Minera Branch where wagons could be exchanged. It is hauling coal for the Limeworks c1900.	*courtesy* George Lerry
48	Drams loaded with clay on a 1ft 8" gauge tramway (opened 1862) from quarry to Caello Brickworks, Minera, in 1962	RSB
49	A substantial embankment on the Sandycroft Plateway leading to Sandycroft Ironworks / Foundry and a wharf on the river Dee.	RSB
50	Edited sketch map of tramways in the Buckley area before the standard gauge steam-hauled railways were built. The original was drawn by John Bentley in 1971 and is reproduced here courtesy of the Buckley Society.	RSB; *courtesy* BS

Fig No	Caption	Provenance
51	Tramways and standard gauge railways meet south of Buckley Old Station. A crossover is avoided by the building of sidings on an interchange wharf where incoming coal – for the brickworks – is exchanged for outgoing bricks.	©RSB
52	The network of railways which constituted the WM&CQR in 1900. Note that Brymbo had two stations by 1900; one owned and operated by WM&CQR and the other by GWR	RSB
53	Buckley Railway, an initiative developed in 1860 by local coal owners, brick-makers and potters to secure enhanced market opportunities via the Chester to Holyhead Railway at Connah's Quay or by boat on the river Dee and the Irish Sea	©RSB
54	Buckley Railway's steep descent to Connah's Quay. The weed and litter-strewn trap siding on the right of the picture was intended to trap and contain runaways.	RSB
55	Gradient profile of Buckley Railway from Buckley (old) Station to Connah's Quay	RSB
56	Connah's Quay railways c 1880.	*courtesy* QWA 2019
57	Sail and steam vessels in Top Dock, Connah's Quay.	*courtesy* Tom Coppack
58	sketch map explaining the complexity of WM&CQR stations to provide passenger access to the L&NWR Chester - Denbigh line and to justify the use of 'Mold' in the WM&CQR Company name.	RSB
59	2-6-0T locomotive No 3 after rebuilding at WM&CQ works at Rhosddu in 1899	JH
60	Cast iron Cheshire Lines notice illustrating the company's thrift in ensuring that only passengers who had paid for a ticket could use at their convenience.	*courtesy* Gordon Biddle
61	Engineering contractor's elevation and plan (not to scale) for the Hawarden Swing Bridge	RSB
62	Sir Edward Watkin in 1891	RSB
63	Ralph Turnbull & Son's *Guide to UK Dock & Port Charges 1904*	MF
64	Developing industries in NE Wales and Deeside – 1760-1850.	RSB
65	Sketch map (not to scale) illustrating the complexities of railways, and stations, at Wrexham c1946 – after the grouping but before British Railways was set up in 1948.	©RSB
66	The network of passenger and mineral railways which were developed to serve the iron works, collieries and brick works NNW of Wrexham.	©RSB
67	Sketch map (not to scale) of the two Brymbo stations and the railway companies working them.	©RSB; BHT
68	View over part of Brymbo Steel Works in 1890 showing railway links	BHT
69	Brymbo West Crossing Halt on the GWR Minera Branch c1910	BHT
70	GWR Timetable by Bradshaw – July 1922. Brymbo West Crossing Halt is marked as a 'Halt'. Brymbo GWR General Station is also a booked stop and will be shown, too, in Table 475. Note that **H** and **K** references for some short workings which show that there is anticipated business to and from Brymbo West Crossing Halt.	RP
71	Brymbo General Station (GWR) c1910 looking towards Minera branch and Mold	BHT
72	Brymbo General Station (GWR) in 1960. The Station closed to passenger services in 1950 but freight traffic continued and the principal building shown in **Fig 71** remains, though somewhat derelict. However, the footbridge has gone.	BHT

Fig No	Caption	Provenance
73	Brymbo Central Station (WM&CQR/GCR) 1935 looking north towards the buffer stops. The Station closed to passengers 1971 but freight traffic continued until 1956 because it was a head-shunt for goods trains reversing into collieries and Brymbo Steel; Works sidings.	BHT
74	**Fig 74a**: A combined special train organised by SLS and the Manchester Locomotive Society (MLS) on 6th September 1952. **Fig 74b**. The working timetable for the train illustrated in **Fig 74a**. The timetable details the route and has been edited from the timings recorded by Ian Clarke (SLS) with Stephen Bragg & Peter Greenough (MLS). **Fig 74c**. Ticket for the SMS / MLS special train illustrated in **Fig 47a**.	*courtesy Railtour Files* 1952
75	7-coach R&CTS special leaving Brymbo General station on 29th April 1967 hauled tender-first (no turntables for large locos at Brymbo) by Class 8F 2-8-0.	*courtesy* MB *BackTrack*
76	Restored GWR steam railmotor No 93 on the Llangollen heritage railway in March 2011. Carrog is a station on the railway.	RSB
77	Edited extract from OS 25" © map of Denbighshire in 1912. The green arrow is the direction of the photograph in **Fig 79** albeit that was taken 48 years after the map was published!	©OS; RSB
78	A view towards Berwig Level Crossing Halt in the early twentieth century.	BHT
79	Site of Berwig Level Crossing Halt in 1960 when the line was still open for mineral traffic.	BHT
80	Gresford Colliery in the 1920s – rail connected as the sidings and wagons show.	BHT
81	Simon Hughes in Speedwell Shaft Minera, c.1928.	WCBC – *History*
82	Gresford Colliery Disaster September 1934. Huge crowds of men and women gathered on a colliery surface after a disaster awaiting news of family and friends. The wagons show the importance of rail connections for big collieries.	RSB
83	Memorial to the Gresford disaster using one of the colliery's head wheels as a visible memory of a colliery, and an industry, that has gone.	RSB
84	Holywell branch.	*courtesy* MB *BackTrack*
85	From 1905 a L&NWR Milnes-Daimler motor bus provided a passenger service from Holywell, on the Chester to Holyhead line, uphill along the Greenfield valley to Holywell town. The route board on the side of the bus, reading 'Holywell Station' was, perhaps, advertising for the planned branch line which did not open to Holywell Station until 1912.	RSB
86	Holywell Junction c1912 with a train for Holywell Town in the bay platform constructed for the branch. Because of the 1 in 27 gradient on the branch the trains were always propelled.	*courtesy* Pat Thomas
87	Postcard view c1912 of the new Holywell Town Station from the terminal buffer stop behind the photographer and the goods yard to the right. The change in gradient is apparent from the relative level of the Station layout downhill towards Holywell Junction 1.5 miles away.	*courtesy* Pat Thomas
88	A comparative 2019 view of **Fig 86** showing the Holywell Station site approached from Holywell Junction on foot. The former goods yard would have been on the left in this view and the platform beyond the bridge on the right.	©RSB

Fig No	Caption	Provenance
89	Working the Holywell goods yard in 1951; No 41270 Ivatt Class 2 2-6-0T shunts a 20--ton brake van to pick up a short goods train for Holywell Junction.	*courtesy* Pat Thomas
90	Edited map of the Dyserth branch.	*courtesy* MB *BackTrack*
91	Twentieth century billboard advertising the output of one of the Dyserth limestone quarries which were rail-served by the Dyserth branch.	RSB
92	Spur to limestone quarry at Dyserth showing the very the tight curve and BR Class 5 45156 *Ayrshire Yeomanry* at LIMIT OF SHUNT (September 1963) and **INSET** – an outbound train of wagons loaded with limestone at Dyserth, September 1961.	*courtesy* MB *BackTrack*
93	Bridge 3 on the Dyserth Branch near Meliden.	©RSB
94	Bridge 7 on the Dyserth branch looking uphill towards Dyserth. This bridge illustrates the quality of the trackside structures built by L&NWR in the 1860s so 150 years earlier.	©RSB
95	Ex-works L&NWR steam railmotor No 1 at Wolverton, where it was built in 1905.	*courtesy* David Jenkinson
96	Extract from an edited OS 6" scale © map showing the elements of the Abergele railway accident between the DOWN Irish Mail passenger express and some runaway goods trucks in 1868.	©OS; RSB
97	L&NWR accident near Abergele when the Irish Mail was struck by some runaway wagons on the same track. The wagons contained casks of paraffin which burst. The released paraffin drenched the de-railed locomotive and was ignited instantly by coals from the loco firebox. This sketch was purportedly made about 90 minutes after the accident.	*courtesy* *Illustrated London News*
98	John Wilkinson (1728 - 1808) – ironmaster and entrepreneur.	BHT
99	Diagram of a typical mid-nineteenth century hot air blast furnace. Pre-heating the blast air made furnace operation more efficient and cost-effective.	RSB
100	Wilkinson's cylinder boring machine was very successful because it was the first such machine which could bore cylinders for steam engines accurately, ensuring the internal diameter was sustained throughout the length so provide an even bore in which the piston precisely fitted.	RSB; WCBC – *History*
101	Bersham Furnace and Foundry 2019; surviving buildings include an octagonal canon foundry, an adjacent probable fettling shop and a boring mill later converted to a corn mill. The site is managed by Wrexham County Borough Museum & Archives Service but is currently closed to the public.	©RSB
102	Sketch map of the railways to Brymbo, Minera and serving other Works and Collieries in the area after developments in 1846.	©RSB
103	Twentieth century remains of 1847 railway link to Brymbo. **A)** Course of 1 in 3.5 Moss Incline or Brake. **B)** Door name plaque for Brake Methodist Chapel, built in 1885 on the 1847 railway trackbed near the entrance to Brymbo Tunnel. Chapel demolished in 2009. **C)** Arch entrance to Summerhill tunnel.	RSB; WCBC – *History*
104	A sketch summary of the railway routes and operating companies serving Brymbo	RSB
105	1912 OS © 25" © map extract showing the network of railways in and around Brymbo Works	BHT
106	The Loco Department at Brymbo Works in 1904 (from *Brymbo [Works] News*)	BHT

Fig No	Caption	Provenance
131	Raw materials required, and delivered by rail, for a week's steel-making at Shotton Steel Works.	TSRC
132	Shotton Steel Works internal rail network and links to BR at Dee Marsh Junction	TSRC
133	Hudswell Clarke 0-4-0 saddle tank shunter JUPITER delivered new to Shotton Steel Works in 1910. The crew, left to right, are: W Hargreaves (driver), C Jones (fireman), W Evans, E Griffiths (shunters)	TSRC
134	VESTA new to the Works in 1916 and presented to NT by the Summers family for display at Penrhyn Castle.	TSRC
135	A diesel-hauled train of iron ore in Summers' Private Owner ore wagons	TSRC
136	Hudswell Clarke 'Badger'-type diesel hydraulic loco for the 2ft 6" gauge internal railway system installed at Shotton Steel Works in 1971. Note driver entrance is only on the left-hand side of the cab	TSRC
137	A website glimpse of a small part of Shotton Records Centre – which has contributed significantly to this book.	
138	Sir Richard Summers on the footplate of BR Class 9F 2-10-0 loco with a train of iron ore bound for Shotton Steel Works in Summers' private owner bogie hopper wagons. Sir Richard was a long-time railway enthusiast and for a time was Chairman of the LMS company.	TSRC
139	EWS Class 66 loco on the remaining main line access rail in the Tata Steels Shotton Works.	TSRC
140	John Summers & Sons General Office for their Shotton Steel Works. It was designed by Manchester architect James France who was one of the 'Manchester School' of architects who favoured the terracotta and redbrick style of which this Listed building is a good example.	TSRC
141	Hawarden Bridge Halt in the 1950s, thronged with men at Shotton Steel Works change-of-shift.	TSRC
142	Modern technology demolishes nineteenth century technology; the final end of Dyserth Quarries.	BHT
143	The end of Brymbo Blast Furnace.	BHT
144	**Fig 66** showed the railways in the Wrexham and Brymbo areas and their ownership before BR. This is the same base map but only two open routes now remain – Shrewsbury to Wrexham via Rhos Junction and thence to Shotton or to Chester.	©RSB
145	BR/Sulzer Class 25 Bo-Bo diesel-electric loco 25165 leaves Brymbo with a train of steel billets from Brymbo Steel Works on 27 September 1977.	GE
146	Holywell Junction Station on the Chester to Holywell Station but no longer serving any railway purposes. It is in the style of an 'Italinate villa' and to the left of the building is the bush-choked bay platform which was used by Holywell Town branch trains until 1930.	GE
147	End of the line to Minera near the former Brymbo West (GWR) Station	HE
148	Changing the landscape at Brymbo – edited © GOOGLE EARTH view of the site of Brymbo Steel Works in 2018 and **INSET** a reduced version of **Fig 110** showing the nineteenth century growth of Brymbo Works on a plateau of tipped slag.	RSB; ©GOOGLE EARTH

Fig No	Caption	Provenance
149	Site of Minera Limestone Quarry re-invigorated by the North Wales Wildlife Trust as a managed nature reserve, open to the public with disabled and push-chair access for walkers and family groups.	BHT
150	The substantial brick and stone bridge by which the Holywell branch crossed the A548. The extensive car-park beside the road is convenient for walkers taking the railway track bed to Holywell Town.	©RSB
151	A bi-lingual interpretation panel at Greenfield Dock, once the Deeside terminus of the Holywell branch railway. Fortunately, the sign has not been spoiled by graffiti, but it is beginning to decay round the edges so is a reminder that such signs must be maintained.	©RSB
152	Original station and Goods Shed at Prestatyn and the mainline junction for the Dyserth branch line. The buildings, supplanted by station larger facilities as the Chester to Holyhead line became busier, were derelict for a number of years but are now carefully restored and a furniture showroom for David Jones' business.	©RSB
153	Dyserth – 1ton 10cwt hand-operated crane rescued from Dyserth Station Goods Shed and installed behind a stone-backed bench alongside the Dyserth walk- and cycle-way along the former railway trackbed.	©RSB
154	Author Rob Shorland-Ball driving Rhyl Miniature Railway (RMR) steam loco '*Joan*' in 2008.	*courtesy* RMR
155	An early impression of Hawarden Bridge Steel Works site from a nineteenth century letterhead.	TSRC
156	Map issued in 2018 to booked visitors for the Tata Steel Records Centre. Compare the view over Hawarden Bridge northwards in **Fig 149** with the site layout on this map	©TSRC
157	BHT have identified a 'Heritage Area' around the remains of John Wilkinson's Iron Works site. Appropriately the BHT office and archive is at present in the new Brymbo Enterprise Centre above and just north of the Works site.	BHT
158	Brymbo Ironworks site derelict in the 1990s. On the left of the picture are the remains of an early blast furnace, perhaps in blast when 'Iron Mad' John Wilkinson owned the site. Compare this view with BHT proposals for the site in the 2020s in **Fig 159**.	BHT
159	BHT proposals for the Brymbo Ironworks site which have secured a National Lottery Heritage Fund grant of £4.7M. **Inset** is an exposed part of the Fossil Forest (and a living dog for scale) which enhances the Brymbo story from trees to coal, iron and steel.	BHT
160	A red hot and heavy ingot on the Brymbo Rolling Mill – the Steel works needed railway connections.	BHT
161	An Airbus 380 wing, built at Broughton factory on Hawarden Aerodrome, Flintshire, NE Wales and *en route* for Queensferry wharf on its road, barge and ship journey to Airbus final assembly line at Blagnac, near Toulouse, in France.	*courtesy* Richard Davies
162	Summerhill Tunnel in the Moss Valley and leading to Brymbo. Hope for the future!	©RSB

SELECT BIBLIOGRAPHY

Anon., *John Summers & Sons Ltd – steel making at Shotton.* Works Relations Dept. 1988

BAUGHAN, Peter E., *Regional History of the Railways GBn XI – North and Mid Wales.* David & Charles. 1980.

BENNETT, John (ed), *Minera Lead Mines and Quarries.* Wrexham Maelor Borough Council. 1995.

BODLANDER, A., HAMBLY, M., LEADBETTER, H., SOUTHERN, D., WAETHERLEY, S., *Wrexham Railways – a collection of pictures. Vols I & II* Bridge Books. 1992 & 1993

BOYD, James I.C., *Wrexham, Mold & Connah's Quay Railway and Buckley Railway.* Oakwood Press. 1991

BSC, *Full Circle – The Story of Steelmaking on Deeside.* Shotton Works, Deeside. 1980

BURT, Roger, WAITE, Peter, BURNLEY, Raymond, *Mines of Flintshire & Denbighshire.* University of Exeter Press. 1992.

CHRISTIANSEN, Rex, *Forgotten Railways 11 – Severn Valley and Welsh Border.* David & Charles. 1988.

COOKE, R.A., *Atlas of the Great Western Railway as at 1947.* Wild Swan Publications Ltd. 1988.

DAVIES, Glyn, *Minera.* 1964.

DAVIES, K., WILLIAMS, C.J., *Greenfield Valley.* Holywell Town Council. 1986.

DAVIES, P.G., DAWSON, C.J., THOMAS, J.R., *Buckley Railway Album & Associated Industries.* The Buckley Society. 2007

DAWSON, Frank, *John Wilkinson – King of the Ironmasters.* History Press. 2012

DODD, S.H., *Industrial Revolution in N Wales.* University of Wales Press. 1933.

EDGAR, Gordon, *Industrial Locomotives and Railways of Wales.* Amberley Publishing. 2020.

JONES, Joan D., *Brymbo Steel Works – a collection of pictures.* Bridge Books. 1991

LERRY, George, *Henry Robertson, Pioneer of Railways into Wales.* Woodalls Ltd. 1949.

MORGAN REES, D., *Mines, Mills and Furnaces – introduction to industrial archaeology in Wales.* HMSO. 1989.

PRITCHARD, A.T.W., *History of the Old Parish of Hawarden.* Bridge Books 2002.

PRITCHARD, A.T.W., *The Making of Buckley and District.* Bridge Books. 2006

REDHEAD, Brian, GOODIE, Sheila, *Summers of Shotton.* Hodder & Stoughton. 1957.

ROGERS, Graham, *Brymbo and its Neighbourhood.* 1991

SMITH, Gordon, *A Century of Shotton Steel (1896-1996) /* British Steel - Strip Products. 1996

THOMAS, J.R., *Tramways and Railways to Holywell.* 1995